A SYNOPSIS
OF AMERICAN
HISTORY

A SYNOPSIS OF AMERICAN HISTORY

THIRD EDITION

CHARLES SELLERS
HENRY MAY
University of California at Berkeley

NEIL R. McMILLEN
University of Southern Mississippi

VOLUME TWO
since the civil war

RAND McNALLY COLLEGE PUBLISHING Company • Chicago

Rand McNally History Series

Fred Harvey Harrington, *Advisory Editor*

Current Printing (last digit)
15 14 13 12 11 10 9 8 7 6 5 4 3 2 1

Third Edition

Preface

A Synopsis of American History is a brief summary, with emphasis on politics, designed for those who are beginning the study of the subject. Our purpose in offering a much briefer book than the average textbook is not to cut down the *amount* a student reads, but to increase its *diversity*. Use of the *Synopsis,* together with the *Berkeley Readings in American History* and other materials, should help a student to get some idea of the vast diversity of American historical writing and to experience some of the excitement of close, first-hand study of historical sources. At the same time he can acquire some control of the chronological order without which history makes no sense. The very brief chapter bibliographies are restricted to books which are both readily available and readable and provide no more than a bare introduction to the study of each period.

In general, we have said little directly about social and intellectual history, not because we consider these fields unimportant, but because they are best studied in sources and specialized books and do not lend themselves to summary. In our opinion, political history affords the clearest organization of American history. Surprisingly often, American politics reflect with fair accuracy the underlying tendencies in economic, social, and intellectual life.

In reducing this big story to such a small space, we have found it impossible to avoid expressing opinions. While we have tried to keep partisanship to a minimum, we have allowed ourselves to suggest interpretations. Appropriate reading in other books—the whole purpose of the *Synopsis*—should enable students to accept or reject our interpretative statements.

We wish to thank Professor Richard B. Morris, who read the whole manuscript, and Professors Harold Hyman, William E. Leuchtenberg, and Martin Sherwin who read parts of it. Professor Richard Abrams read chapters 16–30 in both the original and the second edition, and the latter particularly owes much to his knowledge of recent American history. Despite much discussion and general agreement, each author is responsible for facts and interpretation in his section of the book—Charles Sellers for chapters 1–15 and Henry May for chapters 16–31. For the third edition, Professor Neil R. McMillen has revised the text throughout. Chapter 32 and all the essays on "Conflicting Historical Viewpoints" are the work of Professor McMillen.

A *Synopsis of American History, Third Edition*, is available as a single volume or as a two-volume set. In the two-volume set, chapters 1–16 comprise Volume One, *Through Reconstruction*; chapters 15–32 comprise Volume Two, *Since the Civil War*.

C.S.
H.M.
N.R.M.

Contents

Special Lists

Maps

A SYNOPSIS
OF AMERICAN
HISTORY

1860   **Abraham Lincoln** (Republican) elected over Stephen A. Douglas (Northern Democrat), John C. Breckinridge (Southern Democrat), and John Bell (Constitutional Unionist).

1860–1861   Seven states of the lower South secede and organize the Confederate States of America.

1861   Confederates bombard Fort Sumter, beginning the Civil War.
Virginia, North Carolina, Tennessee, and Arkansas secede and join the Confederacy.
Morrill Tariff. Substantial upward revision of duties, beginning a long period of high protection.
Trent affair. Union naval officer seized two Confederate diplomats from a British vessel.

1862   Homestead Act. Free farms of 160 acres to actual settlers.
Morrill Land Grant Act. Land grants to the states for agricultural and mechanical colleges.
Pacific Railroad Act. Federal subsidies for a railroad from Omaha to California.
Slavery abolished in the territories and the District of Columbia.
Second Confiscation Act. Freeing escaped or captured slaves of Confederates.

1863   Lincoln's Emancipation Proclamation. Declaring free all slaves in Confederate areas.
National Bank Act. With a supplementary act of 1864 establishes a system of banks issuing a uniform paper currency based on holdings of federal bonds.
Turning point of the war in July, when Union forces capture Vicksburg on the Mississippi and stop Lee's invasion at Gettysburg.
Lincoln announces his "ten percent plan" for the easy restoration of the seceded states to the Union.

1864   Lincoln vetoes the Wade-Davis bill, containing a harsher congressional plan for restoration of the seceded states to the Union.
Abraham Lincoln (Republican) reelected over George B. McClellan (Democrat).

1865   Lee surrenders to Grant at Appomattox Courthouse.
Lincoln assassinated.
The Thirteenth Amendment abolishes slavery throughout the United States.

The Civil War
1861-1865

15

When Abraham Lincoln arose to deliver his inaugural address on March 4, 1861, few people had any very clear idea of how the secession problem should be handled. Some voices in the North counseled letting the "erring sisters depart in peace." The abolitionist minority called for a holy war to free the slaves. Majority opinion in the North was increasingly convinced that the Union must somehow be preserved, but there was no clear mandate for military coercion of the seceded states. The war that finally came, like most wars, came not because anyone deliberately willed it, but out of a fortuitous chain of circumstances whose result reflected only imperfectly the conscious collective will of North or South. Insofar as a guiding will affected the outcome, it was the will of Abraham Lincoln.

LINCOLN AND THE SECESSION CRISIS

The new President was known to the country only as a lanky and apparently uncultivated lawyer-politician from the prairies of Illinois. He had won brief notice years earlier when his opposition to the Mexican War caused Illinois voters to repudiate him after a single term in Congress. Not until his debates with Douglas in the senatorial campaign of 1858 had he attracted national attention. Elected president by a minority of the voters, he had given little public indication of his policy in the months between the election and the inauguration. Actually he had blocked all efforts at compromise by privately opposing any arrangement that left the slightest room for the expansion of slavery. But this position could be put down to political expediency—compromise on the territorial question would have left the infant Republican party little reason for existence—and gave no clue as to what he would do when he assumed office.

Certainly Lincoln was not prepared to lead a crusade to free the slaves. He had insisted that slavery was wrong and that its expansion should be stopped so that the country might look forward to its eventual peaceful extinction. But he had repeatedly denied any disposition to interfere with slavery where it already existed. He had also denied in his debates with Douglas that he was "in favor of bringing about in any way the social and political equality of the white and black races." A "physical difference" would prevent the two races from ever living together on equal terms, he had said, and, therefore, "I, as much as any other man, am in favor of having the superior position assigned to the white race." He wanted slavery excluded from the territories so that "white men may find a home—may find some spot where they can . . . settle upon new soil and better their condition in life . . . as an outlet for *free white people everywhere.*"

The inaugural address revealed both a leader of unsuspected stature and a position around which northern opinion could rally. With an eloquence that no president since Jefferson had attained, Lincoln pleaded for preservation of the Union. "The mystic chords of memory," he said, "stretching from every battlefield and every patriot grave to every living heart and hearthstone all over this broad land, will yet swell the chorus of the Union, when again touched, as surely they will be, by the better angels of our nature." In trying to touch these chords, he reassured the South in the most positive terms that he would countenance no act against slavery in the states where it already existed.

But the address also had a vein of iron. The Union, said Lincoln, was perpetual, any violent acts against the authority of the United States were "insurrectionary or revolutionary," and these statements were to be taken "as the declared purpose of the Union that it *will* constitutionally defend and maintain itself." Though the federal government would not initiate hostilities, the President told the South, it would "hold, occupy, and possess" the federal forts and other property in the seceded states and collect the import duties there.

It is clear in retrospect that Lincoln thus committed himself to a course that led directly to one of the bloodiest wars in history. But war was not his purpose. Eight of the fifteen slave states were still in the Union. By refusing to recognize secession while at the same time declining to proceed forcibly against the secessionists, Lincoln was seeking to reinforce the manifest Unionist sentiment in the upper South. Apparently he wanted to keep the upper South from seceding, hoping that latent Unionism would eventually overcome secessionism in the seven seceded states of the lower South.

There were several difficulties with this Union-saving strategy. One was that Lincoln exaggerated the strength of Unionist sentiment in the lower South. Another was the likelihood that the effort to hold the federal forts in the seceded states would lead to armed conflict. Armed conflict was the more likely because many of the secessionists were quite ready to provoke a crisis that would force the upper South to choose sides.

The issue of peace or war came to a focus in the harbor of Charleston, South Carolina. Practically all the federal forts and other property in the lower South had been taken over by the seceding states before Lincoln's inauguration. Of the few posts remaining in federal hands, the unfinished and lightly garrisoned Fort Sumter, located in the entrance to Charleston's harbor, had become the symbolic focus of the whole controversy over federal property. Sumter had sufficient supplies to hold out only six weeks, and a decision about its future could not be postponed. Lincoln finally informed the Confederate authorities that he was sending a naval expedition to reprovision Sumter. They in turn ordered their general at Charleston to demand the fort's immediate evacuation and in case of refusal to bombard it. The demand was made and refused, and on April 12, 1861, the Confederate shore batteries opened fire.

Lincoln responded by calling on the states for seventy-five thousand troops. Rather than make war on their fellow Southerners, four states of the upper South—Virginia, North Carolina, Tennessee, and Arkansas—now reluctantly followed the lower South out of the Union. The four slave states of Delaware, Maryland, Kentucky, and Missouri remained with the Union, though the last two had strong secessionist movements and furnished many soldiers to the Confederacy. The tables were turned on the secessionists when the strongly Unionist western section of Virginia seceded from Virginia and laid the basis for the new state of West Virginia under the aegis of the Union. Meanwhile the Confederacy had acted to consolidate the adhesion of the upper southern states by moving its capital from Montgomery to Richmond.

THE WAR BEGINS

A spirit of martial ardor swept over both sections in the spring of 1861. Northerners expected a short and easy war, while Southerners seemed oblivious of the overwhelming superiority in human and material resources against which they would have to contend. The five and one-half million free people of the eleven Confederate states faced a population of twenty-two million in the twenty-three Union states.

The North had a four-to-one advantage in free males of fighting age and would muster twice as many soldiers. Even if one southern soldier was worth two Yankees (as Southerners loudly proclaimed), how were southern armies to be supplied and transported? The North had 80 percent of the country's factories and most of the coal and iron. Twenty-two thousand miles of railroad traversed the North as compared with nine thousand in the South, and the North's rail network included a series of vital trunk lines between East and West while the sprawling southern regions were but circuitously and inefficiently bound together.

Under the circumstances the South made a remarkable military showing. This was due in part to the advantage of fighting a defensive war. The North was compelled not only to invade but occupy the South, and southern commanders had the additional advantage of shorter interior lines of communication for shifting troops from one front to another. Moreover Jefferson Davis could utilize from the beginning a galaxy of outstanding generals, Albert Sidney Johnston, Joseph E. Johnston, Thomas J. ("Stonewall") Jackson, and, preeminently, Robert E. Lee; while Lincoln spent several years trying a succession of variously unsatisfactory commanders before he found a really able one.

The Appalachian highlands, thrusting deep into the South, divided the theater of war into two zones. Throughout the conflict the greatest public attention was focused on the East, where the rival armies menaced each other's capitals only a hundred miles apart. Here the Confederate armies, magnificently led by Joseph E. Johnston and then by Robert E. Lee, repeatedly repelled Union invasions aimed at Richmond. General Irvin McDowell's army was turned back at Bull Run in northern Virginia in July, 1861. Lincoln's next general, George B. McClellan, tried another tack, ferrying an enormous invasion force down Chesapeake Bay and up the York River to the eastern outskirts of Richmond only to be beaten off in the series of hard-fought battles that constituted the Peninsula Campaign of May–June, 1862. Later that summer Lee trounced another Union army led by John Pope in the second battle at Bull Run and followed up this victory with an audacious advance across the Potomac River into Maryland. McClellan caught up with him at Antietam Creek, some fifty miles northwest of Washington, in September, 1862, and in a closely contested battle inflicted so much damage that the Confederates had to withdraw to Virginia.

Back on his home ground Lee was again invincible, defeating Ambrose E. Burnside at Fredericksburg in December and Joseph E. Hooker at nearby Chancellorsville the following May. Once again the great Confederate general sought to capitalize on his success by invading the North, gambling on the hope of a decisive victory that would cut the east-west trunk railroads in Maryland and Pennsylvania, imperil Washington, and persuade the North to make peace before its superiority in manpower and material became irresistible. On July 1, 1863, Lee's seventy thousand men and the ninety thousand Union soldiers of George G. Meade faced each other from opposing ridges outside the little town of Gettysburg in southern Pennsylvania. For three days wave after wave of Confederates swept up against the strong Unionist position barely failing to flood over it. Lee was again forced to retreat to Virginia, and the South's last hope of victory was gone.

While Lee's brilliant gamble was failing in the East, the Confederacy's military doom was being more plainly spelled out in the West. Here the Mississippi, Tennessee, and Cumberland rivers afforded natural invasion routes for the combined operations of Union gunboats and armies, and here an obscure Union commander Ulysses S. Grant had been steadily and inexorably crunching deeper and deeper into the South. Forts Henry and Donelson, guarding the Tennessee and Cumberland rivers, had fallen in February, 1862. Pressing on south up the Tennessee River, Grant had inflicted a severe blow on the main Confederate army in the west at Shiloh in April and moved on into northern Mississippi. Meanwhile Union gunboats had steamed up the Mississippi from the Gulf to take New Orleans and down the Mississippi from the north to take Memphis. The last Confederate stronghold on the Mississippi, Vicksburg, fell to Grant in July, 1863, while Meade was turning back Lee at Gettysburg, and the Confederacy was cut in two.

THE CONFEDERACY AT WAR

The burden of directing the Confederate war effort fell almost wholly on the shoulders of Jefferson Davis. Lacking able subordinates in his cabinet and in the Confederate Congress, Davis perhaps took on too much of the burden of detailed administration and sometimes exercised poor judgment in decisions about military strategy and commanding officers. But only an able and conscientious executive could have kept the Confederacy operating and its armies in the field under the staggering difficulties that he faced for as long as he did.

At the beginning of the war Davis had high hopes of aid from Europe. France's Napoleon III was openly sympathetic as were the ruling upper classes in Great Britain, and both of these countries went so far as to recognize the Confederacy's belligerent status. But Davis was counting on the economic power of the South's cotton to produce more substantial aid—full diplomatic recognition, financial assistance, and perhaps even military intervention. The South might have built up large credits for the purchase of supplies in Europe by shipping its cotton abroad. Instead the Confederate authorities placed an embargo on cotton exports, expecting that this would force British cotton mills to close and thus bring pressure on the British government to intervene more openly on behalf of the Confederacy. Unfortunately the British mills had a year's surplus of raw cotton on hand, some alternative sources of supply were available, and although some of the cotton mills eventually shut down, their unemployed workers remained sympathetic to the more democratic North and exerted their influence against any aid to the South.

The South's best chance to drive a wedge between Great Britain and the North came in November, 1861, when a United States naval vessel stopped the British ship *Trent* on the high seas and took off the Confederate diplomats James M. Mason and John Slidell. But the United States promptly released Mason and Slidell, and Lincoln's skillful minister in London, Charles Francis Adams, was increasingly successful in preventing the British from aiding the Confederacy either directly or indirectly. And France refused to act without British support.

Meanwhile Lincoln had ordered the Union navy to blockade southern ports; and by the time the Confederacy decided to ship cotton to Europe in exchange for supplies, this was no longer possible. Cut off from all outside goods (except a trickle brought in by swift blockade runners), the Confederacy was increasingly hard put to supply its armies with munitions or its people with the ordinary necessities of life.

As the war wore on and as the Confederacy's prospects dimmed, the early enthusiasm was replaced by growing discouragement, apathy, and disaffection. The Confederate conscription law, which exempted overseers and owners of twenty slaves, was especially resented by poorer Southerners who began to say that this was "a rich man's war and a poor man's fight." Desertions became an increasingly serious problem. The South's state-rights tradition was also a source of weakness as fractious governors like Joseph E. Brown of Georgia and Zebulon B. Vance of North Carolina defied the policies of the Richmond government. It seems fair to conclude that the South's commitment to the war had been less than wholehearted in the beginning and that a growing disenchantment with it was a major factor in the Confederacy's eventual collapse.

LINCOLN AND THE WAR

Lincoln was having his problems too. The North had a large contingent of "Peace Democrats" who as the war dragged unsuccessfully on demanded a negotiated settlement. The draft law of 1863, from which the wealthy could escape by paying $300 or hiring a substitute, provoked a bloody two-day riot in New York City. At the other end of the political spectrum, Lincoln was ceaselessly hounded by a group of "Radical" Republicans who wanted to make the war an antislavery crusade and who advocated a punitive policy toward the South. Under the leadership of men like Senator Charles Sumner of Massachusetts and Representative Thaddeus Stevens of Pennsylvania, the Radicals gained great power in Congress where they set up a Joint Committee on the Conduct of the War, which constantly criticized and interfered with the President's conduct of military operations.

The split between Radical Republicans and moderate or administration Republicans was not related, however, to the series of major laws passed by the wartime Congresses. The Morrill Tariff Act of 1861 marked a turn toward higher protective duties, and subsequent legislation of 1862 and 1864 pushed duties to unprecedented levels, inaugurating an era of extravagant protectionism that would last into the twentieth century. The long fight for free land culminated in the Homestead Act of 1862, granting 160 acres to any family that wished to settle on the public domain. The Morrill Land Grant Act of 1862 donated public lands to the states for support of agricultural and mechanical colleges. In the same year Congress finally authorized the long-projected transcontinental railroad, granting thirty million acres and millions in federal bonds to the Union Pacific and Central Pacific railroad companies to build a line from Omaha to the Sacramento River. By an act of 1863 Congress established a national banking system with member banks issuing a stable currency of uniform national bank notes on the basis of their holdings of federal bonds.

In passing these important measures to serve the interests of northern farmers and business enterprise, the Congress was simply legislating the Republican platform now that the Southerners were no longer there to oppose. None of these measures aroused the controversy in the Republican party that the subject of slavery created. Anxious to mollify the loyal slave states of Delaware, Maryland, Kentucky, and Missouri, Lincoln stoutly resisted doing anything to suggest that abolition of slavery was a northern war aim. In the fall of 1861 he removed the Radicals' favorite general John C. Frémont from command in Missouri for declaring that the slaves of rebels were free. Meanwhile he sought unsuccessfuly to interest Congress and the loyal slave states in a plan of gradual, compensated emancipation with the federal government footing the bill.

The Radicals were determined to force the issue, and in 1862 pushed through Congress legislation abolishing slavery in the territories and in the District of Columbia. More important was the Second Confiscation Act of 1862, declaring forfeit the property of all persons supporting the rebellion and proclaiming escaped or captured slaves to be "forever free." By this time Lincoln was becoming aware of the value of an emancipation policy in helping to win the war, especially by gaining friends for the Union in Europe. Finally, on January 1, 1863, he issued his Emancipation Proclamation. This famous proclamation freed only those slaves living in rebel areas and justified the action on the ground of "military necessity." Only as the Union armies advanced did the freedom proclaimed by the proclamation become an actuality for the slaves. Not until 1865 did the Thirteenth Amendment, forbidding slavery throughout the country, become a part of the Constitution.

The Emancipation Proclamation did not allay the Radicals' suspicion of Lincoln, but they failed to block his renomination for President in 1864. In this wartime election the Lincoln Republicans ran as the Union party, appealing to War Democrats by nominating for vice president Andrew Johnson, the Tennessee Senator who had remained loyal to the Union. The regular Democratic nomination went to General McClellan, many of whose supporters were calling for peace negotiations. The long string of Union defeats in the East had so strengthened antiwar sentiment that Lincoln might have been defeated but for some timely military successes in the West on the eve of the election.

TOWARD APPOMATTOX

It is now clear that the fall of Vicksburg and Lee's failure at Gettysburg in July, 1863, had destroyed the last chances of a Confederate victory. And by this time, after trying a long succession of commanders, Lincoln had finally found a general who would justify his confidence. Ulysses Grant, who had capped his doggedly successful western campaigns with the victory at Vicksburg, was called to the East and in the spring of 1864 made general-in-chief of all the Union armies. Before leaving the West he had consolidated Union control of Tennessee with a victory at Chattanooga. Now his grand strategy was a two-pronged final offensive against the South with General William T. Sherman leading one great Union army south from Chattanooga into

Georgia and himself leading another south from Washington toward Richmond.

The twin offensives were launched simultaneously in May, 1864, the two Union armies of around one hundred thousand men each pressing back Confederate armies of around sixty thousand. In the West Sherman steadily pushed the Confederates south and by September had won the important rail center of Atlanta. Here he made his audacious decision to abandon his line of supply and wage a war of destruction between Atlanta and the sea. Devastating the countryside as he went, he was in Savannah by December, and the Confederacy had been further segmented. Turning north, Sherman reached Columbia, South Carolina, in February, 1865, and by March was in east central North Carolina.

By demoralizing the Confederate areas south of Virginia, Sherman greatly facilitated Grant's advance on Richmond. In the Spotsylvania Wilderness and at Spotsylvania Courthouse in May, 1864, Lee inflicted heavy casualties on the invading Yankees as he had so often done in the past. But this Yankee general did not withdraw to lick his wounds as had all his predecessors. By flanking movements he kept pressing south toward Richmond. At Cold Harbor Lee again inflicted frightful losses on the Union army, but still Grant pushed inexorably south, passing just east of Richmond and crossing the James River. Lee managed to shield Richmond as Grant moved around it to the south and southwest toward Petersburg. By June the two armies were entrenched facing each other in a long line bending from Richmond southward around the southern side of Petersburg.

Grant simply would not let go, and as the siege went on through the summer and fall and winter his superiority in manpower began to tell. Remorselessly he kept extending his line to the west, and Lee's line became steadily thinner and more vulnerable as he had to keep stretching it farther. By April Lee could extend his line no more and had to pull out of his entrenchments, abandoning Richmond and Petersburg. But by this time Grant had cut all the roads leading south over which Lee might effect a junction with the only remaining Confederate army of any strength. On April 9, 1865, at Appomattox Courthouse Lee bowed to the inevitable and surrendered. One month later the fleeing Jefferson Davis was captured in disguise in Georgia and imprisoned at Fortress Monroe. The Confederacy was dead.

LINCOLN AND THE SOUTH

The treatment of the vanquished South had long since become a new bone of contention between Lincoln and the Radicals. Lincoln wished to bring the rebellious states back into full membership in the Union as rapidly and painlessly as possible. By the time Union forces occupied Arkansas in December, 1863, the President was ready with his "ten percent plan" of reconstruction. Under this plan he proposed to extend amnesty and restore confiscated property to all Confederates who would take a simple loyalty oath, excluding only high civil and military officers of the Confederacy or its states. As soon as 10 percent of a state's 1860 electorate had taken the oath, the state could write a new constitution and rejoin the Union.

The Radicals, however, feared with considerable reason that if the southern states were reconstructed on this basis, the old ruling class would return to power and the Negro freedmen would be little better off than they had been under slavery. Anxious for a thoroughgoing reconstruction of southern society, they insisted that black men be given the ballot and that the old rebel leadership be effectively excluded from political life. As a counter to Lincoln's plan they secured the passage in 1864 of the Wade-Davis bill. This measure required a majority, rather than 10 percent, of the 1860 voters to take a loyalty oath before reconstruction could begin and further insisted on disfranchisement of ex-Confederate leaders.

Lincoln allowed the Wade-Davis bill to die by pocket veto, but the Radicals had one tactical advantage. A state would not be fully restored to the Union until its representatives were seated in Congress, and the Radical-controled Congress had full power over the admission of members. This power the Radicals used to deny admission to the first southern representatives who appeared under Lincoln's 10 percent plan. In March, 1865, as the war drew to a close, they gave a further indication of their objectives by creating the Freedmen's Bureau to assist the ex-slaves in adjusting to freedom and to protect their rights in their new state.

The sharpening struggle between Lincoln and the Radicals was suddenly cut short on Good Friday, April 14, 1865, five days after Lee's surrender at Appomattox, when a demented actor and southern sympathizer, John Wilkes Booth, shot a fatal bullet into the President's head as he sat in a box at Ford's Theater.

A grieving nation suddenly discovered its great tragic hero. To Lincoln's strength and humility and eloquence and magnanimity was now added the quality of martyrdom. He had presided over the bloodiest war in the American experience, preserving the Union as the land of liberty and last best hope of man. Hesitantly and grudgingly but nevertheless in the end unmistakably, he had also made the war a struggle to include *all* male Americans within the sphere of American liberty. Yet the Emancipation Proclamation and the Thirteenth Amendment were only a beginning. It was Lincoln's Radical critics who saw most clearly that the task of completing emancipation still lay ahead, and even his great talents could hardly have been equal to this Herculean task. Perhaps it was a timely martyrdom that translated Abraham Lincoln—a man groping toward an ideal only dimly perceptible in his society and age—into the Great Emancipator. For a century and more to come, Lincoln, the symbol, would remind his countrymen that the egalitarian dream was still unfulfilled.

FOR FURTHER READING:

The standard work on the Civil War era is Allan Nevins's *The War for the Union* (4 vols., 1959–1971). Divergent interpretations of the North's reaction to secession are presented in David M. Potter, *Lincoln and His Party in the Secession Crisis* (1950)*; and Kenneth M. Stampp, *And the War Came: The North and the Secession Crisis* (1950)*. The northern conduct of the war is best followed through the biographies of Lincoln, the best single-volume one being Benjamin P. Thomas, *Abraham Lincoln* (1952). For greater detail, see Albert J. Beveridge, *Abraham Lincoln, 1809–1858* (2 vols., 1928); and the chronologically succeeding volumes by James G. Randall (completed by Richard N. Current) on *Lincoln the President* (4 vols., 1945–1955)*. Current has also written a fine interpretive essay on *The Lincoln Nobody Knows* (1958)*. Special aspects of the North during the war are treated in John Hope Franklin, *The Emancipation Proclamation* (1963); George M. Frederickson, *The Inner Civil War* (1965)*; T. Harry Williams, *Lincoln and the Radicals* (1941)*; and T. Harry Williams, *Lincoln and His Generals* (1952)*. Clement Eaton has written a *History of the Southern Confederacy* (1954)*, and Frank E. Vandiver's *Their Tattered Flags* (1970) is a sprightly history of the secession government. Rembert W. Patrick describes *Jefferson Davis and His Cabinet* (1944); and the Confederacy's *King Cotton Diplomacy* (1931) has been analyzed by Frank L. Owsley. The military history of the war from the point of view of the northern armies may be followed in the vivid volumes by Bruce Catton: *Mr. Lincoln's Army* (1951)*, *Glory Road* (1952)*, and *A Stillness at Appomattox* (1954)*. A more detailed and professional evaluation of the northern military effort through 1863, with greater attention to the western campaigns, is Kenneth P. Williams, *Lincoln Finds a General: A Military Study of the Civil War* (5 vols., 1949–1959). *The Gettysburg Campaign* (1968) is examined by Edwin B. Coddington. The fighting as

---

* Available in paperback edition.

viewed from the southern side is best followed in the distinguished studies by Douglas Southall Freeman: *R. E. Lee, a Biography* (4 vols., 1934–1935), and *Lee's Lieutenants* (3 vols., 1942–1944); and Tom Henderson Wells has written an excellent history of *The Confederate Navy* (1971). Also outstanding are two works by Frank E. Vandiver, *Rebel Brass* (1956) and *Mighty Stonewall* (1957). Bell I. Wiley has described the common soldiers in *The Life of Johnny Reb* (1943)* and *The Life of Billy Yank* (1952)*. Of the multitude of personal accounts by contemporaries, two very different ones may be singled out as having special interest: the *Personal Memoirs* (2 vols., 1885–1886)* of General Grant, and *A Diary from Dixie* (1905)* by a Richmond lady, Mary Boykin Chesnut.

EVENTS OF RECONSTRUCTION

National	Date	General Tendency	State
Lincoln Plan announced.	1863	**Presidential Reconstruction**	Governments set up in Louisiana, Arkansas.
Wade-Davis Plan pocket-vetoed by Lincoln.	1864		
Lee surrenders. Lincoln shot. Johnson Plan announced.	1865		Governments partly functioning in Virginia, Tennessee.
Freedmen's Bureau bill and Civil Rights bill vetoed. Fourteenth Amendment submitted to states.	1866		All remaining states reorganized under Johnson Plan.
Congressional elections: Radical gains. Reconstruction Acts. Tenure of Office Act.	1867	**Height of Radical Reconstruction**	Tennessee readmitted. Military Rule in effect.
Impeachment of Johnson. Fourteenth Amendment in effect. Grant elected.	1868		North Carolina, South Carolina, Florida, Alabama, Louisiana, Arkansas, readmitted under Radical governments.
Fifteenth Amendment in effect. First Enforcement Act.	1869		Conservative government restored in Tennessee. Virginia readmitted under moderate government.
Congressional elections: Republican majorities reduced.	1870	**Conflict**	Moderate government restored in North Carolina. Mississippi, Texas, Georgia, readmitted under radical government.
	1871		Conservative government restored in Georgia.
Second and third Enforcement Acts. Grant reelected.	1872		
	1873		
Congressional elections: Democrats gain control of House.	1874	**Restoration of White Rule**	Conservative government restored in Arkansas, Alabama, Texas.
Civil Rights Act (Declared invalid 1883).	1875		Conservative government restored in Mississippi.
Hayes-Tilden disputed election.	1876		Federal troops removed from Louisiana, South Carolina.
	1877		Conservative government restored in Florida, South Carolina, Louisiana.

Reconstructing the Union
1865-1890

16

In the generation after the Civil War economic expansion absorbed most of the nation's energies. The people's attention, however, centered at first on a more traditional kind of problem, the Reconstruction of the Union and the new order in the defeated South.

THE PROBLEM

The problem of Reconstruction was manifold. Most obvious, and easiest, was the physical rebuilding of shelled cities and ruined railroads. Harder to reconstruct was the defeated section's economic life. The South's industry was at a standstill; much of her farming land was lying idle. Her labor system was destroyed, investment capital was lacking, the savings of many people were wiped out by the collapse of Confederate currency and bonds. Beneath every other problem lay that of a new relation for the South's two races. All that was clear about the country's 4,500,000 Negroes was that none of them remained a slave. There were 286,000 in blue uniforms; a few were settled on confiscated plantations in the Sea Islands of the Carolinas, many were simply wandering, drifting from Union army camps to southern cities with great hopes and no means of support. Nearly everybody assumed that they were to continue to work on the land. A few radicals had suggested that they would become landowners and the Sea Islands experiment had raised some hopes. White Southerners assumed that they would work as laborers for white landowners.

In this politically minded country, most people approached such problems in political terms. By 1865 three southern states had already been reconstructed under the easy terms offered by President Lincoln, which demanded only that 10 percent of the citizens take an oath of future loyalty and recognize that slavery was ended. Once this was done, elections could be held for both state governments and federal Congressmen. The difficulty was that Congress refused to admit these delegates.

To settle this kind of difficulty, Americans turned to the Constitution. In this unheard-of situation, however, it offered little help. What was the status of a sovereign state which had seceded and been forced to return to the Union? Was it still a state, since secession had been illegal, or was it merely a conquered province? Who could decide: Congress or the president? The president was commander-in-chief of the armed forces and had the power to pardon. But Congress had the right to admit new states, to make rules for territories, and to judge the qualifications of its own members. Long before Lincoln's death, the two branches of government had been at loggerheads over these issues.

More important in the long run than even the constitutional question was the state of mind of three main groups: the ex-slaves, the defeated southern whites, and the citizens of the victorious North. Though able Negro leaders shortly appeared, most of the ex-slaves were not only illiterate but completely inexperienced, both in politics and in such economic institutions as wages and rent. Many pathetic stories are told about the strange hopes and fears of these displaced people. Yet the basic desires of the freedmen were clear and by no means foolish. What they wanted was real freedom, and the signs of freedom were the right to move around, access to education, and ownership of land.

Right after the war, according to northern travelers in the South, shock rather than bitterness was the most common state of mind among southern whites. With their institutions destroyed, what was to become of them? Most pressing of all, without slavery, how was the cotton going to be picked and planted? At first, many looked northward for their answers.

The third and largest group, the victorious northern whites, were by no means a united body. Nearly half, to begin with, were Democrats. Only a few Democrats had been willing to accept the breakup of the Union, but many had sharply criticized the conduct of the war and had opposed emancipation. The sole purpose of the fighting, the party's leaders had insisted, should have been the restoration of "the Union as it was." In the 1864 elections the Democrats had lost some ground, yet they still mustered a formidable 45 percent of the votes.

Not even the Republicans were sure how much of a change they wanted. The group called "Radicals" agreed that Lincoln had been too weak and lenient, but they agreed on little else. Republicans were divided on such matters as the tariff and finance, and few had thought through the future status of the Negro.

Two paradoxes made constructive action inordinately difficult. First, slavery had been abolished and the ex-slaves armed by a nation which believed overwhelmingly in the inferiority of the Negro race. This belief, now discredited, was centuries old and almost universal. Even among the abolitionists, only a few had accepted the Negro as an intellectual and political equal. Only part of New England permitted Negroes to vote. Starting with Connecticut, Wisconsin, and Minnesota in 1865, one northern state after another continued to turn down Negro suffrage in the years after the war.

Second, in Reconstruction the North had to undertake a program of drastic, even revolutionary measures. Yet nearly all nineteenth-century Americans had been taught that government action should be sharply limited. This had been said by Jefferson, Jackson, and Lincoln. Schools and colleges taught as gospel truth the maxims of *laissez faire* political economy.

The choice faced by the North, in its simplest terms, was the choice offered to every victor: occupation or conciliation. All the feelings of nineteenth-century Americans were against continued military occupation. Somehow, most agreed, the South must be forced to see its errors and govern itself—according to northern ideas.

Yet to whom in the South could government be confided? To the ex-rebels who were, many Northerners believed, still rebels at heart? To the ex-slaves whom most Northerners regarded as members of an inferior race? Even if they were given the vote, the freedmen, inexperienced in politics and a minority in all but two states, could hardly govern alone. They would have to have the support either of a substantial number of southern whites or of sufficient occupying forces. With or without Negro suffrage the same choice would exist: conciliation or occupation.

PRESIDENTIAL RECONSTRUCTION

The first alternative, conciliation, was tried under the authority of presidents Lincoln and Johnson and is often referred to as Presidential Reconstruction. It is hard to tell how Lincoln's "ten percent plan" might have worked if it had been continued. As we have seen, this was already sharply challenged by Congress, and Lincoln himself had said it was only one of many possible devices. The Wade-Davis bill, Congress' somewhat more drastic substitute, had been left unsigned by Lincoln.

Like Lincoln, Andrew Johnson embodied the log-cabin presidential tradition. He had been a tailor by trade and had learned to read only as an adult. A resident of eastern Tennessee, where slaves were few, and a former Jacksonian Democrat, he had been an outspoken opponent of secession and a lifelong enemy of the southern planter class. Yet he had no real commitment either to Negro rights or to the Republican party. Like Lincoln, Johnson was honest and able, but he proved to lack completely Lincoln's gifts for patience and political realism.

Like his predecessor, Johnson started by offering amnesty to those who would sign an oath of allegiance. Exceptions to the offer, more numerous than in Lincoln's plan, included important Confederate officials and Confederates who owned more than $20,000 worth of property. This seemed to exclude the leaders of the Old South. Those who had taken the oath were to vote for a constitutional convention in each state. This must repeal the state's ordinance of secession, abolish slavery, and repudiate the Confederate and state debts. Then the state might elect a new government and send representatives to Washington. By the end of 1865 all the states had actually passed through either the Lincoln or the Johnson version of this process, and in conservative or southern eyes Reconstruction was over.

Government was functioning in the South, and the people, Negro and white, were getting back to work. Yet much in the new order was deeply disturbing to northern opinion. Some of the reconstituted states elected prominent Confederates to state and federal office. Most enacted special "Black Codes" to regulate the conduct of freedmen. To former slaveholders, such rules seemed natural and necessary; to many northerners they looked like the next thing to slavery. In some states Negroes were not allowed to assemble; in others the labor of petty offenders could be sold at auction; in some Negro children could be apprenticed to white men without the consent of indigent parents. Most of the codes provided for strict enforcement of compulsory labor contracts. In South Carolina, the code spelled out the intent of such contracts: Negroes were to engage only in agricultural labor or domestic service.

In 1865–1866 northern opinion was further affronted by outbreaks of racial violence in the South. Responsibility for race riots was of course disputed, but the victims nearly always turned out to be Negroes or pro-Negro whites. To Radical Republicans, it seemed that life was not safe in the South for those who really supported a change in southern society, and this change they were determined to bring about. To some it was a moral duty; to others a political necessity.

In the spring of 1866 Congress extended the life of the Freedmen's Bureau, a wartime organization designed to supervise and aid the ex-slaves, and passed a Civil Rights Act prohibiting many kinds of discriminatory legislation. It also refused to admit the representatives of the new southern state governments. Clearly, the President could not hope to carry forward his policy without regard for such formidable opposition. Yet Johnson, like other presidents in other battles with Congress, seemed to grow steadily more stubborn. He blamed the race riots on Radicals, minimized southern denial of Negro rights, and pardoned thousands of southern leaders. In the spring of 1866 he vetoed both the Freedmen's Bureau bill and the Civil Rights Act.

By this time, Johnson had gained the support of Democrats and solidified the Republican party against him. In the fall he toured the country, violently denouncing his opponents as traitors. In the November election the voters gave their answer. The Republicans won two thirds of both Houses and the Radical leadership moved into key positions of power. A new phase of Reconstruction was clearly at hand.

CONGRESSIONAL RECONSTRUCTION

In Congressional, or Radical, Reconstruction, the other alternative, military occupation, was finally given a trial. The purpose, however, was still reform; the South was to be occupied only until her society could be altered and a new electorate formed. This meant something like social revolution, and it was clear that in this revolution the Negroes must play a major part.

The Freedmen's Bureau and Civil Rights bills, both repassed over the President's veto, established the principle that the former slaves were to be protected by the federal government during a transitional state. (They were not, however, to be given land; in this property-loving age only a few suggested such an extreme measure and local experiments in this direction were abandoned.)

Federal protection for the Negroes already implied a change in the relation of the federal government and the states, and such a change was spelled out in the Fourteenth Amendment submitted to Congress in June, 1866. The first section of this amendment provided that no state should infringe any citizen's "privileges or immunities," nor "deprive any person of life, liberty or property, without due process of law," nor deny to any person "the equal protection of the laws." Thus individuals were guaranteed by the *Union* against oppression by the *states*. (The Bill of Rights already protected individual liberties from the federal govenment.)

The second section of the amendment edged toward Negro suffrage. It provided that if a state denied the vote to any of its male inhabitants, its representation should be reduced accordingly. The third and fourth sections barred leading Confederates from Congress or federal office and forbade states to repudiate the federal or recognize the rebel debt.

Obviously this all-important amendment could not be ratified by three-fourths of the states without some southern support. President Johnson urged southern states not to ratify, and Congress, as it might have anyway, moved on to still more drastic action.

The First Reconstruction Act, passed in March, 1867, divided the South into five military districts, wiping out the existing state governments. Under military supervision, each state was to elect a constitutional convention. Delegates to these conventions would be chosen by vote of the whole male population, including the freedmen and excluding leading Confederates. Each constitution was to be ratified by a majority of the state's new electorate and approved by Congress. When the new state had ratified the Fourteenth Amendment its representatives might be admitted to Congress. This Act was clarified and tightened by further legislation, and in 1870 Radical Reconstruction was completed by the ratification of the Fifteenth Amendment, once and for all forbidding suffrage discrimination on the basis of "race, color, or previous condition of servitude."

All these actions were taken against the firm opposition of the President and in the face of the nearly certain disapproval of the Supreme Court. To safeguard Radical Reconstruction, Congress made the most drastic attempt in American history to establish the dominance of a single branch of government.

To disarm the Court, Congress simply withdrew certain kinds of cases from Supreme Court jurisdiction, and the Court prudently refrained from challenging this action. Johnson, however, could be rendered powerless only by impeachment and conviction for "treason, bribery, or other high crimes or misdemeanors." Failing after much effort to find serious evidence of "crimes," Congress saw its best chance for impeachment in the Tenure of Office Act passed in 1867. This Act, of dubious constitutionality, forbade the removal of cabinet officers without congressional sanction. Johnson challenged it by trying to remove Secretary of War Edwin Stanton, an appointee of Lincoln. In the spring of 1868 the House of Representatives impeached the President in a long, confused, and shaky set of charges. Anger ran so high that his accusers failed by only one vote to secure the two-thirds of the Senate necessary for conviction.

RADICAL RECONSTRUCTION IN ACTION

How did the Radical program actually work in the South? To this crucial question, historians have developed two opposite answers. A generation ago most accounts said that Radical Reconstruction had been a dreadful mistake. Southern state governments, dominated by ignorant Negroes, self-seeking carpetbaggers, and despicable southern "scalawags" ("collaborationists" would be the modern term), had imposed a reign of terror, extravagance, and corruption. Finally, the South, supported by a revival of decent moderate opinion in the North, had risen in revolt and thrown off the yoke.

More recently this version has been challenged by an opposite one. According to this second, neo-Radical view, Radical Reconstruction was a long-overdue attempt to bring justice and progress to the South. It was sustained in the South not only by federal forces but by determined Negro support. Its defeat was brought about by brutal terrorism and northern betrayal.

The truth about this abortive social revolution is various and complex. It is clear that some of the Radical governments were indeed both extravagant and blatantly corrupt. Yet extravagance and corruption were common in this period in northern states and cities. Moreover, the Radical governments scored some real accomplishments, bringing to the South broader suffrage (for whites as well as Negroes), poor relief, and the beginnings of free, popular education.

Perhaps the key question to ask about Radical Reconstruction is whether it ever had a real chance of success: that is, of effecting a permanent change in southern institutions and customs. The answer is complex. Successful Reconstruction would have demanded either prolonged northern occupation or some degree of cooperation between southern whites and Negroes. For the first the northern people proved to have no enduring appetite. The second seemed more promising initially. Many southern whites did make an effort to accept the new situation (though many did not). Contrary to legend, some "scalawags" were well intentioned, just as some carpetbaggers were honest and some Negro leaders well informed and moderate. Yet any permanent alliance among these elements faced great difficulties. The cooperating southern whites were willing to accept Negro voting under white leadership; the Negroes demanded real political equality. Predictably, if not inevitably, the necessary coalition failed.

Violence against the Negroes and their political allies broke out on a larger and larger scale. At first determined to suppress the Ku Klux Klan and other terrorist organizations, Congress grew weary of the attempt. In one state after another, with differing degrees of forcible action, southern whites achieved victory at the polls. In 1877, when President Hayes withdrew the last federal troops, the cycle was complete; the South was under the rule of native whites. At first the new "lily-white" governments, mostly led by members of the prewar planter class, allowed Negroes some token participation in politics.

Then, in the nineties, governments claiming to represent the poor whites of the section came to power. Violently denouncing the alleged alliance of aristocrats and Negroes, these governments drove the southern Negroes almost entirely out of politics. This was done partly by pressure and partly by ingenious suffrage requirements—grandfather clauses, literacy tests, and the like—enforced against Negroes and not against whites.

SOCIAL RECONSTRUCTION

Since the Negroes never received the "forty acres and a mule" for which they had longed in 1865, they had to work for white landowners. Money to pay them was lacking, and the only possible solution was some form of tenantry. The result was the sharecrop and the crop-lien systems. Throughout the South sharecroppers, both white and Negro, received their seed, tools, and staple necessities from landlords to whom they turned over a third or a half of their produce. Most, and often all, of the rest went to pay long-standing debts accumulated by the tenants at country stores with high-monopoly prices and exorbitant rates of interest. The system was not slavery, and it got the crops planted and harvested. Yet the Negro farmer, forever in debt and unable to move, without education or political privileges, subject to white courts and occasionally to white terrorism, could hardly be called free.

In the 1880s the South, under white rule again, put on a spectacular drive for industry. Heavy inducements were offered to capital, and much was accomplished in steel, lumbering, tobacco, and, especially, textiles. Yet by the turn of the century's southern efforts had barely held even: the South's percentage of the nation's industry was about that of 1860. Even this, in a rapidly expanding economy, was a considerable achievement, but the price was heavy. In southern mill towns disease and child labor were endemic. Most of the profits of industry were flowing out of the section. Until World War II, the South remained both poor and overwhelmingly agrarian.

Perhaps the saddest chapter in all American history is the general acceptance, in the North, of the failure of so much effort. Thirty years after the war most people took for granted a southern system which included not only disfranchisement and rigid social segregation of the Negro but also recurrent violence. In 1892 and 1893, for example, more than 150 Negroes were lynched each year, often with sadistic tortures.

How could the people who had defied the Fugitive Slave Act, fought the war, and voted for Radical Reconstruction accept this situation? For one thing, it was easy to emphasize the seamy side—and it was a large one—of Radical Reconstruction, the greed and corruption with which the process had often been executed. Moreover, most people were convinced that racial differences made political equality impossible. Government, according to nineteenth-century science and social science, could do very little to change customs or alter society. There was, moreover, a bright side to the story. A great Civil War had been settled without executions or confiscations, and the two sides were beginning to be reconciled. It was easy to forget that the Negro was paying most of the bill for this reconciliation.

Responsive in its way to the drift of public opinion, the Supreme Court made its peace with the new situation. In the Civil Rights cases (1883) it decided that the Fourteenth Amendment did not prevent *individuals*, as opposed to states, from practicing discrimination. In Plessy *vs.* Ferguson (1896) the Court held that "separate but equal" accommodations for Negroes in trains (and by implication in restaurants, hotels, and the like) did not violate their rights. Few inquired very carefully whether accommodations were indeed equal.

The upshot, then, of the greatest struggle in American history seemed to be a tragic failure. Yet the story had not ended. The Negro had gained a few rights and a great many hopes. And neither in the North nor the South was the national conscience really at ease.

CONFLICTING HISTORICAL VIEWPOINTS

Was Reconstruction a Tragic Era?

Until the 1930s historians generally agreed that Reconstruction was a period characterized by sordid motives and human depravity. It was the "Age of Hate," "The Blackout of Honest Government," "The Dreadful Decade," and "The Tragic Era." In 1939, however, Francis Butler Simkins, a distinguished southern scholar, urged his fellow historians to adopt "a more critical, creative, and tolerant attitude" toward the period. In a notable essay (Journal of Southern History [1939]), Simkins suggested that the traditional interpretation was rooted in "the conviction that the Negro belongs to an innately inferior race."

Until Simkins's time most white students of Reconstruction did in fact approach their work with decidedly racist views. In the first serious history of the era, James Ford Rhodes's enormously influential History of the United States from the Compromise of 1850 (*7 vols., 1893–1906*), *blacks were described as "the most inferior race." Similarly, in John W. Burgess's* Reconstruction and the Constitution (*1902*)

Negroes were characterized as inherently inferior beings incapable of "subjecting passion to reason." Although Rhodes and Burgess were sharply critical of the motives and actions of congressional Radicals, the traditional interpretation of Reconstruction is best identified with the work of William A. Dunning. A Columbia University scholar and the author of Reconstruction, Political and Economic (*1907*), *Dunning and his many students uncovered a wealth of factual information about the period. But their work was seriously marred by their prosouthern and anti-Negro biases. They portrayed the postbellum scene in darkly tragic hues of unrelieved brutality, scandal, corruption, and licentiousness. According to the Dunningites, Reconstruction was not only unnecessary but harshly cruel to the prostrate South and ruthlessly exploitive of the ignorant freedmen.*

Black scholars, most notably W. E. B. Du Bois, author of Black Reconstruction (*1935*), *vigorously disputed Dunning School conclusions. But in an age of virtually unchallenged white supremacy few Caucasians thought to question simplistic characterizations of vindictive Radicals, venal carpetbaggers, reprobate scalawags, and barbarous darkies. A shift in the climate of racial opinion, however, ushered in a new era of Reconstruction historiography. Reflecting a growing national sensitivity to civil rights, historians since the 1930s have turned Dunning's conclusions inside out. First in a series of monographs and biographies, then later in such sweeping syntheses as John Hope Franklin's* Reconstruction After the Civil War (*1961*) *and Kenneth Stampp's* The Era of Reconstruction (*1965*), *revisionists discarded racial stereotypes and viewed the postbellum period in a generally favorable light. According to these modern scholars, traditional studies grossly exaggerated not only the extent of corruption, fraud, and black rule, but even the length of Radical control. Indeed, to both Franklin and Stampp, Reconstruction was a tragic era only in that it failed to insure blacks economic, political, and social equality.*

At present the revisionists are clearly in the ascendancy. But as Stampp has written, the revisionist's "ultimate and inevitable fate is one day to have his own revisions revised."

FOR FURTHER READING:

Herman Belz's *Reconstructing the Union* (1969) is a provocative study of Presidential Reconstruction. Representative traditional interpretations of Congressional Reconstruction include Walter L. Fleming, *The Sequel of Appomattox* (1919) and E. Merton Coulter, *The South During Reconstruction* (1947). H. K. Beale, *The Critical Year* (1930) and E. L.

McKitrick, *Andrew Johnson and Reconstruction* (1960)* offer conflicting views of Lincoln's successor. La Wanda and John Cox, *Politics, Principle, and Prejudice* (1963)* and David Donald's *The Politics of Reconstruction* are noteworthy revisionist works. Robert Cruden focuses on *The Negro in Reconstruction* (1969)* and Hans L. Trefousse sympathetically analyzes *The Radical Republicans* (1969). There are numerous state studies, but F. B. Simkins and R. H. Woody, *South Carolina During Reconstruction* (1932) and V. L. Wharton's *The Negro in Mississippi, 1865–1890* (1947)* are among the best. C. Vann Woodward's justly celebrated trilogy, *Reunion and Reaction* (1951)*, *Origins of the New South* (1951)* and *The Strange Career of Jim Crow* (1955)* are indispensable for understanding the South during the post-Reconstruction period.

Grady McWhiney, *Reconstruction and the Freedmen* (Berkeley Readings in American History, 1963)* is a documentary study.

---

* Available in paperback edition.

VALUE ADDED BY SELECTED INDUSTRIES, IN 1879 PRICES, FROM 1839 TO 1899 (IN BILLIONS OF DOLLARS)

Year	Total	Agricul-ture	Mining	Manufac-turing	Construc-tion
1899	11.75	3.92	0.55	6.26	1.02
1894	10.26	3.27	.39	5.48	1.12
1889	8.66	3.24	.35	4.16	.92
1884	7.30	3.00	.23	3.22	.86
1879	5.30	2.60	.15	1.96	.59
1874	4.30	1.98	.11	1.69	.52
1869	3.27	1.72	.07	1.08	.40
1859	2.69	1.49	.03	.86	.30
1854	2.32	1.32	.03	.68	.30
1849	1.66	.99	.02	.49	.16
1844	1.37	.94	.01	.29	.13
1839	1.09	.79	.01	.19	.11

(Adapted from *Historical Statistics of the United States* [1960], p. 139.)

The Triumph of American Industry
1865-1893

17

Like a vast and bloody wound, the Civil War seems to divide nineteenth-century American history into two parts. Yet America's industrial expansion, the most important tendency of the postwar years, was under way before the war and continued during it. This immense process would have taken place if slavery or secession had never been heard of and still would have transformed world history. American industrial growth was not unique: England had gone through a similar transformation earlier, Germany underwent one about the same time as the United States, and it was under way before the end of the century in Japan and other countries. But American industrialization was larger in scale than that of any other country and perhaps transformed the national culture more profoundly.

"THE SECOND AMERICAN REVOLUTION"

As we have seen, America had long been exploiting her unique advantages for economic growth. Since 1815, the market revolution had been under way. Like no other country, America had within her own borders nearly all necessary raw materials, a rapidly expanding market, and a swelling labor force. By the 1850s she had also an expanding and increasingly mechanized agriculture to feed her city workers, rich sources of capital, demonstrated inventive genius and managerial skill. East of the Mississippi the country was already provided with an adequate transportation network. The American railroad system was the biggest in the world and the country's most important single industry. Yet American trains still ran on British rails.

Many historians have credited America's industrial spurt to the Civil War itself. Yet as we have seen, according to one index, the value added by manufacturing, the century's largest percentage gains took place in prewar decades. Obviously, the war created certain immediate demands: woolen cloth for uniforms, shoes, blankets, and guns. Yet it can be argued that these necessities took productive resources away from more important endeavors. Indeed, one of America's great economic advantages in the nineteenth century was that *except* in the 1860s economic growth did not have to be shaped for military ends.

Another theory, advanced by Charles A. Beard and other historians, is that the Civil War was in reality a Second American Revolution in which industrialists, after several generations of frustrated effort, were able to capture control of the government and force it to do their will. This theory deserves a close look.

Until the Civil War, the theory says, the southern-western agrarian majority prevailed, first in Jefferson's and then again in Jackson's time. Thus industry was unable to achieve either a sufficiently protective tariff, an adequate banking system, or (because of sectional bickering) a transcontinental railroad. Now the industrialists seized control of the government in a three-stage operation. First, the Republican party attracted a part of the pivotal Midwest to the support of high tariffs by conceding free homesteads and other farmer-backed measures. Then, while the South was out of the Union and the agrarian majority correspondingly reduced, the spokesmen of industry jammed through Congress the legislation they had long wanted. Finally, through Radical Reconstruction the South was to be kept out of the national councils while the industrialists' program was perfected and entrenched.

Through this daring seizure of power, American industrialists had achieved: (1) a high protective tariff (beginning 1861); (2) a national banking system (1863) and the destruction of the state banks by punitive taxation (1865); (3) the right to import foreign laborers under contracts, signed abroad, which pledged their first year's wages for their transportation (1864; repealed, 1868; practice outlawed, 1884); and (4) a transcontinental railroad system lavishly supported by government land grants and loans (first legislation, 1861). Somewhat more complicated were the benefits gained from the system of wartime finance. Only a quarter of the costs of war were paid by taxation. The rest was handled by the sale of government bonds and the issuance of fiat money (greenbacks). The bonds, which paid 6 and 7 percent interest, could sometimes be bought in greenbacks which sank, at their lowest, to less than half their face value. Yet the same bonds were redeemed in gold. Thus smart investors could add 100 percent profit to the interest they had already received. Labor suffered severely from wartime inflation since wages lagged behind prices. Farmers suffered in the chronic deflation of the rest of the century. Only bankers and speculators profited throughout, and the result of government policy was, as Hamilton had said it should be, the accumulation of capital for investment in industry.

Careful research has shown that this thesis of a Second American Revolution, carried out consciously in the interest of businessmen and industrialists, is not valid. To begin with, industrialists and business-men were by no means united either on the issues of the Civil War and Reconstruction or on the economic program just mentioned. The system of war finance had grown in response to war emergency against the opposition of many powerful businessmen. Interest on govern-ment bonds was severely cut into by inflation. After the war, few businessmen were in favor of high tariff and financial deflation at the same time. Many of the politicians who demanded military rule for the South, like Thaddeus Stevens, were inflationists, though they were also often protectionists. The western banking community, on the other hand, supported hard money but opposed the high tariff and was generally in favor of a lenient policy toward the South. In short, the myth of an inside group, dictating economic policy in its own interests and using the slogans of war and Reconstruction to further its interests, must be discarded. In the minds of most people, including business-men, the war and Reconstruction were political and not economic struggles.

Yet it remains true that industry, whether or not anybody planned it that way, received important and unprecedented governmental sup-port during the war, reached unprecedented heights in wartime and continued to rise, with few interruptions, for the rest of the century. The railroads, in many ways the key to industrial expansion, were indeed given very heavy support by the federal government and by some states. Much of this aid came in the form of the government's most plentiful asset, land.

The banking and currency systems were, in the long run, unsatisfac-tory. Yet they served their wartime purpose for both government and industry. The greenback inflation helped pull the country out of depression and sparked the wartime boom. The national banking system provided a sound and uniform currency and also a steady market for government bonds, which were the basis for the new bank notes. Thus the government was provided with sufficient wartime revenue and could place with confidence its huge orders for munitions and supplies.

After the war the needs of an expanding economy were less well met. The supply of money was often insufficient and bore no relation to the changing needs of business. The banking system was inflexible, and there was still no central authority with power to damp down booms and prevent panics. Businessmen, divided among themselves and often prisoners, like other Americans, of rigid and obsolete economic theories, by no means agreed on what they wanted in the complex world of money and banking. If they had, they probably would have got it.

The triumph of industry was not, then, a planned and masterful capture of the government, and the war itself may have had little to do with the rate of expansion. Yet by the 1880s, if not earlier, industrial enterprise was playing a new role in America and contemporaries knew it. The change was partly cumulative and partly psychological. Before the war, industry had been a powerful competitor for public favor and attention. Now, its scale and achievements brought it clearly to the center of the stage. The great drama of exploiting, through private enterprise, the natural resources of a continent, dominated the public imagination. For some time Congress, the Supreme Court, the press, and the pulpit gave business enterprise their unstinting support. State banks, or serious sectional bickering about something as important as transcontinental railroads, seemed memories of the distant past. So, for a time, did Jeffersonian prejudices against the growth of cities and factories.

CONDITIONS OF GROWTH

In many areas outside of politics, postwar conditions were even more favorable to industrial expansion than the conditions which had brought about the boom of the fifties. To begin with, the agricultural revolution, which must precede and accompany any industrial revolution, continued to expand. It was becoming possible for fewer people to grow more food. Wheat furnishes a major example. On the prairies of Illinois and Indiana, in the new and booming spring wheat belt of Minnesota and North Dakota, in the great valley of California, and, in good years, even on the dry plains of Montana, new varieties of wheat produced bigger and bigger crops. Farmers learned to use machinery on an ever-increasing scale. The harvester was followed by the twine binder and the steam thresher. Finally, on the biggest and richest farms, great combines pulled by steam engines harvested and threshed at once. Gigantic elevators stored the wheat at railheads and river ports. Some of it went from there to the new roller mills of flour-producing centers; Minneapolis alone shipped over seven million barrels a year. Both wheat and flour were shipped abroad. American wheat became the mainstay of the British industrial population. European countries, worried about dependence on the United States, sent commissions to study American methods. Meanwhile the many expert speculators in American wheat kept an anxious eye on India, Russia, and Argentina.

Much the same story of geographical expansion, mechanization wherever possible, and entrance into an ever-widening market could be told, with important differences, of other American crops. Like Virginia tobacco in colonial times, American wheat, cotton, and cattle were part of a world economy. After 1870, with farm prices in general falling, trouble was in sight for American farmers, and farm problems were again to become a major headache for politicians. But to those interested in increasing industrial production, more and cheaper food seemed nothing but good news.

The mineral resources necessary for industry turned out to be even more plentiful than anybody had suspected. Deposits of coal and iron, the main essentials for heavy industry, were found within transportable range of each other in many places from the Appalachians to the Great Lakes. The center of copper production moved from Michigan to Montana and Arizona. Like the minerals, the timber of Wisconsin and the far Northwest seemed inexhaustible. The problem was not to save resources, but to multiply methods of using them ever faster.

Somewhat backward as yet in basic science, Americans contributed more than their share to the technological advance needed by industrial society. Some crucial improvements in basic industry, like the Bessemer and open-hearth processes for steel production, were of combined European and American origin. Perhaps because of the needs of a continent-sized democracy, Americans excelled in the field of communication, where they produced the telephone, the typewriter, and the linotype. The problems of new cities brought further adaptations of worldwide scientific advance. By the 1890s, electric street railways were taking Americans to work, and electric lights were beginning to brighten their streets and houses.

Population to man the factories and swell the markets continued to pour in from Europe and Asia. Between 1870 and 1900 the population of the United States grew from 38,500,000 to 76,000,000. More than 12,000,000 of this increase came from immigration. Many wondered whether this flood could be absorbed, but the needs of industry for workers, plus the old American commitment to free immigration, beat back the doubters.

Like people, money for investment flowed westward across the Atlantic. Most of the capital needed came, however, from American industry itself. It has been estimated that between 1869 and 1898 about 13 percent of the national income went into further industrial expansion. This high figure is partly explained by profitable and competitive innovation. In part, it reflects the energy and ability of the period's industrial capitalists, many of them more interested in expanding their vast and complex enterprises than in lavish living.

Nearly all conditions seemed to favor large-scale enterprise. Demand at first seemed inexhaustible. New urban populations with rising income needed consumer goods, and expanding agriculture and industry itself needed machines. Better transportation made it possible to concentrate on mechanization, which often meant bigness. In some industries, like steel, equipment became so expensive that only very big units could meet the fixed costs of production. Prices tended downward during the last half of the century, putting a premium on economic efficiency (sometimes, not always associated with large-scale production). Sharp depressions squeezed out weak competitors, underlining the disadvantages of cutthroat competition and suggesting the desirability of bringing rivals together.

Bigness could take many forms. A great firm might seek to monopolize a single product or a complex empire might tie together many related enterprises. (Carnegie's agglomeration, for instance, included iron and coal mines, shipping lines, steel plants, and rail factories.) Though many of the biggest firms were owned by single individuals or partnerships, the corporate form of organization was used more and more after 1875. It could draw most easily on wide sources of capital, and it could best evade regulation. When public hostility to bigness began to be a problem, gentlemen's agreements could take the place of outright mergers or able lawyers could work out new forms like trusts and holding companies.

Finally, a cause and a result of bigness was the country's rich supply of managerial skill. No other profession, in the period, offered so much wealth and prestige, none was as attractive to ability and ambition as the management of industry, whether or not divorced from its ownership.

Except for their daring, one can find little in common among the great industrialists of the period. Some, like Carnegie, exemplified the traditional poor-boy-to-millionaire pattern though most came from families well above the average in income and education. Some were ruthless pirates, indulging in every kind of misrepresentation and bribery, not hesitating to bring about disastrous panics in order to drive down the prices of stocks they wished to buy. Others were scrupulous Boston gentlemen who tolerated no associate whose moral character and probity were not impeccable. Some spent their money on Fifth Avenue palaces and baronial country estates or on Renaissance pictures. Many poured it out in unprecedented gifts for museums, libraries, and, above all, universities. A few hoarded it for future generations, but, most important, enough plowed it back into expanding production. In doing this, they were constantly assured by press and pulpit, they were benefiting the whole civilization.

THE ACHIEVEMENT

There was much reason for the widespread public admiration of the industrial accomplishment. Before the end of the century, industrial growth had scattered factories from Michigan to Georgia; drawn workers for them from the farms and villages of the world; linked them to mines, forests, and ports; and made the United States the greatest producer of wealth the world had ever seen.

The most spectacular accomplishment was railroad construction. The already dense network of the northeastern quarter of the country was consolidated and improved and the wrecked southern roads rebuilt. Daring engineers pushed five different railroads clear to the Pacific Coast, throwing steel bridges across the Mississippi, building tunnels and grades through the Rockies and the Sierras, crossing deserts where wood for ties and food for workers had to be brought from the East. Sometimes a whole population to use the railroad had to be brought from the East, too; railroad corporations played during this generation the role of the Virginia Company or the Ohio Company. Everywhere in the West the course of the railroads determined the future of the region. Towns that were bypassed faded away, while at main junctions and terminals whole new cities appeared. It is not surprising that the railroads dominated the politics of the period as they did its economy.

Steel, in midcentury still a luxury product associated with fine cutlery, became the mainstay of the railroad age. Not only was it used for rails, locomotives, bridges, and cars, but also for mining machinery, oil drilling equipment, and steam turbines, and for ships of the new navy and the girders for the first Chicago skyscrapers. By 1900 the United States produced as much steel as its next two competitors, England and Germany, combined; a year later the industry gave rise to the first billion-dollar merger. In a parallel development, oil, a worthless by-product of the salt industry at the beginning of the period, became the nation's chief illuminant and lubricant as well as the source of the Standard Oil Trust, the Rockefeller fortune, and thereby the University of Chicago.

Change affected most consumers' goods as well as heavy industry. Shoe manufacture, a traditional home of the craftsman and home-worker, became dependent on highly complex machines rented from the monopolistic United Shoe Machinery Company. Chicago slaughterhouses and packing plants put the village butcher out of business. Now long lines of cattle cars moved toward Chicago, refrigerator cars in the opposite direction, and meat millionaires built palaces on the lakefront.

Despite the large share of the new wealth that was plowed back into the industrial process, a great deal of it went to make life easier, more efficient, and more pleasant for millions of people. By the 1890s the rapid rise of sports, the sharp increase in high school education, the flood of cheap magazines and popular novels, even the bicycle craze and the popular song that commemorated it forever, testified to the presence of a large, relatively leisured middle class. As for the industrial workers, their wage rates stayed about the same during the period while the cost of living dropped. Between 1865 and 1900 real wages rose by something like a half, and the average working day inched downward from eleven hours to ten. If one were to disregard the disastrous impact of seasonal and cyclical unemployment, one could easily conclude that the factory worker made important gains.

By the end of the century, the decisive stage in the process of industrialization and urbanization was completed. Forty percent of the people were counted as urban in the 1900 census; that is, they lived in places of 2,500 or more. As the figure suggests, even this vast change can be exaggerated. As late as 1900 most Americans lived either in rural areas or in towns that would seem small and quiet indeed to their descendants today. More of them earned their living on farms than in factories, more of them were owners of businesses—sometimes of very small businesses—than were managerial employees of corporations. Yet nobody, from the most isolated farm in Vermont to the sleepiest village in Mississippi, was wholly unaffected by the power of industry.

Before the 1890s, comparatively few tried to balance the costs of industrialization against its benefits. Most Americans in these years assumed, as Jefferson had not, that factories and cities were not only good in themselves but peculiarly American. In terms of human happiness, the balance sheet can never be accurately drawn up. One can be sure, however, that such a change in a nation's way of life has to be paid for heavily, in one way or another, wherever it occurs, whether in Russia or England or America. Though in some ways industrialization was easier in this rich, expanding, ocean-guarded republic than anywhere else, it had its costs. Soon some people were to conclude that the moral, social, and psychic price of industrialization was on the same scale as its tangible benefits.

Only in the mid-1890s, when the third of the period's racking depressions concentrated attention on all the evils of the new way of life, did many Americans stop to regret the landmarks swept away, the traditional patterns destroyed, the difficult questions raised and not answered. Even then nearly everybody knew that the gigantic process could never be stopped. In terms used by economists, the economy of the United States was now mature. In other terms, there was a lot of maturing still to come.

CONFLICTING HISTORICAL VIEWPOINTS

Were Industrialists Robber Barons?

During the social unrest of the late nineteenth and early twentieth centuries, the American entrepreneur was much-maligned. As a class, one recent scholar has written, businessmen were often viewed in the populist and progressive eras as "avaricious rascals who habitually cheated and robbed investors and consumers, corrupted government, fought ruthlessly among themselves, and in general carried on preda tory activities comparable to those of the robber barons of medieval Europe." Thus, the poet Walt Whitman lamented "the depravity of the business classes of our country" and the journalist Henry D. Lloyd (Wealth Against Commonwealth [*1894*]) *indicted the entire system of American capitalism for greed and graft, and contempt for the common welfare. Among the severest critics of the captains of industry, of course, were such socialist writers as Gustavus Myers. In his indignant* History of Great American Fortunes (1907), *Myers portrayed post-Civil War entrepreneurs as unalloyed villains, grasping, ruthless and unscrupulous buccaneers who corrupted politics and crushed competition. But progressive scholars, although less doctrinaire, were scarcely more complimentary. Frederick Jackson Turner carefully distinguished Western builders of new industry from Eastern speculators in old enterprises, and Charles and Mary Beard scrupulously acknowledged the creative results of business expansion. But the businessman nevertheless fared poorly in progressive writings. In their masterful synthesis of progressive historical interpretation,* The Rise of American Civilization (*2 vols., 1927*), *the Beards compared the industrialists of the Gilded Age to "military captains" and "feudal chieftains" who amassed vast personal fortunes through "highly irregular and sometimes lawless methods, ruthless competition, menacing intrigues, and pitiless destruction of rivals."*

During the depression years of the 1930s, the businessman's reputation sank even lower than the Dow Jones industrial averages. Capitalism, many scholars believed, was morally and fiscally bankrupt and when Matthew Josephson published his brilliant polemic, The Robber Barons, *in 1934, only a few intellectuals thought to quarrel with his epithet.*

But as the memory of the Great Depression faded so too did the concept of the robber baron. Indeed, since World War II the businessman's stock in American historical writing has been decidedly bullish. In John D. Rockefeller: The Heroic Age of American Enterprise (*2 vols., 1940*) *the first major revisionist counterattack, Allan Nevins rehabilitated the reputation of one of the nation's most controversial industrialists. In this admiring study, and in a second biography of the same figure published thirteen years later, Nevins conceded that Rockefeller had engaged in legally and morally questionable conduct, but he praised him nevertheless as a constructive innovator who brought order to the chaotic American industrial scene. Disputing Josephson's charges that greed was the businessman's dominant motive, Nevins argued that post-Civil War industrial giants sought "competitive achievement, self-expression, and the imposition of their wills on a given environment."*

With the notable exception of such New Left scholars as Gabriel Kolko (Railroads and Regulation 1877–1916 [*1965*]), *most business historians have reflected this sympathetic interpretation. Writing in the World War II and Cold War eras, such entrepreneurial historians as Thomas C. Cochran and William*Miller (The Age of Enterprise [*1942*]), Alfred D. Chandler (Strategy and Structure: Chapters in the History of the Industrial Enterprise [*1962*]), and Edward C. Kirkland (Industry Comes of Age [*1961*]) have been generally appreciative of American industrial and technological achievement. Yet, while they clearly admire the entrepreneurial genius, they have shown more interest in analyzing and describing the structure and nature of American industrialism than the moral character of the American industrialist.*

FOR FURTHER READING:

Thomas C. Cochran's *Business in American Life* (1972) is a masterful overview by a mature scholar; and W. W. Rostow's *The Stages of Economic Growth* (1960) places American industrialization in a world perspective. Important histories of selected subjects include T. C. Cochran, *Railroad Leaders, 1845–90* (1953); Peter Temin, *Iron and Steel in Nineteenth-Century America* (1964); and Lee Benson, *Merchants, Farmers, and Railroads* (1955).

WESTERN HISTORY, 1860–1895

Mining Rushes	Indian Wars	Miscellaneous Events	States (in Capitals) and Territories
		1858 Butterfield Overland Express (transcontinental stage route)	
1859 Nevada (gold and silver) Colorado (gold)			1859 OREGON
1860–1866 Idaho (gold)			
1860		1861 Pony Express Pacific Telegraph	**1860**
		1862 Homestead Act	1861 KANSAS, Colorado, Nevada, Dakota
1862 Arizona (gold)	1862 Massacre of whites, Minnesota		1863 Arizona, Idaho
1862–1864 Montana (gold)	1864 Arapaho-Cheyenne War Massacre of Indians, Sand Creek, Colorado		1864 NEVADA, Montana
	1865–1867 War with Western Sioux		
1865		1866 Long Drive to Sedalia, Missouri	**1865**
1867 Wyoming (gold)	1867 Indian Peace Commission		1867 NEBRASKA
	1868 War on Southern Plains		1868 Wyoming
		1869 Union Pacific Railroad completed	
1870	1871 War in Texas Panhandle		**1870**
1873 Deeper portion of Comstock Lode, Nevada (richest strike ever)		1873 Timber Culture Act	
	1874 Red River War	1874 Barbed wire patented	
	1875–1876 War in Black Hills		

WESTERN HISTORY, 1860–1895 (continued)

Mining Rushes	Indian Wars	Miscellaneous Events	States (in Capitals) and Territories
1875			**1875**
1876 Black Hills, Dakota (gold)			1876 COLORADO
1877 Leadville, Colorado (silver, lead)	1877 Nez Percé uprising, Idaho	1877 Desert Land Act	
1879 Tombstone, Arizona (silver)		1878 Timber and Stone Act	
1880			**1880**
1882 Butte, Montana (copper)		1882–1883 Santa Fe, Southern Pacific, and Northern Pacific routes completed	
1885	Capture of Geronimo and end of Apache War	1885–1886 Disastrous winters, end of range cattle industry	**1885**
	1887 Dawes Act	1887 Drought and western farm crisis	
	1889–1890 Ghost Dance, battle of Wounded Knee	1889 First Oklahoma rush	1889 NORTH DAKOTA, SOUTH DAKOTA, MONTANA, WASHINGTON
			1890 WYOMING, IDAHO
1890		1893 Great Northern Railroad completed	**1890**

231

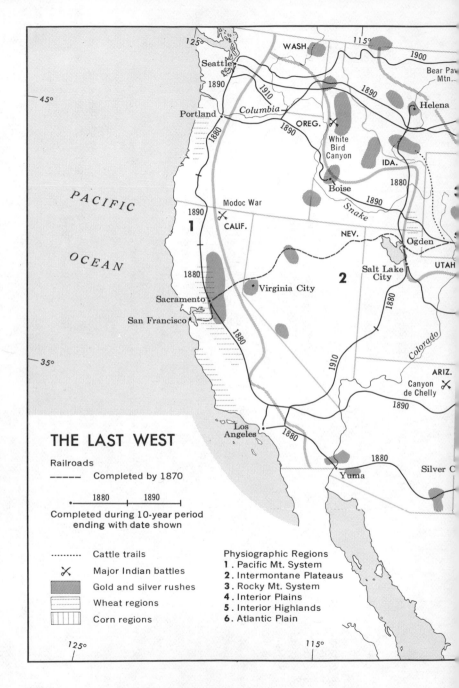

THE LAST WEST

Railroads

– – – – – Completed by 1870

•———1880———|———1890———|

Completed during 10-year period
ending with date shown

.... Cattle trails

✕ Major Indian battles

▓ Gold and silver rushes

▤ Wheat regions

▥ Corn regions

Physiographic Regions
1 . Pacific Mt. System
2 . Intermontane Plateaus
3 . Rocky Mt. System
4 . Interior Plains
5 . Interior Highlands
6 . Atlantic Plain

PACIFIC

OCEAN

WASH.

Seattle

1890

Portland

Columbia

OREG.

White
Bird
Canyon

Boise

Modoc War

CALIF.

1890

1

Sacramento

San Francisco

Virginia City

NEV.

Salt Lake
City

UTAH

Ogden

Helena

Bear Paw
Mtn.

IDA.

1880

Snake

1890

2

1880

Colorado

ARIZ.

Canyon
de Chelly

1890

Los
Angeles

1880

Yuma

1880

Silver C

1910

1880

1890

1880

1910

1900

1890

1890

1890

125°

115°

45°

35°

125°

115°

232

MONT. 1890 N. DAK. MINN.

Big
Mound ✕ Red 1880 Duluth WIS.

1880 Bismarck 1890 S. DAK. St. Paul 45°
MICH.

✕ Little
Bighorn WYO. 1890 1880
Lead
Wounded ✕ Milwaukee
Knee IOWA
Missouri NEBR. ILL. Chicago IND.

Line
of semi-aridity 1880
Cheyenne THE GREAT PLAINS
COLO. R Platte 4 MO.

Denver KANS. Kansas City St. Louis KY.
Abilene
Sand
Creek ✕ Dodge 1880 Arkansas TENN.
City OKLA. 5 ARK. 35°
1880 MISS.
Santa N. MEX. Round ✕ 1880 Mississippi
Fé Mtn. Washita 1880 1880
TEX.
1880 Dallas 1880 LA.
6 Red
El Paso 1890 1880 1880
New Orleans
Austin Houston
1890 1880 Galveston
San Rio Grande
Antonio Gulf of Mexico

0 100 200 300
MILES

105°

95°

233

The Last West
1860-1890

18

While the United States was struggling with the tragic heritage of an old region, it was also confronting the problems of a new one. Between 1860 and 1890, with no time out for the Civil War, half the present area of the country was occupied and exploited. In 1860 settlers were fast filling up the eastern parts of Kansas and Nebraska. San Francisco and Sacramento were bustling towns and farming was well established in the Willamette Valley of Oregon. Between these two distant borders, the Pacific settlements and the states just west of the Mississippi, lay a vast region of plains and mountains barely penetrated by European civilization.

Two things make this last and greatest West different from all earlier frontier regions. First, far more than ever before, this West was the frontier of an urban and industrial country. Second, its geography made it much less hospitable to settlers than any earlier American frontier.

PLAINS AND MOUNTAINS

From Jamestown to the Mississippi, however hard the conditions of frontier life, there had normally been enough rainfall for farming. Long accustomed to forest, pioneers of the last generation had encountered all the way from northeastern Illinois to eastern Kansas rich prairies covered with tall grass. They had learned to overcome their suspicion of treeless land. This was a lesson they were going to have to unlearn a little farther west.

Beyond the prairies lay the Great Plains, beginning at the invisible line of semiaridity. This runs a wavering course, more or less close to the ninety-eighth meridian, from eastern North Dakota to the Texas

Panhandle. Some of the area west of this line, particularly in its north-eastern parts, can profitably be farmed by those who know its ways. As one moves westward toward the Rockies, however, the Plains grow steadily higher, drier, and less fertile. In 1860 nothing grew there but the short native grass, and aside from the soldiers who guarded the wagon trails at a few forts, it remained in the possession of its ancient inhabitants. These included the jack rabbit, antelope, coyote, and buffalo, all biologically adapted to live in arid country, and the Plains Indian, culturally adapted to live on the buffalo.

Beyond the Plains lay the Rockies, rich in minerals and long penetrated by fur trappers, and beyond them the intermountain plateaus, mostly made up of sage-brush desert, jagged mountain ranges, and, in the Southwest, true desert dotted with cactus and mesquite. Some of the land in this forbidding province could be irrigated as had been demonstrated by Spaniards on the Mexican borderlands and Mormons near the Great Salt Lake. Beyond these plateaus lay the Pacific mountain chains, first the Sierra Nevada and the Cascades, then the Coast Ranges, with rich valleys between.

The whole area had been given the bad name of the Great American Desert. Only the strongest motives could draw settlers into it. The motives that did were the same as those which had first drawn Europeans across the Atlantic: religious freedom (in the case of the Mormons), adventure, independence from one's neighbors, and, most commonly of all, desire for land and gold.

THE MINERS

Between 1859 and 1864 gold rushes occurred at scattered points in what later became the states of Nevada, Colorado, Idaho, Montana, and Arizona. One more major rush, to the Black Hills of South Dakota, took place in 1876. In each case, the boom went through the same stages. First, when a strike was reported, thousands of prospective miners, some greenhorns, some veterans of other mining booms, rushed to the spot. Within a short time merchants, gamblers, prostitutes, and plain bandits appeared to divert some of the wealth from the lucky minority. A certain amount of murder might be tolerated, but claim jumping had to be prevented, and these remote communities soon worked out their own codes of mining law. Sometimes respectable citizens organized vigilante groups to bring about a semblance of rough justice. Before long the diggings were worked out, at least as far as they could be with the picks or washing pans or sluice boxes of the first comers. Sometimes they would close permanently, leaving only ghost towns. Sometimes a second metal would be found, and a second rush take place as in the cases of Colorado silver or Montana copper. Sometimes, as in Nevada in 1873, deeper digging would produce another bonanza. Often after the raw surface metal was gone, organized exploitation with expensive machinery and deeper drilling would produce richer results. Meantime the original prospectors, nearly always broke, would travel to some other likely wilderness, if not in the United States in Canada or Alaska or farther.

This haphazard but intense exploration of mineral resources doubled the world's gold supply with important results for American political history. Silver production, also sharply increased, created in a few western states a special economic interest that held its political power for more than half a century. In many cases, towns created to serve the needs of miners found other means of livelihood and survived when the mines closed. New populations, now present at scattered points in the West, raised new problems, particularly those of transportation and protection against Indians.

TRANSPORTATION

The Oregon migrants and California gold seekers had gone either around the Horn, across the Isthmus of Panama, or over the plains. Beginning in 1861, stage lines and wagon trains reached across the country. At the end of the 1850s, the enterprising firm of Russell, Majors and Waddell developed the spectacular pony express which actually got letters from Independence, Missouri, to San Francisco in ten days of fast relay riding. In 1861 this was displaced by a coast-to-coast telegraph line.

Meantime, the secession of the South had settled the old arguments about the route for a railway and in 1862 work was started under heavy government subsidy. The Central Pacific climbed painfully through the Sierra from Sacramento while the Union Pacific drove along the wagon train route from Omaha via Cheyenne to South Pass. In 1869 while the nation celebrated, top-hatted dignitaries met at Promontory Point, Utah, to watch the driving of the golden spike linking the two roads. For the next decade and a half, much of it a time of depression, the Union Pacific-Central Pacific remained the only through route from coast to coast. Then in the prosperous early 1880s three more lines were completed: the Southern Pacific and the Santa Fe systems through the Southwest and the Northern Pacific from St. Paul to Portland. In 1893 a fourth road, the Great Northern, connected St. Paul and Seattle by a route still further north. This last road, unlike its competitors, got along without governmental subsidy, chiefly by promoting the development of its region.

THE INDIAN TRAGEDY

Penetration of the plains and mountains by miners, migrants, and stage coaches had long since made Indian troubles inevitable. The long and bloody struggle for the last West is one of the least pleasant stories in American history. Probably no peaceful solution was possible of this conflict between an aggressive, expanding nineteenth-century civilization and a nomadic, stone-age culture dependent on vast hunting spaces. Yet, as in the case of Reconstruction, mistakes made a hard problem worse. Part of the fault lay with divided councils, civilian administrators squabbling with soldiers, soldiers disagreeing among themselves, settlers arguing with eastern humanitarians. Part of the long tragedy arose from inevitable anger over traditional Indian methods of war. Yet no Indian atrocity is more grisly than such white actions as the Sand Creek massacre of 1864 when several hundred men, women, and children of a tribe trying to surrender were exterminated and their bodies mutilated by a detachment of United States troops.

Many Indians, from the Utes of the Great Basin and the Nez Percés of Idaho to the Modocs of northern California, fought the white man at one time or another. But the most serious opponents of frontier advance were the Sioux of the Northern Plains and the Apache of the Southwest. Divided into small, efficient war bands led by such resourceful leaders as Red Cloud and Crazy Horse, the Sioux proved remarkably adept at highspeed, mounted warfare. In position on their swift ponies, they were expert with the short bow and later with rifles, and they confronted their white enemies with little more target than a heel and a hand. The Apache, who had been fighting Mexicans for years, were equally dangerous and still more elusive in their own country of desert and rocky canyon.

The long struggle with the Plains Indians began with a Sioux massacre of whites in Minnesota in 1862. Fierce fighting with Sioux and many other tribes continued through the Civil War years and sporadically in the 1870s. The last serious Sioux war broke out in 1876 when the Dakota gold rush penetrated the Black Hills, recently guaranteed to the Indians. But as late as 1890, the ghost dance frenzy on the Northern Sioux reservation led to an uprising and one last tragic slaughter at Wounded Knee, South Dakota. Long before this the Plains Indian cause had become hopeless with the slaughter of the buffalo. The animals, once among the most numerous in the world, were almost exterminated in the decade after 1870 by meat hunters, sportsmen, and finally by professionals catering to the eastern demand for hides. Meantime the Apache wars in the Southwest dragged on until Geronimo, the last important chief, was captured in 1885.

Ever since the Monroe administration, the government's official policy had been to move the Indians beyond the reach of the white frontier. Once not only Oklahoma but the whole plains had been talked about as permanent Indian country. Inevitably, reservations had become smaller and more crowded with the advance of the settlers, and forced resettlement had been supplemented with doles of beef, staples, and clothing.

As always in American history foolish and cruel policies eventually produced protest campaigns, some of them effective. As the Indian menace ebbed, eastern friends of the Indian argued with increasing effectiveness that a policy amounting to conquest and pauperization was not tolerable. The Indian, reformers argued, should be civilized and assimilated rather than maintained in primitive tribal condition. This accorded well with nineteenth-century social theory and also, at times, with the wish of western settlers to break up reservations. After a number of minor reforms the Dawes Act of 1887 reversed Indian policy. Tribal authority and ownership of land was gradually to be extinguished, and reservation land was to be parceled out to individual Indians, each head of family receiving 160 acres. Such allotments were to be held in trust pending complete ownership after twenty-five years. Indians living in nontribal fashion were to become citizens. Land not so parceled out could be sold by the government to individual settlers with the proceeds going toward Indian education.

This well-intentioned statute proved disastrous to the Indians. Most of the reservation land went to white settlers. Tribal authority was destroyed, and individual Indians were often victimized by white neighbors. Some received allotments too soon; others were deprived of incentive by the waiting period. In 1934 government policy was reversed again by the Indian Reorganization Act, designed to protect what remained of tribal life.

THE OPEN RANGE

Before the Indians and buffaloes had quite vanished, the plains began to be occupied by the advance guard of the expanding American economy in the form of cattle. The range cattle industry, so much the staple of legend that it is hard to see the reality, was actually a boom-and-bust episode typical of the period's economic history.

Longhorn cattle were developed in Texas, and there, too, the Anglo-American cowboy got his distinctive dress, his high-backed saddle, and some of his vocabulary. Feed was free on the unoccupied grassland and the only thing lacking was a market. This was provided when railroads reached Kansas in the 1860s. Huge herds of steers could now be driven fifteen hundred miles across the plains from Texas to

Sedalia, Missouri, or Abilene and Dodge City, Kansas. Thence they could be shipped to packing centers. The long drive north from Texas was a dangerous and difficult business beset by Indians, angry homesteaders, diseases, drought, and the tendency of the animals themselves to panic and stampede. It is not surprising that when the herds were safely penned in the railhead towns the cowboys sometimes behaved like sailors in from a long voyage.

Texas longhorns were wiry beasts, and soon it proved more profitable to drive them still farther and fatten them up on the open grasslands of western Kansas and Nebraska, the Dakotas, Wyoming, and even Montana. Sometimes the strain was improved by bulls shipped in from further east. For a while free grass, cheap cattle, and rising demand brought about boom conditions. Romance attracted such eastern dudes as Theodore Roosevelt, who had his fling as a rancher in South Dakota, and 30 percent dividends attracted English syndicates. Soon, inevitably, even the vast plains became overcrowded. As in the mining camps, competition was regulated by semilegal codes. Cattlemen's associations divided up the government-owned unfenced range, regulated the annual roundup when new calves were separated and branded, and dealt summarily with rustlers.

By the early 1880s, two new enemies of the cattle industry appeared. The first of these was the prairie farmer advancing hopefully onto the dry plains and fencing the land. The second was sheep. The sheep industry had spread from the New Mexico plateaus via the Colorado parks and Utah tablelands to the western plains. According to cattlemen, sheep cropped the range too close, destroyed turf with their hooves, and drove away by their lowly presence the superior and first-coming cattle.

The end of the open-range cattle industry came with the disastrous winters of 1885–1886 and 1886–1887 when the grass was hidden under deep snow and millions of cattle froze and starved. From this point on the successful cattleman abandoned the old wide-open ways, fenced his range, scientifically improved his herd, and put his indignant cowboys to growing feed for the winter.

THE FARMERS

In the thirty years after the Civil War more land was settled than in the whole of American history before that time. This great movement of population belonged only in part to the history of the Great Plains. Much of the new population completed the job of settling the fertile prairies. Yet when the farmers solidly occupied eastern Kansas, Nebraska, and the Dakotas up to the line of semiaridity, they inevitably spilled over it. Some tried their luck as far west as Wyoming and Montana. In many ways, the experience of these western settlers was like that of prairie farmers in the past generation. In other ways, both the new kind of country and the changing national economy made this last chapter of frontier farming different.

This was the first migration of farmers to take place since that great farmer victory, the passage of the Homestead Act of 1862. Under this law any head of family who lived on and cultivated his claim for five years could get title to 160 acres free. This amount of land seemed generous to legislators familiar with conditions farther east, but on the Great Plains, where farming cost more and was more risky, it was not enough to make a profitable venture. Later legislation made some attempt at adaptation to western realities. The Timber Culture Act of 1873 allowed a homesteader another 160 acres if he planted at least a quarter of it in trees. The Desert Land Act of 1877, lobbied through by cattlemen, allowed a prospective irrigator of dry lands to buy 649 acres. He was to pay twenty-five cents an acre down and would get title in three years on payment of the balance, provided he could prove he had irrigated a portion of the land. The Stone and Timber Act permitted the purchase of western lands not suitable for farming but valuable—sometimes very valuable—for timber or stone at the absurdly low price of $2.50 an acre.

All these laws, like many earlier American land laws, played into the hands of speculators, and many of them invited fraud. Cattle, lumber, and land companies used their employees as false homesteaders and hired new immigrants for the same purpose. The country was simply too big for the government to check up on everything that was happening. In the end, all but a small part of the land settled by farmers in this period was acquired not from the federal government directly but from intermediaries. Some of it came from land companies and some from western states which had received land under the Morrill Act for the purpose of promoting education.

The biggest of all the land sellers, however, were the railroads. The first transcontinentals and some other roads had received enormous grants along their rights of way. Their main interest was not in revenue from direct sale of this land but in building population in the areas they served. Thus they offered favorable terms, free inspection trips, agricultural information, and credit. They also advertised, and it is not surprising that the Great Plains sounded, in their promotional litera- ture, a good deal like the Land of Canaan. Railroad agents together with state immigration bureaus and steamship line employees flooded Europe with leaflets about the low prices, phenomenal yields, and easy profits of western farming. In 1882, the peak year for this kind of migration, 105,000 Scandinavians and 250,000 Germans crossed the ocean, most of the former and many of the latter heading for western farms.

As farmers, whether from Illinois or Norway, moved farther west they confronted a host of new problems. Where there were no trees, they had to spend their first winters in dugouts or houses made of thick plains sod. To keep warm they had to burn buffalo or cattle dung, corncobs, or hay. Fencing presented a worse problem until the invention of barbed wire in 1874 and its rapid spread. To make wells, they had to dig down hundreds of feet in the drier areas. To save what surface moisture there was, they had to learn to plow very deep and then harrow over the top to make a dust mulch. Finally, machines were needed to harvest large areas fast in this region of dangerously changeable weather.

For fencing, for well machinery and windmills to pump the water once found, for steel or chilled-iron plows to break tough sod, for harvesters, threshers, and binders, as well as for land itself, the farmer needed credit. Fortunately or unfortunately, in the good times of the early 1880s, plenty of credit was available at high rates of interest.

In the Red River Valley of Dakota as in the San Joaquin Valley of California, wheat ranches of scores of thousands of acres gave an early foretaste of industrialized agriculture. Elsewhere in the new areas, a more modest prosperity prevailed. Farmers built better houses; farming towns paved their streets and improved their schools. The price of land skyrocketed.

To many, it seemed that the Great American Desert had at last been conquered. Advances had been made in techniques of "dry farming," and in the use of new varieties of wheat which could resist drought and cold. As always, the American farmer hoped that good times would continue indefinitely. Experts appeared who said that the climate of the plains was changing: tree planting, irrigation, even the building of railroads and telegraphs were somehow bringing more rain.

Actually, the Great Plains were nearing the end of one of their regular cycles of relatively greater rainfall. In 1887 the first of a series of dry summers withered the crops in the fields. With this grim warning of trouble, credit stopped flowing westward and the boom collapsed. Many of those who had moved beyond the line of semiaridity hastened back in despair. Half the population of western Kansas disappeared in four years, and whole towns were deserted as Colorado mining towns had been when the vein ran out. This disaster, peculiar to the new region in its origins, ushered in a general agricultural depression which in turn gave place to an over-all financial collapse. And unlike other farm crises, this one could not be solved by opening new land at low prices. There was nowhere to go.

THE HERITAGE OF THE FRONTIER

In 1893 the historian Frederick Jackson Turner said that a period of American history had ended in 1890 with the disappearance of the frontier. So far, the frontier had molded American character. It had also, Turner and his followers believed, served as a safety valve for urban discontents. Without it, America would be very different.

Much of this "frontier theory" has been disputed. For instance, it has been pointed out that more government land was disposed of in the decade after 1890 than in the decade before. "Free land," moreover, had always been something of a delusion. Much had gone to speculators rather than directly to small farmers. It had always been particularly difficult for a city worker, without training, equipment, or credit, to "go west." In fact, since the Civil War at least, most people seeking to escape poverty had moved in the opposite direction, from the farm to the city.

Yet it was true, as Turner said, that the 1890 census for the first time found no continuous border beyond which the country was unsettled. It was true also that a great many people in the 1890s *felt* that a period was ending with the filling up of the West and that American problems in the future would be different and perhaps more difficult. While few historians agree with Turner that American individualism, equalitarianism, and nationalism come entirely from the West, few would deny that the American temperament owes something to both the reality and the legend of the frontier.

One obvious legacy of the West, and of this last West in particular, was a habit of violence. From vigilantes, frontier sheriffs, and cattlemen's associations the West drew a tradition of rough justice. From mining camps and cowtowns and end-of-track railroad settlements it drew another of just plain roughhouse. And in the twentieth century, violence sometimes hung on in still less attractive forms like the bloody labor wars of Colorado or the persistently high homicide rates of some western states. Perhaps violence was inseparable from some of the more attractive traits of the frontier legend—the devotion to individual freedom and equality we like to think of as western.

In politics the West has shown certain consistent traits. Sometimes the western liking for innovation has made easterners think it radical. Four far-western states pioneered in women's suffrage. The Initiative and Referendum came from the West and so did that last extreme of equalitarianism, the popular recall of judicial decisions. Yet such vigorous ultraconservatives as senators McCarran of Nevada and Goldwater of Arizona are also characteristically western. Sometimes western radicalism and western conservatism are inextricably blended in the same people. What Westerners have in common, perhaps, is a fierce devotion to individual independence, a contempt for tradition, a willingness to try something new, a delight above all in defying whatever mysterious forces are currently meant by the term "the East."

FOR FURTHER READING:

R. A. Billington, *Westward Expansion* (1949), is a usable general history of the West, and his *America's Frontier Heritage* (1966) offers a reappraisal of the Turner hypothesis. L. R. Hafen and C. C. Rister, *Western America* (1941), is a detailed account of the trans-Mississippi region. Walter P. Webb, *The Great Plains* (1931)*, is a fascinating and controversial interpretation of the region by a devoted native. Rodman Paul's *Mining Frontiers of the Far West, 1848–1880* (1963)* is the most scholarly overview of the subject but it does not supplant Mark Twain's *Roughing It* (1872)*. J. D. W. Guice, *The Rocky Mountain Bench* (1972), comments on the quality of frontier justice. Summaries of United States Indian policy in the period are L. B. Priest, *Uncle Sam's Stepchildren* (1942), and Wilcomb E. Washburn, *Red Man's Land— White Man's Law: A Study of the Past and Present Status of the American Indian* (1971). Angie Debo's *A History of the Indians in the United States* (1970) is an excellent survey; and Dee Brown's *Bury My Heart at Wounded Knee* (1971) is a passionate account of the Indian wars. There are many books on the cattle kingdom, including E. S. Osgood, *The Day of the Cattleman* (1929)*; E. E. Dale, *The Range Cattle Industry* (1930); and Louis Pelzer, *The Cattleman's Frontier* (1936). Joe B. Frantz and Julian E. Choate, Jr. examine *The American Cowboy* (1955); and Philip Durham and Everett L. Jones focus on *The Negro Cowboys* (1965). The problems of the plains farmer are authoritatively discussed by F. A. Shannon, *The Farmer's Last Frontier* (1945); and effectively portrayed in the works of Hamlin Garland, especially *Main Travelled Roads* (1891)*. The social history of the northern plains is discussed by Everett Dick, *The Sod-House Frontier* (1937), and the special problems of the Scandinavian immigrant are depicted in Ole Rolvaag, *Giants in the Earth* (1927). R. M. Robbins, *Our Landed Heritage* (1942)*, is a survey of public land policy. Henry Nash Smith, *Virgin Land: The American West as Symbol and Myth* (1950)*, is an important and highly sophisticated interpretation of the effect of the West on American thought and emotion.

---

* Available in paperback edition.

The Political Parade
1868-1892
19

The politics of the generation after the Civil War are generally considered one of the least important and most sordid topics in American history. During this period, we have often been assured, the American people were concentrating on industrial development. Politics became a meaningless side show in which second-rate statesmen made pompous speeches while special interests maneuvered for advantage behind the scenes. This picture has much truth in it, but it is not complete. Much was at stake, though the campaign slogans did not always reflect the real issues.

THE STAKES OF THE GAME

Politics were, for instance, deeply affected by the period's three depressions: the major one from 1873 to 1879, the minor one of the mid-1880s, and the collapse initiated by the panic of 1893. These depressions and related events such as the fall of farm prices in 1869 and 1887 greatly influenced people's political behavior. They did not, however, produce effective governmental action. Only in the depression of the mid-1890s did demands for relief and remedy absorb political argument briefly, and even then the call for action was temporarily rejected. Throughout the period, depressions affected people mainly by making them vote for the party out of power. They also influenced their attitude toward the two big economic arguments of the period, those over the tariff and the currency.

According to the period's dominant economic theory, it was not part of the government's duty to interfere with the business cycle. Distress would always be remedied in the long run by the action of the invisible, all-powerful laws of political economy. The government's role in the economic sphere was simple: (1) it should raise enough money for its own modest wants by equitable means; (2) it should provide a sound currency; and (3) perhaps (there was disagreement on this point) it should seek to advance the national products in the international market. The trouble was that the Civil War had thrown these traditional economic functions way out of kilter. In its great need the government had raised huge sums by any means available. It had placed internal taxes on everything in sight from coal and iron to billiard tables. It had, for the first time, taxed incomes. Partly to make up for these taxes, it had increased the moderate prewar protective tariff. It had issued $450 million worth of fiat money, the greenbacks, and floated immense loans. Now, most people agreed, the problem was to get rid of these burdens and go back to the simple old ways. This proved harder than it sounded.

It was easy enough to remove the income tax and other internal taxes, and this was largely accomplished by 1872. This being done, it seemed obvious that the tariff came next. Many people thought that the high wartime rates constituted unfair favors to special interests and placed a heavy burden on consumers. At first, most politicians took it for granted that the rates must go down. Somehow, though, tariff reduction bills that passed one house tended to be amended piecemeal in the other and then again in conference committee until they were no longer reduction bills.

Part of the difficulty lay in the nature of Congress in which each member represented his constituents and, consequently, very often a geographical and economic special interest. Each commodity was likely to have its own powerful spokesman. It soon developed that the easiest way to compromise between two conflicting interests, such as raw wool and woolen textiles or raw sugar and refined sugar, was to do some kind of favor for each. Thus, despite many attempts, wartime rates were never substantially and permanently lowered. By 1890 the Republican party and a minority of the Democrats were openly committed to raising protection still higher, though the opposition continued to be both sizable and fervent. Certainly this issue was a real one: the rates on steel rails or woolens mattered a great deal to some people and the price of sugar, for instance, to others.

A problem which the high tariff brought with it—a strange one for modern readers—was the treasury surplus. Governmental functions were so comparatively simple that increased revenues could not easily be spent. Consequently too much of the limited supply of money accumulated in the treasury. One way to handle this problem was suggested by Grover Cleveland in 1888: lower the protective tariff. Other suggestions, however, proved more politically appealing. One could, for instance, lower the nonprotective tariff rates on articles like coffee, tea, or sugar which were not made in this country. This was done in 1872 and again in 1890. It had the advantage of reducing the income of the government only and not of private interests. Or there were always veterans' pensions, river and harbor improvements, and subsidies to silver miners, railroad builders, and other powerful groups.

The other main economic argument arising from Civil War finance centered upon inflation. Right after the war, as we have seen, businessmen were deeply divided on this matter and so were the still prosperous farmers. Gradually, however, as farm prices sank in the 1870s and then again in the late 1880s and 1890s, farm opinion turned toward inflation. At the same time, bankers, eastern editors, and some businessmen became more and more convinced that tampering with the value of money was dishonest and invited disaster. Many economists today would agree that the country's money supply during the whole period was insufficient and inflexible. Certainly many contemporaries believed this as a result of their own bitter experiences.

Three main methods of inflation attracted widespread support. The first was the suggestion, sometimes called the Ohio Idea and incorporated in the Democratic platform in 1868, that the government bonds be paid in the fluctuating greenback currency instead of in gold. Congress turned down this suggestion decidedly in 1869, resolving to pay the bondholders in "coin or its equivalent." It proved possible, however, to refund the bonds at lower rates of interest.

The next method centered upon the greenbacks, toward which there were three different attitudes. One group said more of the "money of the people" should be issued to relieve financial tightness. Another said that the existing greenbacks should be retired as fast as possible. A third, the one which won the argument, said that existing greenbacks should remain in circulation but no more should be issued. In 1875 Congress resolved that $300 million in greenbacks should be left in circulation, but that on January 1, 1879, greenbacks should be made redeemable in gold. Despite a rise, during the depression of the late 1870s, of angry demands for more greenbacks, this policy was carried out on time. In the good times of the early 1880s, agitation against this accomplished fact gradually declined.

The third proposal to get a big following was the demand for "free" coinage of silver. Traditionally, gold and silver had been the basis of American money, and since 1834 the official ratio between the value of the two metals had been sixteen to one. Since this undervalued silver in terms of world prices, people hoarded the silver dollars and they gradually disappeared. In accordance with Gresham's Law, the "cheap money drove out the dear." In 1873 the coinage of silver was quietly ended. In the decade after this, however, the huge silver strikes of the Far West greatly increased the supply of silver. Now, if the silver dollar had been coined at the old ratio, it would have been the cheaper, and therefore the dominant, coin. This would have expanded the currency and also helped the silver-mining interests, strategically located in underpopulated western states and therefore disproportionately strong in the Senate.

The gold standard, the money of imperial Britain and of international bankers, was blamed for all the farmer's troubles. Pressure to go back to free coinage of silver at sixteen to one became almost irresistible, and twice Congress was forced to make a half-hearted concession to the silver forces. In 1878 the Bland-Allison Act directed the Treasury to purchase $2 to $4 million worth of silver bullion a month at market prices and to coin it into dollars. In 1890 the Sherman Silver Purchase Act required the purchase of the whole output of the silver mines and the issuance thereon of treasury notes. However, by action of the Secretary of the Treasury, these notes, like the silver dollars coined under the previous legislation, remained convertible into gold on demand so the gold standard was still intact. Despite their lack of major victories, the inflationists remained strong in the West and in Congress.

Aside from the tariff and money, the main recurrent issue was political reform. From the late 1870s on, it became painfully clear that the government did not, as standard theory said it should, stay out of economic competition. Its favors in terms of tariffs and tax remissions and subsidies were bought by influence and even money. Some members of the well-established eastern middle class became deeply aroused on moral grounds. Perhaps they were alarmed also by the power of the new rich, who did not share their own traditions of public service. In any case these essentially conservative reformers, Republican by normal allegiance but independent by conviction, became a surprisingly powerful influence. With parties as evenly balanced as they were, professional politicians might hate the unreliable "mugwumps," but they could not ignore them.

The chief proposal of these reformers was the development of a federal civil service. This would end bribery and corruption, take the power of appointment away from unscrupulous politicians, and perhaps create a class of devoted, impartial public servants like those said to exist in England and Germany.

"Snivel service," as the indignant professional politicians called the movement, never achieved its ideal of completely just, impartial administration. It did, however, make it harder to get away with the kind of outright fraud and theft that had become common in the Grant administration. Some of the most powerful politicians of the day were kept out of the presidency because their records were not pure enough to satisfy the reform element. And after many frustrations the civil service movement did finally secure, in 1883, the passage of the Pendleton Act. Under this some federal offices were filled by competitive examination. Since that time presidents have frequently added to the number of offices under civil service, especially when the opposing party has been about to come to power. The increase of federal employees has, however, prevented reform from destroying traditional political methods.

Tariff, money, and reform were the most important of the obvious political issues, and, underlying these, business depressions played a big part in politics. On the surface, however, campaigns were fought over whatever false issue lent itself best to emotional slogans, torchlight parades, and bitter hatreds more or less forgotten between elections. The first of these false issues, sadly enough, was Reconstruction—a real and tragic problem subordinated to the political battle. While people lost interest in the fate of the southern Negro, Republican politicians "waved the bloody shirt," blaming their opponents for all the horrors of war. Conversely, southerners and Democrats dwelt on the horrors of Negro rule.

After attacks on rebels, Negroes, and carpetbaggers began to pall, there were always Catholics, immigrants, and foreigners in general. One big section of the population could be counted on to respond to fear of the Pope, and another always cheered an attack on Great Britain. Finally, the war records, drinking habits, appearance, and marital life of leading candidates could be attacked.

THE RULES AND THE PLAYERS

Part of the explanation of the character of post-Civil War politics lies in two great political facts: the overwhelming power of Congress and the even division between the two great parties. In Reconstruction, Congress had broken the power of the executive. Real power was centered in the Senate. Powerful and arrogant, some leading Senators had built nearly unbeatable personal machines in their home states. Both state and federal officeholders, appointed at their behest, could be assessed for campaign contributions. When this was theoretically outlawed by the Pendleton Act, local business interests could still be heavily tapped. Thus the right kind of governors and Congressmen would be elected, and a subservient legislature would send the real ruler of the state back again and again to the Senate. With the presidency weakened, there was no powerful advocate for general national needs, and politics had to be carried on by log-rolling, that is, by the trading of one particular favor for another.

The Civil War and Reconstruction demoralized the Democratic party, but by no means destroyed it. Though the Republicans held the presidency during most of the period, the Democrats actually won a popular plurality more often and controlled the lower House more than half the time. National elections often depended on a few thousand well-distributed votes.

Since no single interest group commanded a majority, each party had to appeal to many elements. The Republicans could count on the Union veterans and the Negroes, when and where they could vote. Those businessmen who favored the high protective tariff voted Republican and so, usually, did believers in the gold standard (though many western Republicans were inflationists). In good times, midwestern farmers could be counted on for Republican votes. To a large group of respectable middle-class Protestants, it was unthinkable to vote Democratic. The clergyman who said in 1884 that the Democrats were the party of "Rum, Romanism, and Rebellion" went too far and may have lost the election for his candidate, but he voiced a stereotype many took for granted.

After Reconstruction, the Democrats could start with the Solid South. Most immigrants in the coastal cities, neglected by Anglo-Saxon Republicans and helped by efficient Democratic bosses, were also safely Democratic. Western farmers and much of labor tended to vote Democratic when times were bad. Thus the Democrats were always potentially a party of moderate protest, of agitation for low tariffs, and of cheap money. Yet in the East and Midwest as well as the South, some of the party leaders were ultrarespectable lawyers and businessmen. This kind of conservative Democrat, often interested in foreign trade, might favor a low tariff but oppose any other kind of change as vigorously as any Republican.

Thus each party was divided. The Republican factions were three. The "Stalwarts" were all-out believers in party regularity and the bloody shirt. At the opposite extreme were the many Republican reformers. Between these two were the "Half-Breeds," much like the Stalwarts but less blatant. The Democrats included Bourbon reactionaries and near radicals. In presidential years, therefore, each party tended to select a colorless compromise candidate and write a meaningless platform. Precisely because it was necessary to play down divisive issues, it was necessary to play up personalities, scandals, and party regularity. In crucial states in tight years even bribery and violence were not rare.

Did the system work well? The country and its industry expanded; the presidents and some other politicians were honest and reasonably able men. Party discipline, growing stronger through this period, got the government's essential business done and usually kept the most divisive issues out of politics. Interest groups were able to influence government, though seldom to dominate it altogether.

The system made for stability rather than innovation. In relatively peaceful times it satisfied most people; when discontent raised its head, political habits had to change.

THE GRANT ERA

When Grant was elected in 1868, many people expected a dignified, masterly administration in the Washington tradition. Naturally, the chief national hero was flattered by politicians and big businessmen. Equally naturally Grant, who before the war had had little interest in politics and no experience of success, enjoyed the flattery. Originally inclined toward a lenient Reconstruction policy, he was skillfully maneuvered by the Radicals into their camp. His appointments dismayed his admirers. Though they included real statesmen like Hamilton Fish, the New York aristocrat who became Secretary of State, they also included routine politicians, incompetents, seedy relatives of the Grants, military men out of jobs, and plain crooks. Grant's own honesty made his political naiveté all the more tragic.

In financial matters Grant was moderately conservative, vetoing a measure to increase the greenbacks but battling the Supreme Court to defend the validity of those in circulation. Secretary Fish handled foreign affairs with surprising effectiveness. In 1871, the difficult issues arising out of England's wartime friendliness to the Confederacy were sensibly settled by arbitration. To placate reformers, a Civil Service commission was set up, but it was not allowed to interfere with serious politics.

By 1872 the reformers were tired of Radical Reconstruction, irritated by the failure of tariff reduction, and disgusted by the administration's moral laxity. Determined to block Grant's reelection, they held a separate Liberal Republican convention and nominated for the presidency the veteran reformer and crusading editor Horace Greeley. Hoping to make a "new departure" and end the constant attacks on their patriotism, the Democrats nominated Greeley also. As a former Whig, Republican and abolitionist, Greeley was a strange Democratic candidate. Vulnerable to ridicule for his many and sometimes contradictory causes, somehow a relic of the prewar past, Greeley was disastrously beaten.

With Grant reelected and reformers discredited, the way seemed clear for Stalwart domination. However, the Democrats captured the House of Representatives in the depression year 1874 and used their victory to investigate the administration. A sinister pattern seemed to repeat itself in one department after another: the purchase of political favors for money. Corruption of this sort touched great causes like the building of the Union Pacific; it honeycombed the Indian Service, the Freedmen's Bureau, and the collection of internal revenue; it touched ambassadors, cabinet members, and even the President's private secretary. Before the end the hero of Appomattox realized that something was the matter and apologized on the ground of his own political inexperience.

THE DISPUTED ELECTION

By 1876 Republican regimes remained in power in only three southern states. With the South back on their side and many northerners hostile to the administration, it seemed likely that the Democrats would return to power. To prevent this unthinkable disaster, the Republicans nominated the honest and able, though rather uninspiring, Rutherford B. Hayes of Ohio. The Democrats also bid for the reformers by nominating Samuel J. Tilden, who as governor of New York had destroyed the grafting Boss Tweed ring in New York City.

Tilden, with a sizable popular plurality, captured New York and several other northern states in addition to the South. It seemed clear that he had won. The Republicans, however, claimed the votes of the three southern states still under carpetbagger rule: Florida, South Carolina, and Louisiana. In each of these states the Democrats had indeed intimidated Negroes and both parties had been guilty of other dubious practices. After a long and bitter dispute, the conflicting returns from these states were referred to an electoral commission which, acting on strictly party lines, gave the election to Hayes by one vote.

Actually, certain Republicans had approached certain Democrats in advance to make sure the result would be accepted. The Compromise of 1877, as this has been called, somewhat resembles the prewar compromises. Like them, it was made by conservatives for the purpose of preventing trouble. Southern Democratic leaders were assured that, if they accepted Hayes's election, he would remove the troops from the remaining southern states and that the South would receive its share of railroad subsidies and similar federal favors. Actually, conservative southern Democrats, many of them former Whigs who believed in supporting industry, had no love for the agrarian Democrats of the Northwest. The Republican conservatives, on the other hand, hoped to build up their party in the southern states. This hope did not mature, and by the next election the bloody shirt was again waving in the breeze. One result of the compromise stood: the North was through intervening on behalf of the southern Negro. Once more white Southerners controlled the South.

THE PRESIDENTIAL SEESAW

Hayes made a serious effort to reform the federal bureaucracy, an effort which involved him in a bitter fight with the Stalwarts of his party but did not go far enough to please the reformers. A financial conservative, he stood firm against inflation. A believer in the principle of a single presidential term, Hayes had made too many enemies to be renominated even if he had changed his mind. After a stalemate between the Stalwart backers of a third term for Grant and the partisans of James G. Blaine, the oratorically gifted but somewhat tarnished "Plumed Knight" of the Half-Breeds, the nomination went to the moderately reform-minded James A. Garfield of Ohio. To placate the defeated Stalwarts, the Republicans gave the second place on the ticket to Chester A. Arthur of the New York Customs House, a perfect representative of machine politics. Garfield won a close election against General Winfield Scott Hancock and, like his predecessor, began struggling with the Stalwarts over patronage. On September 29, 1881, this promising president was shot by a crazy Stalwart office-seeker.

To the surprise and dismay of some of his friends, Vice President Arthur made a good president. Turning against his old cronies, he fought against corruption in the post office and machine politics in his own bailiwick. He backed the Pendleton Act, the first real civil service law, and even attempted to put through a thorough revision of the tariff. In this he failed and the so-called Mongrel Tariff of 1882 was amended out of all reform meaning.

In 1884 the Half-Breeds finally pushed through the nomination of their hero, Blaine. The Democrats nominated Grover Cleveland, the stout and solid governor of New York, who had a reputation for honesty and independence. In a campaign that reached a peak of colorful scandal-mongering on both sides, Cleveland won. To the deep disgust of devoted Republicans, a number of "mugwump" reformers switched parties to support him.

To the horror of many Republicans, a Democrat was in power—for the first time since 1860. Actually no disaster ensued; Cleveland dealt fairly effectively with the most obvious and immediate problems facing the government. One of these was the rising treasury surplus. Instead of allowing it to be dissipated by continually bigger pensions for veterans, which he courageously opposed, Cleveland insisted on tariff reduction. In 1887, using the most forthright language employed by any president since the war, he attacked the high tariff as the creator of oppressive monopolies and managed to push a tariff reform bill through the House of Representatives though not the Senate.

The protective tariff, therefore, was the one national issue that played a big part in the campaign of 1888. The Republicans nominated the cold and correct Benjamin Harrison of Indiana, grandson of Old Tippecanoe. Since it was clear what was at stake, they were able to go farther than usual in "frying the fat," that is, wringing campaign contributions out of protected industries. Despite these and less savory tactics, Cleveland won a popular plurality, but Harrison secured a majority of the electoral votes.

For some reason, the Harrison administration took this doubtful mandate as a green light for an extreme program along Stalwart lines. With liberal pension acts and rich pork-barrel appropriations for rivers and harbors, post offices, and the like, the new Congress launched a successful assault on the surplus in the old-fashioned manner. The administration leaders gave their cordial support to the complex and ultraprotectionist McKinley Tariff of 1890. To put this across, it was necessary to make several gestures toward the Western critics of the administration. For the first time, the tariff offered protection to farm products as well as manufactures. The administration supported both the Sherman Silver-Purchase Act and the Sherman Anti-Trust Act (see p. 260). The admission of six western states and an unsuccessful attempt to give Congress power to control southern elections completed the strategy of the administration high command.

In 1890 the Republicans were repudiated overwhelmingly in Congress and in 1892 Cleveland was vindicated by reelection. Despite the reappearance, however, of his corpulent and familiar figure, there were signs that the conventional pattern of politics was changing. In the heavily Democratic Congress there were several members of a new third party calling itself the People's party and demanding a whole list of radical reforms. Shortly after Cleveland's inauguration a severe financial panic alarmed businessmen. This was only the beginning; the second Cleveland administration was to face a host of new problems at home and abroad. Or, more accurately, it would encounter old problems that could no longer be ignored.

FOR FURTHER READING:

Matthew Josephson, *The Politicos* (1938), is dated but still fascinating; as is Herbert Agar, *The Price of Union* (1950). The best overview of the period is John A. Garraty, *The New Commonwealth, 1877–1890* (1968).

H. Wayne Morgan's *From Hayes to McKinley* (1969) is an able synthesis of party politics in the gilded age; and Robert D. Marcus has offered an illuminating study of the *Grand Old Party* (1971). Daniel J. Rothman, *Politics and Power* (1966) takes a close look at the Senate. Irwin Unger, *The Greenback Era* (1964) skillfully relates financial controversy to political and ideological divisions. For the Grant administration, two biographies are very helpful: William B. Hesseltine, *Ulysses S. Grant, Politician* (1935), and Allan Nevins, *Hamilton Fish: The Inner History of the Grant Administration* (1936). The disputed election is convincingly interpreted by C. Vann Woodward, *Reunion and Reaction* (1951)*. A full but rather uncritical account of a major figure of the period is Allan Nevins, *Grover Cleveland* (1932).

Ari Hoogenboom, *Spoilsmen and Reformers* (Berkeley Readings in American History, 1964)*, is a collection of documents dealing with one of his period's major political issues.

---

* Available in paperback edition.

THE INS VERSUS THE OUTS: AMERICAN POLITICS, 1868-1896

President	Presidential Vote (in thousands) R	D	Representatives Elected R	D	other	Major Tariff Legislation	Financial and Other Important Legislation	Business Conditions	
1868 Grant R	3,013	2,707	149	63		1867 Reduction narrowly beaten.		To 1869 Moderate prosperity for agriculture. Moderate depression for industry.	1868
1870			134	104	5	Slight reductions.	1869 Resolution to pay bonds in coin. Bonds refunded at lower rates.	1869 Collapse of farm prices.	1870
1872 Grant R	3,597	2,843	194	92	14	Ten percent off protected articles. Coffee, tea, free.		1869–1873 Moderate prosperity for industry.	1872
1874			109	169	14		Most remaining internal taxes repealed. 1873 End of silver coinage. Greenback expansion vetoed. 1875 Resumption Act (greenbacks to be convertible 1879).	1873 Panic.	1874
1876 Hayes R	4,037	4,284	140	153		1875 Ten percent cut restored.		DEPRESSION	1876

Year	President	Popular vote	House seats	Tariff	Legislation	Economic conditions
1878			130 149 14		Bland-Allison Act. 1879 Resumption (greenbacks convertible).	1879 Recovery.
1880	Garfield *R*	4,453 4,414	147 135 11			PROSPERITY
1882			118 199 10	1883 "Mongrel Tariff."	1883 Pendleton Act.	
1884	Cleveland *D*	4,850	140 183 2			Panic and depresion.
1886			152 169 4			1885 Partial recovery.
1888	Harrison *R*	5,447 5,538	166 159	1887 Cleveland Tariff Message. Mills bill (reduction) passes House.	1887 Interstate Commerce Act.	1887 Collapse of farm prices. UNEVEN PROSPERITY
1890			88 235 9	McKinley Tariff (increase).	1889 Omnibus bill (4 western states). Sherman Anti-Trust Act and Sherman Silver Purchase Act.	Minor panic.
1892	Cleveland *D*	5,183 5,555	127 218 11			1893 Major panic.
1894			244 105 7	Wilson-Gorman Tariff (slight reduction).	1893 Repeal of Sherman Silver Purchase Act.	
1896	McKinley *R*	7,102 6,493	204 113 40			DEPRESSION

The Ripening of Protest
1870-1896

20

In the 1890s, more than in any period before the 1930s, sharp criticism of American industrial and capitalist society broke through the bland surface of American political life. For a few years conservative Americans were deeply alarmed and talked about the menace of revolution. It is hard for present-day Americans to understand the intensity of these fears. Most of the radical demands were for redress and not revolution; many were far from new.

One reason political feelings were so intense was that the two sides in most of the arguments did not speak each other's language. The spokesmen of discontent felt that they had been ignored and frustrated too long. Insistent on being heard, they often sounded more radical than they were. The conservatives, on the other hand, had long taken it for granted that serious discontent in America was impossible. When it appeared they were deeply shocked.

DEFENDERS OF "LAISSEZ FAIRE"

The starting point, for educated Americans of the nineteenth century, was the belief that human affairs were ruled by immutable law. The central law of political economy was that the general good would be best served by the pursuit of individual self-interest. If, under competition, there were difficulties or suffering in society, these were necessary spurs to effort. Rewards went to those who worked hard and deserved them, while poverty was almost always a punishment for vice and laziness. It would be both foolish and immoral for the state or for any private organization to intervene in economic affairs.

These laws of political economy were, said the textbooks, the laws of God. They were also, for those who accepted the new lessons of

Darwinian evolution, the laws of biology. The struggle for existence was the means by which the human race had reached its present high development. Interference would simply help the weak and unfit, injure the strong, and thereby weaken the race. Often spokesmen of *laissez faire* combined the two sources of authority: free competition was the means by which evolution took place under Divine superintendence.

This doctrine of *laissez faire* was taught by political economists, preached every Sunday by clergymen, and invoked by lawyers and judges. During the 1880s and 1890s, the Supreme Court gradually worked out an interpretation of the Fourteenth Amendment which made it a bastion of *laissez faire.* The amendment prohibited states from depriving "any person of life, liberty, or property, without due process of law." "Liberty," the Court said, included freedom of contract and "person" could mean a corporation. "Without due process of law" covered any sort of unreasonable or unnatural regulation (for example of hours of labor or railway rates). What was reasonable depended, of course, on the general knowledge of all educated men, that is on the doctrine of *laissez faire.*

THE REVIVAL OF REFORM

Individualists by tradition, Americans were also reformers. If bad conditions existed, most people believed they could and should be changed. At first, the end of slavery and secession seemed to mean that all was well; gradually, with shocked surprise, many came to realize that this was not the case.

Some of the evils of the period, like recurrent corruption in government and fraud in business, raised no new moral problems; these things were evil and should be punished. Yet, under the new conditions, the line between legitimate competition and dishonesty was not easy to draw. Bribery was wrong, but tips to helpful public officials about likely investments and agreements to give special prices to favored insiders were borderline cases. Closely related to such problems was the old question of monopoly. Since Jackson's day or earlier, most Americans had disliked great accumulations of power. Many businessmen as well as farmers began in the post-Civil War period to feel that great corporations were shutting the door to opportunity and endangering *laissez faire* itself. Understandably the railroads, with their life-and-death power over shippers, drew the earliest fire. By the mid-1880s, when the Supreme Court began to strike down state regulatory laws, demand for national railroad legislation became overwhelming. In 1887 the Interstate Commerce Act forbade certain unfair practices, required that rates be both openly published and "reasonable," and set up a commission to investigate abuses and appeal to the courts for redress.

In 1890, mounting demand for general antimonopoly legislation was met by the Sherman Anti-Trust Act. This law prohibited all contracts, combinations, or conspiracies in restraint of interstate or foreign trade. Anglo-Saxon common law had long prohibited harmful restraint of trade, and some lawyers and businessmen could not believe, despite the language of the Sherman Act, that Congress had intended to go far beyond this traditional position. Thus argument continued as to what kinds of action were prohibited by the Sherman Act, and for the rest of the century this statute, like the Interstate Commerce Act, remained ineffective. Yet each involved that interesting paradox which was to become increasingly common: government intervention to preserve *laissez faire.*

Perhaps the biggest step in the revival of reform was the discovery of the city. Even for those who believed that poverty was the fault of the poor, it was impossible to ignore the epidemics that periodically spread from the slums or the fires that began in jerry-built tenements and spread to business blocks. Looking a little further, some middle-class Americans were amazed to find whole families living in single, airless, lightless rooms with unspeakable sanitation.

Insofar as they did know about slum conditions, many were at first inclined to blame them on the slum dwellers, that is, the new immigrants. In one of the great migrations of all history, about fourteen million immigrants came to the United States in the last four decades of the century. Through the 1870s, most immigrants continued to come from northwestern Europe, particularly the British Isles, Germany, and Scandinavia. In the 1880s, however, southern and eastern Europeans started to appear in great numbers, and by the 1890s these new sources furnished the majority. Slavs from the Austro-Hungarian Empire, Italians from the poverty-stricken south, and Jews fleeing savage Russian persecution came, like all earlier American immigrants back to the Pilgrims, looking for liberty and opportunity. This was certainly in the best tradition of *laissez faire,* and, moreover, immigration was beneficial to expanding industry.

Many insisted that immigration, like other national problems, be left alone. Yet more and more voices were raised in favor of regulation. Some of the demand for a change in immigration policy was an expression of the ugliest forms of racial prejudice, but much came from other sources. Organized labor feared competition from destitute and hard-to-organize newcomers. Some conservatives worried about the menace to established tradition. To middle-class reformers, the new immigrants presented a perplexing picture. Often destitute, knowing no English, and disoriented by a sudden move from a familiar village to a raw metropolis, the newcomers tended naturally to stick together and to maintain their languages and customs. Equally naturally, they were easily organized for political purposes by bosses who could speak their language and attend to some of their immediate needs. Thus sections of New York and Chicago became, to middle-class Americans, as alien as Naples or Prague. Many people tended to approach the new immigrants with a curious mixture of emotions: compassion, missionary desire to uplift, fear, and resentment.

Whether demand for immigration restriction came from reformist or conservative sources or (as often) from both at once, the inevitable result was government action in a new area. In 1882 Congress excluded Chinese laborers, a group especially disliked by organized labor. In the same year convicts, paupers, and criminals were banned—the list was later to include anarchists and other "undesirables." In 1885 the importation of contract labor was forbidden.

Fear of aliens, resentment of big business, and concern for the urban poor all increased sharply in periods of depression. When thousands of unemployed roamed the streets it became harder to believe that poverty was always a punishment for vice or even that prices and production adjusted themselves automatically to social needs.

In each depression period social violence dramatized the existence of discontent. In the railroad strikes of 1877, mobs took over and looted Pittsburgh and Baltimore until President Hayes sent troops. In 1886 a bomb thrown in the Chicago Haymarket provoked police reprisals and set off a public "anarchist scare." In 1892 the Homestead steel strike turned into a pitched battle between strikers and Pinkerton detectives. Horrified at such episodes, many shocked citizens demanded swift action to restore order and punish violence. This they got, but some went on to ask difficult questions. How could such things happen in America where everyone had an equal opportunity? What had gone wrong with the laws of free competition and inevitable progress?

Among the first flatly to challenge *laissez faire* were certain Protestant ministers. Reacting to personal experiences of city conditions or social violence, some Christians found themselves unable to square the ethics of *laissez faire* with the Gospel injunctions to love one's neighbor. By the early 1890s many urban, middle-class congregations heard, to their surprise, that they should apply the law of love to labor relations and the relief of poverty. Some ministers went further than these general injunctions, urging that society be radically reconstructed according to what they considered Christian principles.

Up to this time charitable relief had been either a matter of individual handouts or crowded and inadequate poorhouses. By the mid-century, firm believers in *laissez faire* were organizing to secure charitable efficiency and make sure that the unworthy poor got nothing and that nobody got enough to spoil his character. By 1890, however, a new group had appeared—the settlement workers. These men and women, of whom Jane Addams was the most famous, actually lived and worked in slum neighborhoods. Being "neighbors to the poor" tended to change their attitudes toward the causes and relief of poverty. At the same time, shocking descriptions of immigrant slums began to be spread by talented reporters like Jacob Riis, author of *How the Other Half Lives* (1890).

By the early 1890s, then, many middle-class Americans were finding it hard to accept altogether the theories of *laissez faire*. On the left of this group were believers in drastic social change, like Edward Bellamy, the author of the Utopian socialist novel *Looking Backward* (1888). Somewhat less radical was Henry George, perhaps the most influential American social theorist of the period. George traced all social evils to one single source, the private appropriation of the increase in land values. If this "unearned increment" were taken away from the landlord and used by society, it could be spent for social improvement. At the same time labor and capital would be freed from an unjust burden and true individualism revived.

To the right of George were a host of academic theorists who denied that *laissez faire* and unchecked individual competition had to be the sole law of social evolution. Still to the right of such theorists, and much more numerous, were people who had no answers to current problems and who still believed deeply in individualism, but who found it harder and harder to believe that all was well.

ORGANIZED LABOR

Industrial workers did not need to be told that society was imperfect. It is true that real wages advanced during the period, largely because of falling food prices. Yet $1 to $1.50 a day (a common wage for unskilled labor) was hardly lavish, and it left absolutely no margin for illness, accident, or unemployment.

Yet would-be organizers faced great difficulties. Most managers of industry were frankly hostile to all labor unions, and large sections of the press and public shared this hostility. Frequent depressions made labor activity dangerous—there were thousands of unemployed to replace those who were fired and black-listed. Above all immigration meant the yearly arrival of thousands of new recruits to industry who were poor and inexperienced in the American labor market, often willing to work for what they could get.

The first major postwar organizations attacked these problems in the idealistic spirit inherited from prewar reform movements. Up to about 1873 the most important organization was the National Labor Union which was interested in greenback inflation and many other nonlabor causes. Not really sure whether they accepted the wage system or not, some of its leaders tried to start producers' cooperatives and made vague commitments to socialism. Others placed all their hopes on the eight-hour day. Its energies scattered, the NLU ceased to exist in the depression of the 1870s.

In the prosperous early 1880s, national attention was caught by the Knights of Labor, an organization which had existed since 1869 but had now suddenly grown to three quarters of a million. Like its predecessor, the organization was interested in a host of causes including cooperatives and inflation. Though they officially disliked strikes and preferred arbitration, the loosely organized Knights found themselves involved in a series of major railroad strikes in 1884–1886. At first they scored surprising victories, but they ended by losing disastrously. Unfairly, they were associated by the alarmed public with the Haymarket bombing. In the depression of the 1890s, the organization perished. It had already failed to meet the competition of a new rival, the American Federation of Labor.

Samuel Gompers, founder of the new organization, was a cigar-maker who had absorbed the craft tradition of his trade. Observing the Knights, he blamed their defeat on loose organization and political involvement. The A. F. of L., which he founded under another name in 1881 and gave permanent structure in 1886, was organized strictly on craft lines and, deliberately or not, appealed mostly to skilled workers. Gompers emphasized what he called "pure and simple unionism," which meant the pursuit of higher wages, shorter hours, and union protection, including if possible the closed shop. The proper methods by which to reach these goals were the strike and the boycott. From the government, the A. F. of L. primarily wanted protection of these methods, not ameliorative legislation. The organization did not oppose capitalism, refusing to come out for any overall social theory.

By adapting to existing conditions rather than fighting them, the A. F. of L. survived in the hostile world of the nineteenth century. It weathered the depression of the 1890s, and by 1900 had one-half million members and a limited measure of public recognition. It proved unable, however, to organize the large groups of immigrant workers in heavy industry. Many members of the labor movement, including a strong minority within the A. F. of L. itself, wanted to change the organization's nature—to add political activity to trade union methods, to abandon craft for industrial unions, and, above all, to "organize the unorganized." In the disturbed mid-1890s, this opposition got so strong that Gompers lost the leadership of the A. F. of L. for a year and only narrowly prevented the adoption of a socialist program.

THE FARMERS AND POPULISM

The basic problem of the farmers was the general decline of farm prices from 1870 to 1895. It took more and more cotton, corn, or wheat to pay the farmer's costs, including interest on his debts. Part of the reason for declining prices was that vast areas of the world—Russia, Argentina, and Australia—were coming into competition with America. The farmer, however, tended to blame conditions closer to home. In the first place, he said, the money supply was inadequate and inflexible. It had been wrong to retire the greenbacks, to decrease the number of bank notes in circulation, and, above all, to take silver out of the currency. Second, farmers blamed exploitation by middlemen. Railroad and elevator rates were high and arbitrary, interest rates were going up, and the farmer was being milked by the farm implement trust. Protective tariffs (some farmers said) merely raised the farmer's expenses without helping him.

In two regions, as we have seen, these chronic ills were augmented by local conditions. The overexpanded wheat farmers of the plains were hit by devastating droughts and in 1887 an especially sharp price fall toppled their inflated credit structure. The South, in addition to suffering most of the ills of the West, had to bear the sharecrop and crop-lien system fastened on the section during the postwar shortage of capital. The southern farmer, moreover, suffered from the biracial system, though he did not usually see it that way. Only occasionally, and in only a few southern states, did white agrarian radicals make common cause with Negro farmers against railroads and landlords. More often the discontented white man blamed his troubles partly on his Negro neighbor and accused his conservative enemy of being pro-Negro.

Farmers in the North and South often believed, as their ancestors had for centuries, that the small farmer was by nature an especially valuable and virtuous citizen, that at some time in the past things had been much better for him, and that his troubles were the result of deliberate Wall Street plots. Though conservative in many ways, farmers had an old tradition of calling on the government for help when they felt oppressed. In the late nineteenth century their demands took two main forms: inflation to bring their prices up and regulation to bring their costs down. In the 1860s the midwestern Grangers had helped secure state laws regulating railroads and elevators, some of which were invalidated in the 1880s by the Supreme Court. Farmers took part in many kinds of inflationary movements, including the greenback and silver struggles and various proposals to issue national currency on the basis of land or crops and lend it at low rates.

When acute farm crises hit at the end of the 1880s, the greatest existing farmer organizations were the two Farmers' Alliances of the North and South. In 1890 two senators and eight representatives were elected on straight Alliance tickets, in addition to a considerable number of closely sympathetic congressmen. Encouraged, representatives of the northern and southern Alliances drew together during the next two years to form the People's party.

In their first national convention in Omaha in 1892 the Populists, as they were called, drew up a platform which summarized, in angry and dramatic language, most of the discontent of the period. It called for inflation by legal tender notes, silver, and other methods. Railroad land grants were to be recovered, and aliens were to be forbidden land ownership. Railroads, and also telephone and telegraph industries, were to be nationalized. In an effort to attract labor support, the platform called for the eight-hour day, immigration restriction, and the abolition of Pinkerton industrial detectives. Miscellaneous radical sentiment was cultivated by denunciation of land monopoly, demand for the income tax, and a general statement that the powers of government should be extended as much as was necessary to secure the end of injustice and poverty. Finally, expressing the deep confidence in increased democracy of most American radicalism, the platform praised the initiative and referendum and called for direct election of senators. Running on this platform, General James B. Weaver, the first Populist candidate for the presidency, received a million votes.

Stirred by this promising first effort, some hopeful radicals believed that the Populist movement was going to sweep to power, uniting all the diverse kinds of discontent, upsetting the two-party system as the Republicans had in 1856–1860, and driving out the monopolists and gold bugs.

CLEVELAND'S LAST STAND

Nothing could have been farther from the intentions of the man actually elected to the presidency in 1892. Grover Cleveland incarnated more completely than any politician of the period the doctrine of *laissez faire*. When the Panic of 1893 swept banks and railroads into bankruptcy, when depression set in and unemployment mounted, he had no doubt of his duty. He must fight against the high tariff as always, but still harder against inflation. At all costs demagogues and tamperers must be defeated so as to allow natural forces a chance to bring recovery.

The immediate problem facing the administration was the danger of a lack of gold in the treasury to meet its obligations. Gold had been drained away by the policies of the previous administration. The prohibitive rates of the McKinley Tariff had cut income. Outgo had been increased by political appropriations for rivers, harbors, pensions, and above all, payments for silver under the Sherman Silver Purchase Act. Cleveland put the administration's whole weight behind a drive to repeal this compromise measure. He won his objective, but thereby permanently alienated the western wing of his party. As a result he lacked the power to force tariff reduction through Congress. The Wilson-Gorman bill, thoroughly amended as usual in the Senate, brought little reduction in existing rates.

With the Silver Purchase Act repealed, the government was no longer obligated to buy the output of the silver mines, but it still had to exchange gold for the outstanding greenbacks and silver certificates. To meet the continuing gold drain, the administration resorted to selling government bonds for gold. Two issues were sold, with difficulty, on the open market. For the third, in February, 1895, the administration sought help in the same quarter that great corporations appealed to in time of stress. This was the international banking syndicate of Morgan, Belmont, and Rothschild. This group was accustomed to performing some of the functions carried out in other countries by central banks. It dealt with governments as equals and demanded high prices for its services. Drawing much of the necessary gold from abroad, the banking syndicate bought the entire bond issue on very profitable terms. The treasury reserve was saved for another year, when another public issue became necessary.

Naturally, this episode raised the pitch of popular emotion, which was already mounting fast. In the congressional elections of 1894, the Republican opposition swept Congress and the Populists increased their popular vote by 40 percent. In the same year the most serious strike of the period broke out in the model company town of Pullman, Illinois. While Pullman dividends remained high, wages were cut as much as 30 to 40 percent and employees' rents not reduced. When the desperate Pullman employees appealed for help they received it from the American Railway Union, a new industrial union led by Eugene V. Debs. Around Chicago, A.R.U. men started cutting Pullman cars out of trains and the public began to fear a tie-up in its essential means of transportation.

Welcoming a showdown, the railroad General Managers' Association appealed to the administration. Cleveland's Attorney General, Richard Olney, himself a former railroad lawyer, secured an injunction (invoking among other laws the Sherman Anti-Trust Act) which forbade practically all strike activity. Under this injunction Debs went to jail. Meantime Cleveland sent federal troops to Chicago to maintain order, though the liberal governor of Illinois John P. Altgeld said this was unnecessary. When the troops arrived, riots did indeed break out.

Conservative fears were further roused by the unemployed "armies" which converged on Washington under the leadership of "general" Jacob Coxey and others. Actually these groups were not very large, and their intention was to demand such measures of relief as government loans to finance public work. This proposal seemed to the conservative press the height of extremism and absurdity. In Washington, Coxey was arrested for walking on the grass and the armies peaceably melted away.

As if to complete the anger and frustration of the discontented, the Supreme Court in 1895 sustained the Debs injunction, threw out the very moderate income tax which had been attached to the Wilson-Gorman Tariff, and (in the Knight case) almost completely nullified, for the present, the Sherman Anti-Trust Act.

Still confident in his principles of *laissez faire*, Cleveland spent much of his last two years in office fighting against a more active foreign policy. Shortly before the end of his term, he vetoed a bill requiring a literacy test for immigrants. Denounced as a traitor by western and southern Democrats, he was a hero to many eastern Republicans. Nevertheless, the Republican party looked forward to the election of 1896, expecting the President's unpopularity to give it an easy return to power.

THE BATTLE OF 1896

William McKinley, nominated by the Republicans on a gold-standard, high-tariff platform, seemed the typical Republican statesman. A former governor of Ohio and a war veteran with impeccable moral principles, he was known mainly for the high tariff that bore his name. His candidacy was managed by his friend Mark Hanna, an Ohio manufacturer with great political gifts. Meeting in Chicago, the Democrats were swept off their feet by the famous "Cross-of-Gold" speech of William Jennings Bryan of Nebraska. Bryan was nominated and a platform adopted calling for free coinage of silver and a number of other reform measures.

For the first time since 1860, the parties were clearly divided on a single issue, and on that issue all the emotions of the period were focused. To one side Bryan was a knight in armor rescuing the people. By the other he was painted as an anarchist, an atheist, and a bringer of revolution. Actually Bryan, in 1896 and throughout his career, reflected accurately the feelings of millions of Westerners, thoroughly traditional in religion and morality and by no means radical in politics. In 1896, in some areas, such solid and conventional citizens felt that they had been cheated out of their rights.

Yet when the votes were counted, the Republicans had won. Bryan had carried only the Solid South, the Great Plains, and the mountain West, losing the border states and the northern Mississippi Valley. There have been many explanations for this result, including a rise in farm prices just before the election and Republican pressure on factory workers. It seems to indicate, however, that the forces of discontent in 1896 were either not large enough or not united enough to win against a determined and skillful opponent. To some conservatives, McKinley's victory seemed a narrow victory for sound principles, the end of a strange aberration, and a green light for prosperity. This impression was deepened when prosperity actually did return soon after the election. Discoveries in South Africa and Alaska increased the supply of gold. European crop failures and rising industrial production helped to raise the farmer's prices. For the next couple of decades, many farmers were comparatively well off. Those that were not usually sought redress through organization and bargaining rather than crusades.

In the South, similarly, normality of a sort returned. In North Carolina at the height of the Populist excitement some Negroes had achieved political office. Now the frustrated agrarian radicals nearly all returned to militant segregationism, a position many of them had never left. For another two generations Southerners stood united in defense of white supremacy.

In other respects, however, the forces of change were not as roundly defeated as it seemed. A small minority of determined radicals emerged from the Pullman strike and other defeats of the 1890s to provide articulate criticism of American society in the next generation. The Socialist party, formed in 1900, became for the next generation something close to a coalition of American radicals under the leadership of Eugene V. Debs.

Few of the middle-class reformers who had been aroused by late-nineteenth-century problems returned immediately to a belief in *laissez faire*. Though they did not agree on any overall social analysis or program, they continued to press for particular governmental actions to redress grievances. Thus the 1890s laid down the lines on which conservatives, liberals, and radicals would argue for the next half-century. In domestic controversy, and, also, as we shall see, in foreign policy, the second Cleveland administration marked both an end and a beginning.

CONFLICTING HISTORICAL VIEWPOINTS

Was Populism Constructive?

Until after World War II historians were generally sympathetic to Populism. Openly critical of the values and excesses of a business civilization, such early scholars as Solon Buck (The Agrarian Crusade *[1920]) and John D. Hicks* (The Populist Revolt *[1931]) saw much to admire in the Populist critique of industrializing America. In his enormously influential synthesis, Hicks portrayed the Populists as constructive liberal reformers in the tradition of Jefferson and Jackson. Although their programs failed and their movement disintegrated, Hicks concluded that they not only focused the nation's attention on many of its gravest problems but offered an agenda for twentieth-century reform.*

Hicks's classic study remains the best point at which to begin a serious study of Populism. Comprehensive and insightful, it has never been surpassed as a general account of agrarian discontent. But during the 1950s, numerous revisionists questioned its interpretation. Disturbed by wartime fascism abroad and postwar McCarthyism at home, these scholars probed the darker side of Populism. Unlike Hicks, they fastened on its antisocial and negative rather than its constructive and positive features. In Populism they discovered the antecedents of much that was distasteful and evil in American society. In an essay in The Radical Right, *Daniel Bell, ed., (1963)* Peter Vierick, for example, found in Populism "a mania of xenophobia, Jew-baiting, intellectual-baiting, and thought-controlling lynch-spirit;" and Victor Ferkiss uncovered "Populist Influences on American Fascism"* (Western Political Quarterly *[June 1957]). The behaviorial scientists were generally the most critical, but it was the historian Richard Hofstadter who offered the most persuasive revision of the Hicks thesis. In his Pulitzer Prize-winning* Age of Reform *(1955) this distinguished scholar acknowledged "much that is good and usable in our Populist past." Yet he noted much more that was retrograde and sinister. He faulted the benighted Populists for their chimerical remedies and romantic long-*

ings for a "lost agrarian Eden," as well as for their nativism, anti-Semitism, and paranoia—irrational obsessions that he believed foreshadowed twentieth-century authoritarianism.

At its best, as in Hofstadter's work, revisionism presented a subtle and suggestive argument that enriched our knowledge of agrarian unrest. More often, however, Populism's critics were neither temperate nor convincing. Yet, while their conclusions said more about their fears for the present than about their understanding of the past, they did provoke a reexamination of the nature of Populism. Thus, in the 1960s, a decade of reawakened interest in radical causes, a body of widely varying studies emerged to rehabilitate the Populist image in scholarly literature. Among the first of these was C. Vann Woodward's "The Populist Heritage and the Intellectual" (American Scholar [1959]), a moderate and judicious essay which praised the southern Populists for their noble, but abortive, experiment in racial accommodation. Similarly, Walter Nugent's The Tolerant Populists (1963) celebrated broadminded Kansas agrarian reformers, and Norman Pollack's The Populist Response to Industrial America (1962) portrayed essentially humane and truly radical midwestern farmers who sought realistic solutions to the evils of industrialism. Robert F. Durden's The Climax of Populism (1965) denied that Populists were radical, but he absolved them of retrogressive and nativist tendencies; and Michael Rogin's The Intellectuals and McCarthy (1967) used statistical methods to prove that Populism was not the ancestor of McCarthyism.

FOR FURTHER READING:

The most complete survey of the period's social thought is Sidney Fine, Laissez Faire and the General Welfare State (1956). Daniel Aaron, Men of Good Hope (1951)*, is a series of essays on reformers. H. F. May, Protestant Churches and Industrial America (1949)*, discusses the development of Protestant social criticism; and Jacob Henry Dorn's Washington Gladden (1967) examines a leading social critic. The starting place for city problems is A. M. Schlesinger, Sr., The Rise of the City (1933). Oscar Handlin, The Uprooted (1951)* and Philip Taylor, The Distant Magnant (1971) convey the immigrants point of view. John Higham, Strangers in the Land (1955)*, analyzes native hostility to immigrants; John S. Haller, Jr., Outcasts from Evolution (1971), surveys scientific racism during the period; and both Paul F. Boller, Jr., American Thought in Transition (1969), and Richard Hofstadter, Social

---

* Available in paperback edition.

Darwinism in American Thought (1944), consider the impact of evolution on the Gilded Age. A crucial farm problem is examined in George H. Miller, *Railroads and the Granger Laws* (1971). The campaign of 1896 is examined in several of the works in the essay above, but see also Paul W. Glad, *McKinley, Bryan, and the People* (1964)*. Among the many fine autobiographies see especially those of Jane Addams, Samuel Gompers, and William Allen White. The following are a sampling of innumerable biographies: C. A. Barker, *Henry George* (1955); Paolo E. Coletta, *William Jennings Bryan* (3 vols., 1964–1971); C. Vann Woodward, *Tom Watson* (1938), on Southern Populism; and Ray Ginger, *The Bending Cross* (1949)* on Eugene V. Debs. Robert H. Wiebe, *The Search for Order, 1877–1920* (1967) is a penetrating analysis, useful for this chapter and the four following.

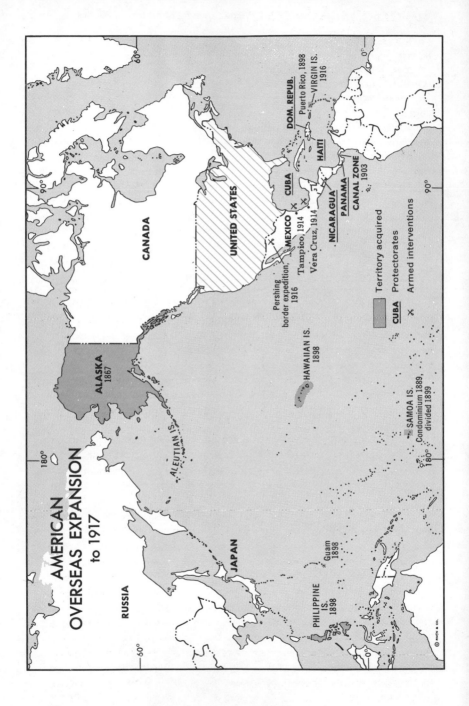

AMERICAN
OVERSEAS EXPANSION
to 1917

RUSSIA

JAPAN

PHILIPPINE
IS.
1898

Guam
1898

SAMOA IS.
Condominium 1889,
divided 1899

180°

50°

ALEUTIAN IS.

ALASKA
1867

HAWAIIAN IS.
1898

CANADA

UNITED STATES

60°

90°

90°

Pershing
border expedition,
1916

Tampico, 1914
Vera Cruz, 1914

MEXICO

NICARAGUA

PANAMA

HAITI

CUBA

DOM. REPUB.

Puerto Rico, 1898
VIRGIN IS.
1916

CANAL ZONE
1903

Territory acquired

Protectorates

CUBA

X Armed interventions

© RAND M & CO.

Overseas Adventure
1898-1900

21

From the Peace of Ghent in 1814 until almost the end of the nineteenth century, the United States remained aloof from international power politics. She was enabled to do so by a fortunate combination of circumstances: the European balance of power, British control of the high seas, and her own growing *potential* for armed resistance. Very few nineteenth-century Americans realized the transitory nature of this combination. Most believed that American freedom from foreign danger was permanent and "natural." The United States, Americans believed, was the greatest nation on earth. Following the advice of the founding fathers, she chose to demonstrate this greatness only by peaceful growth.

Once colonial expansion was completed, public interest in foreign affairs, where it existed at all, concentrated on four traditional concerns. The first was a general sympathy for republican and constitutional institutions and a belief that the world was moving toward free government. The second was the special concern of the United States with the Western Hemisphere under the Monroe Doctrine, and within this an increasing claim to dominance in the Caribbean. The third was a special, and highly ambivalent, relation to England. This led to frequent clashes over such issues as the boundaries of New World British possessions, American sympathy for Canadian rebellion, use of the Newfoundland fishing grounds, and British interest in Central America. These clashes often led to violent denunciation from both sides, but all were settled peaceably, usually by British concessions made partly in the interest of commerce. The fourth concern was the expansion of foreign trade, especially in the Far East. Partly the unrealized dream of a commercial minority, this yet led to concrete results: the establishment of relations with Japan, China, and Korea, the acquisition of a few tiny Pacific islands, and the development of a protectorate in Hawaii.

THE END OF ISOLATION

In the Spanish-American War of 1898, historians have often seen a break with the past and the full emergence of the United States into world politics. Yet the extent of the change can be exaggerated. All four of the traditional concerns mentioned above were involved in the crisis of the 1890s. There was no sudden increase of American might: since industrialization the United States had been a potential great power. Nor did 1898 mark a sudden, permanent shift in popular interest. After a flurry of argument over imperialism most Americans resumed, in the early twentieth century, their habitual concentration on home affairs. However, 1898 did mark something of a change in American commitments. From this point on both the United States and the European powers assumed that America had some interest in world crises ranging from North Africa to the Far East. In the latter area, America's new status was symbolized by a vulnerable and dangerously located colonial possession.

Many reasons have been given for this change. The most obvious suggestion embodies the traditional economic interpretation of imperialism: that the American economy had reached maturity and that therefore America, like other advanced industrial countries, needed raw materials and foreign markets. Actually the colossal, varied, and still growing American economy absorbed most productive energy. Yet during the second half of the nineteenth century, and particularly after the onset of depression in 1893, a rising chorus pointed to the crucial connection between prosperity and foreign markets. Most businessmen, like most Americans, were however anticolonialists. They believed that government should promote foreign trade by all peaceful means, and protect it from the encroachment of foreign empires.

Another explanation for the new departures in foreign policy was the revival and restatement of the traditional idea of America's "manifest destiny" of expansion. A change from continental to overseas expansionism needed new arguments. One of the most common arguments of late nineteenth-century expansionists was the idea of Anglo-Saxon "racial" superiority. In the 1890s this was argued in relation to southern Negroes and new immigrants; it could easily be extended to subject races overseas. Sometimes racialism was linked to a bastard variety of Darwinism. Strong races, it was alleged, needed warlike competition to maintain their virility. Expansion was urged as a religious duty by many, among them the Reverend Josiah Strong, whose best-selling *Our Country* (1886) called for the far-flung physical expansion of American Protestantism, the religion of the future, and of the moral, democratic society that went with it. Another special variety of expansionism was the navalism preached by Captain Alfred Thayer Mahan. Mahan argued that throughout history national greatness had depended on overseas commerce with naval might to protect it. This demanded not only the building of warships but also the acquisition of overseas harbors and coaling stations.

Some of these doctrines were advocated with great force by a group of able, highly placed young men, mostly of upper-class eastern background, typified by Senator Henry Cabot Lodge of Massachusetts and Theodore Roosevelt. Roosevelt, a rising Republican politician, had already played spectacular roles as Civil Service Commissioner and then as Police Commissioner of New York City. In 1897 McKinley appointed him Assistant Secretary of the Navy. At this time Roosevelt, a historian of American naval and Indian fighting, wholeheartedly believed that war—almost any war—might have its uses. It would unite the country, take its mind off sordid issues, and develop the manly virtues in its young men.

A third, less obvious cause of the change in American policy was the actual situation in great power politics. The European empires had already divided up Africa and were eying the last two remaining areas for expansion: the Near East, occupied by the weak Turkish Empire, and the Far East, occupied by the still weaker empire of China. Each of these was too important to fall to any single power so the leading nations uneasily supported the independence of both, watching each other and staking out spheres of economic influence.

Since the German victory over France in 1871, the European continent had been dominated by Germany and its allies while Britain ruled the seas. Now, however, this pattern was breaking up. Germany, under its ambitious young ruler Wilhelm II, was challenging Britain by a program of naval expansion. Britain, worried by this new menace and sensitive about many threats to her exposed, worldwide empire, was emerging from her stately isolation and looking around for allies. A new great power, Japan, was taking a hand in Far Eastern affairs and challenging traditional Russian interests in Korea and Manchuria. Everywhere the situation was fluid and dangerous. If a country with the potential might of the United States were to show an interest in world politics, she would inevitably be seen as a menace by some powers and as a potential ally by others, whatever her own intentions.

What happened in 1898 reflected all these forces. The United States first became involved in a minor war for a quite traditional objective: political liberty in the Western Hemisphere. When the theater of war shifted to the Far East, the old dream of Oriental commerce was reawakened along with the newer arguments for imperial expansion. Finally, against her will and without quite realizing it, the United States by her Far Eastern acquisitions became involved in great power politics.

FORERUNNERS OF EXPANSION, 1867–1890

Though most of the people in this period had not been much interested in overseas adventure, some active statesmen as well as some propagandists had promoted it. Most of this early expansionist activity involved the Caribbean or the Pacific.

William H. Seward, Johnson's Secretary of State and a vigorous expansionist since prewar days, had bought Alaska from the Russian Empire in 1867. He had also managed to secure for the United States the tiny Pacific island of Midway but had failed in his attempt to acquire Caribbean bases. In the next administration Grant had passionately sought to annex the Dominican Republic. This dream had been frustrated by his conservative Secretary of State, Hamilton Fish, who had also narrowly prevented the country from intervening in the bloody ten years' revolt in Cuba (1868–1878).

Probably the peak of popular isolationism was reached in the complacent 1880s. Yet it was also in this decade that the United States acquired a formidable, modern "steel navy," supported in Congress as a means of coastal defense. One statesman who struggled to reverse the isolationist trend was the Republican James G. Blaine, who served as Secretary of State under Garfield (1881) and Harrison (1889–1892). In both administrations he wrangled with Britain, first over rights to build an Isthmian canal and then over protection of the fur seal herd in the Bering Sea. Like Seward, he tried unsuccessfully to acquire Caribbean bases.

More originally, Blaine broached the idea of Pan-Americanism which meant unity of the Western Hemisphere republics under American leadership. In 1885 he called the first Pan-American Conference, which actually met in 1889. This conference was ineffective and the whole Pan-American venture was damaged by Blaine's high-handed efforts to settle South American disputes. It was still more seriously impaired when the United States, in 1891, seemed to threaten war with Chile over a waterfront riot in which two American sailors were killed.

The most important of this period's ventures took place in the Pacific. American interest in the distant and primitive Samoan archipelago was mainly naval. A clash with Germany led, in 1889, to the establishment of a peculiar Anglo-German-American condominium in Samoa.

American involvement in the Hawaiian Islands was far more serious. Since the beginning of the century the islands had been visited by American traders, whalers, and missionaries (in that order). Their descendants had become prosperous sugar planters who held actual power in a picturesque native monarchy. From 1842 on, the United States repeatedly made it clear that she would resent European attempts on Hawaiian sovereignty. A treaty of 1875 allowed Hawaiian sugar free entry into the rich American market, yet American contract labor laws did not affect the islands and it was possible to make use of cheap Oriental workers. This idyllic situation, known affectionately in the islands as the Old Monarchy Days, was clearly too good to last.

In 1890 the McKinley Tariff put sugar on the free list, exposing Hawaiian producers to Caribbean competition, and gave a bounty to domestic sugar producers. In January, 1893, a strong-minded Hawaiian queen made a sudden effort to put the American oligarchy out of power and restore autocracy. This gave rise to a revolution. A republic was established which promptly requested annexation to the United States.

The next month, however, Grover Cleveland became president. A staunch defender of tradition, in both foreign and domestic affairs, Cleveland disliked anything which smacked of colonialism. When a presidential commission reported that the Hawaiian revolution had been improperly aided by Americans, Cleveland withdrew the annexation treaty from the Senate. Amid loud cries of outrage from thwarted expansionists, the Hawaiian Republic was forced to wait just outside the gate, much as the Texas Republic had been a half-century earlier.

The Venezuelan Affair of 1895 showed Cleveland in another traditional role, combining the old motifs of Anglophobia, anticolonialism, and American dominance of the Caribbean. For some time the British had been trying to redraw a disputed boundary line between British Guiana and Venezuela. In 1895, when Britain rejected American pressure to submit to arbitration, Secretary of State Richard Olney sent her a surprising note. The British were informed that any permanent union between a European and an American state was unnatural, that the United States was "practically sovereign in this hemisphere," and that on certain subjects defined by America her "fiat" was law. Anglophobes began calling for war, and for once the Cleveland administration found itself almost popular.

Preoccupied with the South African crisis and concerned about her lack of friends, Britain swallowed her pride and consented to arbitrate the issue. In the long run, she got about what she had wanted. The episode hardly indicated that the United States was sovereign in the whole hemisphere. It did suggest, however, that in the existing state of world politics, American power in the Caribbean might soon come to equal American sensitivity about that area.

In the long run, the most important problem of the Cleveland administration lay still closer, in Cuba. One of the few remnants of Spain's great American empire, Cuba was chronically rebellious yet no Spanish government could afford to let it go. After her Ten Years' War ended in 1878, Cuba entered an interlude of comparative prosperity based in large part on sugar production for the American market. Cuban prosperity was assisted by the McKinley Tariff of 1890 which put sugar on the free list and was impaired by the Wilson-Gorman Tariff's restoration of sugar duties in 1894. In 1895, a time of depression in Cuba as in the United States, another insurrection broke out. Far too insecure to handle wisely this difficult situation, the Spanish government talked of eventual concession and embarked on immediate repression. In Cuba, guerrilla methods were met by increasingly drastic reprisals.

Then as now, it was hard for the United States to ignore what went on so close to her shores. The Cuban rebels issued propaganda, raised money, and fitted out illegal expeditions from the United States. The United States had asserted special interest in Cuba since the days of Jefferson. Moreover, the American people throughout the nineteenth century had considered themselves the special patrons of antimonarchical revolutions. Spanish atrocities and Cuban suffering, exaggerated but not altogether false, became a mainstay of the new, ultrasensational newspapers of Joseph Pulitzer and William Randolph Hearst. Patriotic organizations, some labor groups, some reformers, and many congressmen began to demand American action to end Spanish oppression in Cuba. Grimly, as it hung on to the gold standard, the Cleveland administration resisted the pressure for war, meanwhile pressing Spain to grant Cuban autonomy.

McKINLEY AND CUBA

William McKinley, inaugurated in 1897, represented the more expansionist party. Yet he was sincerely devoted to peace on religious grounds, and his administration was responsive to the wishes of the business community. Many conservative businessmen, feeling that sound government had been narrowly rescued from Bryanism, were heartily opposed to any further crusades, for instance for Cuban liberty. The administration, after giving its first attention to securing the passage of the ultraprotectionist Dingley Tariff, turned toward an effort to calm the Cuban waters. For the moment, the outlook seemed promising. A new ministry in Spain was making gestures toward conciliation and autonomy. Both McKinley and the American minister at Madrid were optimistic when two accidents ended the possibility of peace.

First, Cubans intercepted and gave to the American press a letter from the Spanish minister in Washington, de Lome, incautiously (and inaccurately) describing McKinley as a cheap popularity seeker. Second, and far more important, the American consul at Havana, disturbed at anti-American riots by pro-Spanish loyalists, persuaded the government to send the battleship *Maine* on a "courtesy visit." On February 16, 1898, McKinley received the appalling news that the *Maine* had blown up and sunk in Havana harbor with a loss of over 260 American lives.

While the press and Congress screamed for vengeance and de-nounced the President for cowardly subservience to big business, McKinley still tried to preserve peace. The Spanish, who had every-thing to lose by war, expressed sympathy and regret and denied all knowledge of the disaster. On American demand, Spain abandoned its concentration camps for Cuban civilians, a method particularly dis-tasteful to American opinion, and said it was willing to conclude an armistice with the rebels. At first, however, the Spanish government could not bring itself to *request* such a truce, nor would it agree to American mediation if negotiations failed. Desperate, Spain tried to secure intervention by the European powers, some of whose rulers sympathized with her and disliked the republican upstart. American power, European disunion, and British opposition put serious interna-tional action out of the question. The powers appealed to McKinley for moderation, and both the Pope and the powers put pressure on Spain for further concessions. Finally Spain agreed to request an armistice though not to accept American mediation.

It was too late. Alarmed at a sudden swelling of public passion, reluctant to divide the country, and afraid that Congress might declare war against his will, McKinley on April 11 requested authority to use American troops to create stable government in Cuba. The final Spanish concession, which he had learned of the day before, was reported in an unnoticed sentence of his message. In a mood of patriotic exultation, Congress declared Cuba independent and de-manded Spanish withdrawal. Then, to show the purity of American intentions, it added the "Teller resolution" binding the United States not to annex Cuba.

VICTORY

Most Americans, watching Cuba with passionate indignation, did not know much about Spain's larger colony in the Far East, the Philippine Islands, where another colonial rebellion was under way. Theodore Roosevelt, as Assistant Secretary of the Navy, had directed Commodore George Dewey to assemble the United States Asiatic Squadron at Hong Kong and prepare, in the event of war, to attack the Spanish fleet in Manila Bay. Apparently Roosevelt's purpose had been military rather than expansionist: American rule of the Philippines was a possibility beyond even his imagination.

On May 1 Dewey attacked the Spanish fleet in Manila Harbor, destroying it without the loss of an American life. This astounding victory brought the Philippine question into being; it also left Dewey's squadron in a difficult position. Both friendly Britain and less friendly Germany also had naval forces in Manila Bay. Ashore, insurgent Filipinos confronted Spanish garrisons. The American fleet had brought the exiled leader Aguinaldo to the Philippines, but no American policy toward the rebellion had been defined. Finally a small American land force arrived. On the day after the war actually ended, the city of Manila surrendered to American troops, leaving insurgents and Spaniards disputing the rest of the archipelago.

Meantime in its original theater, the war went far less well at first. American coastal cities panicked at mythical rumors of Spanish raids, and mobilization proceeded with lamentable inefficiency. Still worse confusion marred the encampment of American forces in Florida and their embarkation for Cuba. Fortunately for the United States, Spanish equipment, tactics, and morale were in still worse shape.

After many misadventures, the remaining Spanish fleet was finally cornered in Santiago Bay and an American force, including Roosevelt's famous volunteer regiment the Rough Riders, was landed nearby without opposition. A number of small but bloody engagements in the approaches to Santiago gave Americans, including Roosevelt, a chance to prove their courage under fire. On July 3 the decrepit Spanish fleet sailed bravely out of the harbor to meet certain destruction by naval gunfire and on July 17 the city of Santiago surrendered, leaving the United States in control of Eastern Cuba. In early August General Nelson A. Miles completed a nearly bloodless conqest of Spain's other American island, Puerto Rico, and the fighting ended.

Actually, the United States was not in an easy position. American forces occupied only one end of Cuba and one city in the Philippines. Dressed in blue winter uniforms and fed on hardtack and repulsive canned meat (called by the press "embalmed beef"), American forces in Cuba were ridden with dysentery and malaria and threatened with yellow fever. Lieutenant Colonel Roosevelt, among others, was loudly demanding their recall. Even at home in the Florida camps, because of disgraceful neglect of sanitation, disease was spreading. (Eventually many times more lives were lost by disease than by enemy action.) Fortunately, Spain, without a navy, had no hope of continuing hostilities, and on August 12 an armistice was signed.

PEACE AND EMPIRE

As armistice terms, the United States insisted that Spain withdraw from Cuba and cede to the United States Puerto Rico, an island in the Ladrones (Guam), and the city and harbor of Manila. The fate of the rest of the Philippines (more than seven thousand large and small islands with about eight million people) was left for the peace conference to determine. At first reluctant to annex so much distant territory, McKinley feared another upsurge of public opinion like that which had swept the country into war. Finally he convinced himself that it was the duty of the United States to "uplift and civilize" the Philippines. Very reluctantly, Spain agreed to cede them in return for a payment of $20 million.

In the Senate, the treaty faced serious opposition from the antiimperialists. This diverse coalition included most northern Democrats and the familiar minority of eastern, reform-minded Republicans. It brought together such contrasting individuals as Bryan, Cleveland, Andrew Carnegie, Samuel Gompers, and Mark Twain. Libertarians argued passionately that empire over subject peoples would violate the Declaration of Independence and the Monroe Doctrine. Others pointed out that the Constitution provided no way of governing territories never destined to become states. Racists insisted that Filipinos were unassimilable, and strategists argued, more persuasively, that a Far Eastern possession would endanger American security.

On the other side, it was argued that the flag, once planted overseas, should not be pulled down, that annexation represented the obvious will of God, and that it was America's duty to Christianize the Philippines (which were actually one of the principal outposts of Christianity in the Far East). The strong interest of Japan and Germany in the spoils of the Spanish empire furnished another argument (Germany eventually picked up the Caroline Islands and all the Ladrones or Marianas but Guam).

The business community, generally opposed to war and colonialism but concerned for the expansion and protection of foreign trade, now tended to favor retention of the Philippines. This was partly for strategic reasons; both Hawaii and the Philippines would be useful if the United States was to resist European encroachment on China. Reluctantly the conservative Senate leadership agreed to go along with the President. Yet the two sides remained fairly even, and the treaty would not have passed had not Bryan, as head of the Democratic party, decided to support the treaty and fight the issue of annexation in the coming election.

In their 1900 convention the Democrats declared that antiimperialism was the "paramount issue," and the Republicans accepted the challenge. Theodore Roosevelt, one of the war's principal heroes, campaigned as McKinley's running mate. Actually, however, it cannot be proved that McKinley's solid victory constituted an endorsement of annexation. Many voted once more for the gold standard, the high tariff, and prosperity.

Perhaps the strongest real reason for retaining the Philippines was the lack of a clear alternative. It was obviously out of the question to suppress the revolt and return them to Spain, and nobody wanted to hand them to Germany or Japan. Disunited and in places uncivilized, the islands seemed hardly able to sustain independence without at least the protection of the United States. Yet many continued to feel that annexation was a mistake, both moral and strategic. If this was correct, perhaps the biggest mistake had been the initial occupation of Manila.

The imperialist tide, such as it was, carried with it not only the Philippines, Puerto Rico, and Guam, but also Hawaii and Samoa. McKinley had supported Hawaiian annexation since 1897, but this was accomplished, by joint resolution of Congress rather than by treaty, only in August 1898. Increased Far Eastern concern in general, Japanese interest in the islands in particular, and Hawaii's usefulness in wartime had furnished the decisive arguments. In 1900 the Samoan condominium was ended and the islands divided between Germany and the United States.

Meanwhile in Cuba, which the United States had sworn *not* to annex, American forces performed a heroic job of cleaning up yellow fever. They also quarreled with their Cuban allies. In 1902 they were withdrawn, but not before the Platt Amendment making Cuba a virtual American protectorate was incorporated in American legislation, the Cuban constitution, and a Cuban-American treaty. This provided that Cuba might not impair its own independence or increase its public debt beyond its capacity. To safeguard either Cuban independence or a government which could maintain "life, property, and individual liberty" the United States was given the right to intervene, which it did in 1906 and several times thereafter. Finally, Cuba was required to sell or lease a naval station to the United States. Not until the Franklin Roosevelt administration was the Platt Amendment finally abrogated, leaving Cuba politically independent but linked to the American economy.

America's imperial experience started unpleasantly when the Filipino insurgents, bitterly disappointed at not receiving independence, turned their guerrilla warfare against the United States. In the ensuing war, which lasted until 1902, Americans suffered more casualties than in the war with Spain. Like most troops fighting guerrilla enemies, American forces sometimes resorted to devastation, concentration camps, and even torture—the same methods for which America had denounced Spain. In a series of complex decisions the Supreme Court underlined one of the antiimperialist arguments by deciding that the Constitution did not necessarily apply in full vigor in "unincorporated territories" and that it was possible to levy tariffs on their products.

Despite these ironies, in the long run the American colonial record was a relatively good one. Everywhere strenuous work in education and sanitation was undertaken, and, despite the Court decision, substantial free trade established. Movement toward popular government began with the establishment of a legislature in Puerto Rico in 1900. In 1901 civil government replaced military in the Philippines, which received an elective assembly in 1907. Thus the worst predictions of the antiimperialists were not carried out: the United States did not turn, like Rome, from a Republic to an Empire. Neither did the hopes of the imperialists blossom: the resources of the Philippines remained substantially undeveloped, and poverty, in the Philippines and Puerto Rico, was ameliorated but by no means ended. In the twentieth century, most of the American people apparently gave little thought to their new acquisitions. In 1934, partly for ideological reasons and partly because of pressure from competing economic interests, Congress voted to give the Philippines their independence in ten years, and after World War II this pledge was carried out.

WORLD POWER

Thus the American venture into empire seems to have been a temporary enthusiasm. Yet its effects on foreign policy were profound and permanent. American hegemony in the Caribbean, already an accomplished fact, was underlined, and Britain, long the chief rival claimant, was glad to acknowledge it. In the second Hay-Pauncefote Treaty of 1901, England gave in to American demands for exclusive control of the proposed Isthmian canal, abrogating her own treaty rights to equality in this venture. Shortly afterward, Britain cheerfully cut her heavy overseas commitments by reducing her West Indian forces.

Caribbean hegemony was almost inevitable in this era of frank great-power policing of the world. America's ventures in the Far East were far more controversial. To the old, vague, more or less sentimental interest in commercial equality and the independence of Asian states was added a large and vulnerable Far Eastern colony, menaced particularly by the rising power of Japan. Despite her growing naval strength, the United States lacked power to defend these distant commitments.

Since 1895 Japan and the European powers had been forcing China to surrender leased territories and establishing large additional spheres of economic influence. In 1899 Secretary of State John Hay, a friend of Roosevelt and a partisan of the new "large policy," stated traditional American policy in a fresh manner. Partly at the prompting of American commercial interests, he addressed identical notes to the six leading powers asking them to affirm equal treatment for foreign commerce within their spheres of interest in China. Though the answers were ambiguous, Hay announced that the world had accepted this Open Door policy.

In 1900, when the antiforeign Boxer Rebellion endangered the lives of foreigners in Peking, the United States joined an international rescue expedition. At this time Hay broadened the Open Door policy by sending a second note affirming American support of Chinese territorial integrity and calling for commercial equality in all parts of the Chinese Empire, not just the spheres of European influence.

The Open Door policy pleased Americans and seemed far more in line with tradition than the acquisition of the Philippines. Yet the integrity of the huge, crumbling Chinese Empire added to the safety of the Philippines were big commitments, well beyond the actual, developed military power of the United States.

Inevitably, though tacitly, the course of events had drawn the nation closer to its old rival, Great Britain. During the Spanish War, when most European countries had resented America's chastisement of a proud European nation, Britain had supported the United States and Rudyard Kipling, then the most popular Anglo-Saxon author, had urged America to "take up the white man's burden" of empire. Like the United States, Britain wanted the *status quo* maintained in the Far East as well as the Caribbean and welcomed help in achieving this objective. In many American circles, especially in the eastern upper class, the turn of the century saw a revival of sentiment for British friendship on cultural and even racial grounds. The pro-British tendency was by no means shared, however, by the whole American public, large sections of which disliked British policies in Ireland, India, and South Africa and still thought of England as the stronghold of monarchy and aristocracy. Yet as the great powers chose up sides for the world conflict of the twentieth century, there was probably never much doubt that a showdown would find America on the side of the Atlantic, rather than the Central European, powers.

After the turn of the century most Americans were proud of the nation's new empire, fleet, and prestige and were glad that Washington was more often consulted in times of international crisis. They by no means realized, however, that active world politics demanded serious—in the long run even tragic—commitments. And for the first decade and a half of the twentieth century American interest shifted back, for the most part, to its traditional concentration on economic growth and domestic political controversy.

FOR FURTHER READING:

An informative, reliable history of recent American foreign policy is Richard W. Leopold, *The Growth of American Foreign Policy* (1962). The ideology of expansion is described by J. W. Pratt, *Expansionists of 1898* (1936). The best account of the emergence of the United States into power politics is Ernest R. May, *Imperial Democracy* (1961). Walter LaFeber, *The New Empire* (1963)* argues that the search for foreign markets played a central role in American foreign policy from 1860 to 1898. R. L. Beisner, *Twelve Against Empire* (1968) and E. B. Tompkins, *Anti-Imperialism in the United States* (1970) focus on the opponents of expansion. A lively and sometimes penetrating history of the McKinley administration is Margaret Leech, *In the Days of McKinley* (1959). It should be compared to Howard Wayne Morgan's provocative but not influential biography, *William McKinley and His America* (1963). Both Walter Millis, *The Martial Spirit* (1931), and Graham A. Comas, *An Army for Empire* (1971) are useful studies of the Spanish-American War; and Frank Freidel, *The Splendid Little War* (1958)*, is a highly entertaining pictorial history. The biographies of Theodore Roosevelt listed in later chapters will also prove useful for this topic.

---

* Available in paperback edition.

Roosevelt and
the Progressive Era
1901-1908

22

On September 6, 1901, President William McKinley, a moderately conservative statesman, was shot by an anarchist. When he died a week later the young and dynamic Theodore Roosevelt became president. This tragic incident is often taken to be the beginning of a new period of progressive reform which lasted until World War I. Actually, of course, the Progressive Era was not brought on by the assassin's bullet. Its sources lay deep in the economic, social, and moral history of the country.

THE MATURE ECONOMY

By 1900 the American economy was relatively mature. It was no longer necessary to concentrate all resources and efforts on the expansion of productive capacity. Production continued to increase fairly rapidly in the new century, but not at the fantastic rate of the previous period.

Progressivism owed some of its nature, if not its existence, to the fact that the period 1901–1914 was one of relatively stable prosperity. There was no prolonged depression like those of the 1870s or 1890s, but only two brief financial panics (1903 and 1907). The farmer, that perennial stepchild of the American economy, entered one of his few periods of relative contentment. Of course many farmers were continually having a hard struggle, and some farm evils like tenancy were still increasing. But average farm income, for a change, was moving upward. This was partly because city population, at home and abroad, was increasing faster than farm acreage. By 1900, only 35 percent of Americans lived on farms.

For some of the new urban population, crowded into slums and immigrant ghettoes, things were less than cheerful. Real wages for industrial labor rose more slowly than in earlier decades. Never were social contrasts more extreme, from the still uninhibited multimillionaire, with his Fifth Avenue palace and his fifty-room Newport cottage, to the tubercular child in the cotton mill or the garment worker in his tenement sweatshop. America as before led the world in industrial accidents. Thus it is only with careful qualification that one can call the Progressive Era a time of contentment. It is more nearly correct to call it a period of hope, especially for the politically articulate middle class.

Business consolidation reached a peak at about the turn of the century. Contrary to progressive fears, monopoly did not stifle competition; innovation and expansion kept it in check. During the Progressive Era, the largest firms retained but did not increase their share of the nation's industry. This was enough to make big business the main target of criticism. Its defenders could argue that not all consequences of bigness were bad; one for instance was more money for such advances as electrification and research laboratories. Public relations and advertising received much attention and so did the "Scientific Management" movement of Frederick W. Taylor. Taylor, originally an engineer, urged that each movement of each worker be made as efficient as possible through close study, minute division of function, and rigorous supervision. Working toward similar objectives with less theory, Henry Ford began production of his Model T in 1909. By 1914 he was producing a quarter of a million cars a year.

One aspect of business consolidation that received a great deal of attention was the tendency toward banker control. Only a dozen great investment houses, led by that of J. P. Morgan, could float the securities necessary for one of the period's gigantic mergers, like that of U.S. Steel in 1901. These private bankers, controlling insurance and trust companies as well as industries and railroads, could draw on a large part of the national savings. When necessary, they could supplement their resources with those of their foreign connections. Thus they could perform many of the functions of supervision and stabilization traditionally carried out by official central banks; in a sense Morgan was the successor of Nicholas Biddle. Conscientiously, Morgan and his allies tried to end cutthroat competition, prevent risky investment, and rescue sick industries before their financial collapse. In return they exacted not only high fees but control. Through seats on the governing boards of railroads, steel companies, and many other corporations they could enforce their own ideas of sound operation on a large part of American business.

These functions, however useful, were not without their costs.

Sometimes the regnant bankers were unimaginative and unenterprising (they were very reluctant, for instance, to back automobile manufacturers). They did not worry much about working conditions in the industries they controlled. And, as the period's two panics testify, they did not always achieve the stability they aimed at. Even if the bankers of the age of Morgan had been perfect, however, they would not have been popular. The main single complaint of progressives was directed against what they regarded as immoral and irresponsible power, and this was personified by the mighty, invisible "Money Trust."

THE PROGRESSIVE MIND

Antimonopoly feelings were as old as the Republic, and most of the rest of the progressive ideology was a continuation of the previous period's social criticism. Settlement workers were still discovering urban poverty; ministers were still reinterpreting Christianity in terms of social reform; social scientists were still challenging the basis of nineteenth-century individualist morality. But the discontent of the early twentieth century had a new tone, and this tone was set by a cheerful, though not a complacent, middle class. Careful study has shown that the leaders of early twentieth-century progressivism tended to be fairly prosperous professional or businessmen in their early forties, usually Anglo-Saxon and Protestant, often motivated by personal ambition as well as moral indignation.

Side by side with progressivism, radicalism was also flourishing. In the century's first decade the Socialist party elected many local officials and one congressman. In 1912 its presidential candidate, Eugene Debs, got 6 percent of the popular vote. Such Socialist intellectuals as Upton Sinclair and Jack London confidently predicted a socialist America in the near future. On the far left, the syndicalist Industrial Workers of the World, uncompromising advocates of class conflict, organized western miners and lumbermen. In 1912 the IWW began to spread to eastern textile towns.

Except when frightened by such episodes as the Colorado mine wars or the *Los Angeles Times* bombing of 1911, middle-class progressives refused to be deeply alarmed by the rise of radicalism. Only a few of the most hopeful and fearful Americans believed that revolution was close. Theodore Roosevelt, who had stormed about the menace of anarchism in 1896, could find a good word in 1908 for some socialists. The Socialist party itself was sharply divided between advocates of gradual and immediate change.

Neither fear nor personal suffering played much part in the motives of progressive leaders. Doubtless, concern about the high cost of living helped to turn the thoughts of some toward the trusts and the tariff. Many sympathized with the plight of the urban poor. Yet even such obvious evils as child labor and slums looked different in a period without major depressions. Problems like this were not proofs of society's failure, but calls to action. And for most progressives, the most pressing questions were not humanitarian but moral and political.

First, progressives wanted to end corruption, to throw out the crooks and return power to "good citizens" like themselves. Second, they wanted to control "big business," not in the interest of socialism but in that of free enterprise. Some of them wanted to break up large combinations. Others concluded that "the trusts" should be allowed to exist under close supervision, or that the future lay with some kind of partnership between government and business.

Because they found life in America good, progressives wanted to preserve its promise for the future. They rejected the determinism that had been common in the late nineteenth century. Science, government, the public morality were all changing, and changing for the better. There were no such things as immutable laws, except (for most progressives) concerning moral fundamentals. Following William James, who died in 1910, the pragmatic school of philosophy argued that particular judgments should be made on the basis of concrete consequences rather than according to general metaphysical principles. In educational theory, John Dewey and his followers insisted that children should be taught to solve the problems which arose in their own environment instead of being instructed in the wisdom of the past. The law and even the Constitution were reinterpreted as guides to action rather than unchanging codes. At the height of the Progressive Era, people talked not only of the New Freedom of Woodrow Wilson or the New Nationalism of Theodore Roosevelt, but also of the new literature, the new psychology, even the "new woman."

Optimism gave these middle-class reformers much of their confidence and courage. It also blinded many of them to some of the most difficult contemporary problems. Most progressives seemed strangely unconcerned, for example, about racial injustice. A few of them, including Oswald Villard, Lillian Wald, Jane Addams, and Clarence Darrow agitated openly for Negro rights and even joined the black militant W. E. B. Du Bois in organizing the National Association for the Advancement of Colored People in 1909. But progressivism was largely for whites only and most of its adherents shared the nearly universal belief that blacks were inherently inferior and socially unassimilable. A similar attitude applied to the new immigrants who flowed after 1890 in a great human tide from southern and eastern Europe into the nation's cities. Although appalled by conditions in the urban slums, these otherwise humane and tolerant reformers rarely questioned nativistic assumptions and some of them were in fact in the vanguard of the immigrant restriction movement.

THE PROGRESSIVE ACCOMPLISHMENT

Reform started with the exposure of crying evil. The vogue for sensational accounts of corruption and monopoly began with books like Henry Demarest Lloyd's attack on Standard Oil (*Wealth against Commonwealth*, 1894). The new fashion was taken up by sensational newspapers like those of Hearst and by a new crop of popular, cheap, ably-edited magazines led by *McClure's*. For a while one could hardly pick up a periodical without running into a heavily documented exposure of the city traction ring or the patent medicine trust. Muckrakers, as Roosevelt called the new journalists, attacked big business, the unions, the churches, the press itself, state and city government, and finally the United States Senate. While many people read the muckrakers for sheer excitement, some were stirred to action.

Some of the most important progressive crusades started outside politics in such fields as charity organization, education reform, or juvenile courts (concern for the young was characteristic). Sooner or later, however, most concrete accomplishments had to be registered in political action.

The first progressive political offensive was directed against the most obvious target: America's swollen cities, where grafting utilities and protected vice were all too obvious. City reform got under way in the 1890s, and in the first decade of the century many cities moved from boss rule to reform. Some moved back soon enough, but often the cycle left a heritage of public waterworks, public or highly regulated street railways, tenement laws, and playgrounds. Sometimes new charters tried to take city affairs out of politics by means of a commission or city manager system.

Still more was accomplished in the states, perhaps the most important laboratories of reform. In 1900 Robert M. La Follette, one of the most militant and uncompromising progressive leaders, became governor of Wisconsin. Working closely with experts from the state university, he made Wisconsin a "laboratory of democracy." Reformers won control of one state after another in the Middle West and then in the Far West and East. Even in the South, where reform was often allied with anti-Negro demagoguery, the progressive movement demonstrated vitality. Typical state reforms included a great many devices intended to keep the bosses and railroads out of power and "the people" in control. These included the direct primary, the secret ballot, and even preferential popular choice of United States senators, still officially chosen by legislatures. Woman suffrage was adopted by thirteen states, mostly in the West, by 1914. Beginning in Oregon, a number of western states put lawmaking directly in the hands of the people through the initiative and referendum.

States were pioneers in such economic measures as close regulation of railroads, utilities, and trusts; progressive taxation; and conservation of natural resources. Labor legislation passed by states included workmen's compensation laws for accident cases, child labor laws, and laws establishing maximum hours and minimum wages for women. (Laws regulating men's labor conditions were sometimes overturned by the courts and always strongly opposed as interference with individual liberty.) By 1917 two-thirds of the states, pushed by fervent reformers, had prohibited alcoholic liquors.

Obviously, many of these measures needed to be completed by federal action, and ambitious progressive leaders were eager to move from state capitals to Washington. In 1906 La Follette himself joined what muckrakers called the "millionaire's club," the United States Senate. With other progressive senators, he played a major part in pushing presidents toward reform.

THE PROGRESSIVE HERO

Theodore Roosevelt's inauguration did not cause the Progressive Era, but it was a major event. For the first time since Jackson, a president became the most popular American. For the first time since Lincoln a president stretched the powers of his office. Like Jefferson and Franklin Roosevelt, Theodore Roosevelt was harder to understand than he seemed. On the surface he was noisy, impulsive, and even violent, given to dramatic phrases like "the square deal" and "the strenuous life." He liked to lay down the law about literature, science, or personal morality. At times he acted rashly, as when he discharged without honor three divisions of highly decorated black soldiers on unfounded charges of rioting at Brownsville, Texas. Yet most of his impulsiveness came either early or late in his career or was confined to minor issues. His major decisions as president were usually shrewd compromises.

An informal, confident aristocrat, Roosevelt could indulge in pillow fights with his children or drag sweating diplomats on rocky scrambles. This delighted the public and by no means compromised the dignity of the presidential office. A consistent nationalist, Roosevelt took it for granted that the president of the United States was the equal not only of foreign emperors but of domestic millionaires. A born politician, he never quite lost touch either with radicals like Lincoln Steffens or extreme conservatives like Senator Nelson Aldrich. To each he managed to appear as a defender against the other. Like all good politicians, Roosevelt as president was a master of timing. When he became president, he reassured shocked conservatives by announcing his continuance of McKinley's policies and cabinet. At the same time he put out a trial balloon by denouncing the trusts and moved further in that direction when public response was favorable. In 1904, he easily defeated a conservative Democrat, Judge Alton B. Parker, for reelection. President in his own right and conscious of the progressive tide throughout the country, he moved further toward reform objectives. Then in 1907, when the financial panic seemed to demand caution, he followed the suggestions of J. P. Morgan. Finally, in 1908–1909, about to leave office, he called for a host of drastic reform measures. This accomplished nothing immediately, but left a program which his successors could not ignore.

The actual domestic accomplishments of Roosevelt were important, but less important than his demonstration of the possibilities of the presidency. Despite his reputation as a trust buster, Roosevelt was never hostile to big business as such. He disliked practices he considered dishonest and deeply resented defiance of the federal government. His first request in his December, 1901, message to Congress was for the creation of a Department of Commerce and Labor, including a Bureau of Corporations which would collect information about abuses committed by interstate industries. This moderate measure passed against heavy opposition. In 1902 Wall Street was startled to learn that the administration was going to sue the Northern Securities Company, a typical Morgan-sponsored railroad merger, under the neglected and emasculated Anti-Trust Law. Though the administration won this suit and later others, Roosevelt never placed much confidence in sudden punitive assaults against particular mergers. Wanting to prevent unethical practice rather than sheer bigness, he would have preferred (but did not get) legislation providing for the registration and more orderly regulation of all interstate business.

In 1902 the administration had to deal with a bitter anthracite coal strike. Though bituminous supplies were ample, the press played up the prospects of a desperate fuel shortage. Instead of simply sending the troops to the coal fields to "restore order" after the manner of Cleveland, Roosevelt called both parties to the White House. Unwilling to concede equality to their opponents, the operators adamantly refused to discuss concessions. This angered Roosevelt, who began looking into the possibilities of using the army to mine coal, a threat which went well beyond any known presidential powers. After much pressure, the operators agreed to the appointment of a mixed arbitration commission, and in March, 1903, this group made its award. It gave the miners a 10 percent raise but denied them several of their other objectives, including union recognition. Trouble in the coal fields was long to continue, but a precedent had been established for a new kind of presidential action.

In his second administration Roosevelt had to deal with the demands of the growing group of midwestern Progressive Republicans in Congress. Of all these, the most overdue was railroad regulation. The Elkins Act of 1903, supported by the railroads themselves, had forbidden special rebates to large customers, but the Interstate Commerce Commission was still hamstrung in any effort to regulate rates. After a long process of presidential pressure and compromise, Congress passed the Hepburn Act in 1906. This measure gave the Commission power to set aside existing schedules and determine reasonable rates pending court review. The Commission could also prescribe uniform bookkeeping practices to enable it to keep track of operations, and its jurisdiction was strengthened in other ways. It did not, however, receive the power to make an evaluation of railroad property as a basis for rate-making, an omission which bitterly disappointed Senator La Follette. Similarly, the Federal Pure Food and Drug Act and Meat Inspection Act of the same year gave progressives only part of what they wanted. Some of the worst practices of packers and patent medicine producers were ended, but fraudulent advertising was not prohibited.

Roosevelt, a believer in outdoor life and a vigorous champion of the national interest, prided himself most of all on his efforts for conservation of natural resources. For three centuries Americans had devoted themselves to exploiting their lumber, minerals, and other wealth as rapidly as possible. Now many were becoming conscious of the possibilities of exhaustion as well as the inefficiency and im-morality of indiscriminate private appropriation. Under an act passed in 1891 but so far used only a moderate amount, Roosevelt withdrew enormous areas from public entry and set them aside as National Forests. Water power and mineral sites were also withdrawn, and Roosevelt gave his backing to federal construction of irrigation works under the Newlands Act (1902).

Here as elsewhere, however, the President's chief service was probably the exercise of his talent for publicity. A White House conference of notables and a well-staffed national commission re-ported on the complex problems of land, water, forest, timber, and mineral conservation. A devoted core of conservationists was built up, led by Roosevelt's friend Gifford Pinchot, head of the Federal Forestry Service. Yet opposition by western interests accustomed to private use

of public resources continued formidable, and conservationists secured only a start toward their goals.

The considerable list of reforms *not* undertaken by the Roosevelt
administration was headed by tariff reform. This was increasingly
demanded by midwestern progressives, whose constituents had always
been divided in their opinions on the tariff, and were now hurt by
foreign reprisals against American agricultural products. The President,
however, could never really interest himself passionately in the tariff.
Besides, any move in the matter was sure to split the Republican party.
So this, with much other unfinished business, was left to Roosevelt's
unlucky successor.

IN DANGEROUS WATERS

In foreign policy, Roosevelt seemed to be in his element. An old
expansionist, he was both better informed about foreign policy than
any recent president and more interested in it. More than most
progressives, he seemed to understand the relation between power
and objectives. Yet here, more often than in his domestic policy, he
betrayed a tendency to rashness. In contradiction to his much quoted
adage, Roosevelt did not always speak softly and his stick was
sometimes not big enough.

Roosevelt, like many European contemporaries, believed that the
world had to be benevolently but firmly supervised by the enlightened
great powers. Though he was occasionally irritated by the British, he
took it for granted that the Anglo-Saxon powers, as equals and friends,
should lead the procession. Then came the other Western European
nations, and then a newcomer Roosevelt greatly respected for its
martial virtues, Japan.

Part of the job of the enlightened nations was to prevent major
wars. Roosevelt still believed that a manly willingness to fight was part
of the essential moral equipment of nations and individuals. Force was
still justified to enfore "progress" on backward peoples, and each great
nation must retain the right to protect its vital interests. With these
important qualifications, Roosevelt could support some of the goals of
the contemporary peace movement. He furthered the work of The
Hague conferences on world peace, the establishment of a world
court, and the negotiation of treaties for the arbitration of most
disputes.

The most obvious accomplishment of the administration was its
continued and rapid movement toward American domination of the
Central American and Caribbean areas. The Hay-Pauncefote negotiations, under way before Roosevelt took office, cleared away British

objections to an American-controlled Isthmian canal. Congress had decided that the best route lay through Nicaragua where the United States had obtained treaty rights to build a canal. However, powerful and somewhat shabby private interests, concerned in part with protecting the investment of the nearly defunct French Panama Canal Company, persuaded the Senate to shift to the Panama route. When the Republic of Colombia, which owned Panama, refused to accept American terms, Roosevelt regarded it as an inadmissible blocking of progress by a backward nation.

A revolution in the Isthmus, carried out with American cognizance and naval protection, made Panama an independent republic. With the new country, the United States immediately negotiated a very favorable treaty providing for American "use, occupation, and control" of a Canal Zone. The French company got its money, Panama got $10 million, work started on the canal, and Roosevelt saw the whole affair as one of his great successes. His critics have said, however, that the episode left deep resentment in Latin America, that the canal could have been built in Nicaragua, and that it could have been built in Panama without a revolution if Roosevelt had shown a little more patience in his negotiations with Colombia.

In 1902 Venezuela, once more the center of an international incident, refused to pay its international debts. Britain and Germany both reacted as great powers usually did in such circumstances. Their ships blockaded and even bombarded Venezuelan ports until the Venezuelan dictator agreed to arbitrate his government's obligations. Secretly but forcefully Roosevelt warned the powers to end their naval action. When Germany was slow in complying, Roosevelt backed his warning with a display of naval force.

In Roosevelt's view, if the United States objected to intervention by others in the Caribbean, it was her duty when necessary to police that area herself. In 1904, when the Dominican Republic found itself in similar financial straits, Roosevelt moved in. Against the Senate's opposition, he made an arrangement under which the United States collected Dominican customs, paid the country's creditors, and put its government on an allowance. This was done so successfully and even tactfully that neither Europe nor Latin America objected. However, Roosevelt accompanied his action with a series of characteristic and sweeping statements constituting a new corollary to the Monroe Doctrine and claiming the right of intervention to prevent "chronic wrong-doing" in the Western Hemisphere.

Under Roosevelt's immediate successors, this "Roosevelt Corollary" was interpreted with less restraint. The relatively conservative Taft administration tried to push American capital into Caribbean countries with the idea of subsequent protection by force. The liberal Wilson administration repudiated this kind of "Dollar Diplomacy," but itself intervened far more forcibly to secure good government. By World War I, the Caribbean was clearly an American lake. The United States owned Puerto Rico and the Virgin Islands (bought from Denmark in 1917), controlled the Canal Zone, had a formal protectorate over Cuba under the Platt Amendment, and had liberal precedent for armed intervention elsewhere in the area. Later during the Hoover and Franklin Roosevelt administrations, the United States gradually modified its policies in an effort to overcome Latin American resentment, formally abandoning all claims to the right of unilateral intervention.

The other area of increased American activity was the Far East. China, unmilitary and unprogressive, did not meet Roosevelt's standards for being a civilized nation. Thus he had no objection in principle to foreign enterprise there. Like Hay, however, he objected to exclusive control by foreign powers of commercial opportunity in any part of Chinese territory. His suspicion was deeply aroused by Russian domination of Manchuria. When Russia and Japan went to war in 1905 over rival interests in Korea and Manchuria, Roosevelt gave strong diplomatic support to Japan.

The Russo-Japanese War, like the Spanish-American War, was a smashing defeat of a European by a non-European power with considerable effects on the world balance. With the Russian fleets destroyed and Russia facing revolution, Japan yet lacked resources for continuing the war until Russia surrendered completely. Thus both powers accepted Roosevelt's mediation and gathered to make peace at Portsmouth, New Hampshire. Delighted at his novel role, Roosevelt handled the negotiations with considerable skill. Yet the Peace of Portsmouth, which gave Japan important territorial gains but denied her a money indemnity, proved unpopular in the victorious country.

Thus Roosevelt's hopes for a stable balance in the Far East were defeated, and his major Far Eastern problem during the rest of his term in office was the rising power of Japan. His policies were a characteristic compound of realism, tact, and bravado. Since he could not prevent it, he accepted Japanese domination in Korea and took no action when Japan began to divide actual control of Manchuria with her defeated enemy, Russia. When California and particularly San Francisco started discriminating harshly against Japanese immigrants, Roosevelt put federal pressure on them to desist. At the same time, he negotiated the "Gentlemen's Agreement" (1907) whereby Japan barred emigration of laborers to America. In 1906 he sent the United States fleet, by now the world's third largest, on a trip around the world. Its stop in Tokyo Bay, a daring and imaginative gesture, was a complete social success. More or less in return for all this hard work, Roosevelt was able to secure the Root-Takahira Agreement of 1908. In this both countries agreed to respect equal opportunity for foreign commerce in China, Chinese territorial integrity, and each other's Far Eastern possessions. For the present, this certainly seemed to guarantee the Philippines. How far it protected Japanese mainland gains was not clear.

In 1906, when France and Germany were at loggerheads over Morocco, Roosevelt helped persuade his friend the German kaiser to accept a settlement which left France dominant.

Never had the United States been taken so seriously in world politics. Yet despite Roosevelt's imagination and skill, it is not clear that in the long run his work greatly advanced either American interests or world peace. United States hegemony in Central America, a fact in any case, had been underlined with unnecessary roughness. In the Far East, Japan had replaced Russia as the principal potential threat, and neither the Open Door nor the integrity of China looked much more secure. American commitments in this area still exceeded American power. Throughout the world, the United States had swung a little further toward alignment with the developing Anglo-French-Russian-Japanese entente. The American people, delighted with the country's increased prestige, still often ignored the dangerous realities of foreign policy.

Such carping, however, was little heard at the end of Roosevelt's term of office in 1908–1909. In an unguarded moment at the time of his election in 1904, he had promised not to seek another term. Undoubtedly regretting this, he easily forced the Republican party to accept as his successor his friend and Secretary of War, William Howard Taft. Campaigning against the two-time loser Bryan on a platform of the Roosevelt policies, Taft won easily. Saying goodbye to his "tennis cabinet" and his ambassadorial cronies but not to the nation's affections, Roosevelt departed on an African big-game hunt to be followed by a triumphal tour of European capitals.

CONFLICTING HISTORICAL VIEWPOINTS

Who Were the Progressives?

In his analysis of The Progressive Movement *(1915), Parke De Witt, the first scholar to study progressivism, accepted the interpretation offered by the reformers themselves. Like them, he viewed their movement as an uncompromising onslaught against big business. The period, he concluded, was one of conflict between "the people" and "the interests." Essentially the same idea pervaded the two most famous historical studies written during the 1920s. Vernon L. Parrington's* Main Currents in American Thought *(3 vols., 1927–30) and Charles and Mary Beard's* The Rise of American Civilization *(1927) viewed progressivism as the lineal descendant of a reform tradition that stretched back in American history to the age of Jefferson and Jackson. Pitting the masses against business moguls and crooked politicians, the movement was the twentieth-century phase of the age-old struggle between democracy and aristocracy, equality and privilege.*

Writing from within the progressive frame of reference, such scholars as De Witt, Parrington and Beard were, in effect, involved participants whose sympathetic and simplistic analysis of progressivism was not shared by historians of subsequent generations. The events of the 1920s and 1930s offered new historical vantage points from which to view the movement. To those who lived through the political reaction of "Normalcy" and the economic crisis of the Great Depression, progressivism generally seemed less idealistic and much less effective than earlier scholars assumed. As early as 1932, John Chamberlain, a young Marxist, studied the era closely and then bade Farewell to Reform. *The progressives, he concluded, were nostalgic conservatives seeking to restore a simpler past, not liberal reformers responding to the challenges of industrialism and urbanism. Although Harold U. Faulkner could still celebrate progressivism as* The Quest for Social Justice *(1931), most scholars from Chamberlain's time forward shared his doubts about the nature of the movement.*

Thus, both George Mowry's The California Progressives *(1951) and Richard Hofstadter's* The Age of Reform *(1955) portrayed the era as one in which the urban middle class sought to restore its position of leadership. The progressives were not selfless crusaders for popular democracy, these scholars affirmed, but bourgeois victims of status anxiety. Drawn from the old and established professional elite (lawyers, educators, ministers, editors), whose influence had been eclipsed by a rising new class of industrial and financial plutocrats, the progressives struggled to regain their lost power and deference.*

In a somewhat different vein, Samuel P. Hays's The Response to Industrialism, 1885–1914 *(1957) and Robert Wiebe's* Businessmen and Reform *(1962) cast additional doubts on the traditional view that progressivism was basically a people's crusade against big business. In fact, both argued that so-called "special interests" often favored meaningful reforms that "the people" opposed. In their view, the progressives were neither disinterested do-gooders nor disquieted bourgeois, but realistic conservatives who sought to bring order and efficiency to a chaotic and wasteful society.* The Search for Order, 1877–1920 *(1967), Wiebe's second book and the most systematic expression of this interpretation, suggested that in their quest for* stability and system the "new middle class" progressives often found ready allies in big corporate managers.

Since World War II, then, historians have redefined the sources of progressivism and its relationship to the business community. Although delineating the conservative tendencies inherent in the progressive mind, most scholars still accept the traditional equation of progressivism with reform. New Left historians, however, have denied even that. Gabriel Kolko, for example, has described the movement as The Triumph of Conservatism (1963). In his view, the progressives were not reformers at all and the chief characteristic of the era was not orderly change in the public interest, but complete control by business interests. Clearly, Kolko's is a minority view. But his total inversion of the traditional interpretation serves as a telling reminder that history is art, not science.

FOR FURTHER READING:

George Mowry, The Era of Theodore Roosevelt (1958)* is a good survey. The best single book on Roosevelt himself is probably still H. F. Pringle, Theodore Roosevelt (1931)*. It can be supplemented by Roosevelt's Autobiography (1921), J. M. Blum's penetrating sketch, The Republican Roosevelt (1954)*, and W. H. Harbaugh's Power and Responsibility (1961). Other specimens of the very rich biographical literature are Lincoln Steffens' fascinating and untrustworthy Autobiography (2 vols., 1931); William Allen White's solid and revealing Autobiography (1946); Daniel Levine's Jane Addams and the Liberal Tradition (1971); and William F. Holmes, The White Chief: James Kimble Vardaman (1970). The Socialist Party of America (1955) is David Shannon's subject; and in We Shall Be All (1969) Melvin Dubofsky dissects the IWW. Important statements on race relations in an age of reform include: R. S. Baker, Following the Color Line (1908)*; Temple Kirby, Darkness at the Dawning (1972); Ann J. Lane, The Brownsville Affair (1971); August Meier, Negro Thought in America, 1880–1915 (1963); and David W. Southern, The Malignant Heritage (1968). The intellectual history of the period is outlined in H. S. Commager, The American Mind (1952)*, and some important aspects of it are interpreted in M. G. White, Social Thought in America, The Revolt Against Formalism (1949)*. Roosevelt's foreign policy is examined by H. K. Beale: Theodore Roosevelt and the Rise of America to World Power (1956)*.

---

* Available in paperback edition.

One major facet of progressivism is illustrated and examined in Richard M. Abrams, *The Issue of Federal Regulation in the Progressive Era* (Berkeley Readings in American History, 1963)*.

THE PROGRESSIVE ERA

	President	Domestic Events	Foreign Policy: Europe, Asia	Foreign Policy: Latin America
1898			Spanish-American War. 1899 Open Door Policy. Boxer Rebellion.	
1900	McKinley *R* (September 6, 1901, assassinated)	Gold Standard Act.		
1902		Newlands Reclamation Act. 1903 Elkins Act. Coal strike settled. Northern Securities case.		1901 Platt Amendment. Venezuela Incident. 1903 Panama Affair.
1904	Roosevelt *R*		1905 Russo-Japanese War and Peace of Portsmouth. Algeciras Conference on Morocco.	"Roosevelt Corollary"
1906	Taft *R*	Hepburn Act. Pure Food and Drug Act. 1907 Panic	1907 "Gentlemen's Agreement" on Japanese immigration. Root-Takahira Agreement.	
1908		Conservation conference. 1909 Payne-Aldrich Tariff. Mann-Elkins Act. 1911 "Rule of Reason" decisions.		
1910	Wilson *D*		1911 Chinese Railway Consortium.	Mexican Revolution.
1912		1913 Underwood Tariff. Federal Trade Commission Act. Clayton Act.		1913 "Watchful Waiting" in Mexico.
1914	Wilson *D*		(August) War in Europe.	Tampico and Vera Cruz incidents.
1916		Federal Farm Loan Act. Adamson Act.	1915 (May) *Lusitania* sunk. (May) United States threat and German concession on submarine warfare.	Mexican border warfare.

The Peak of Progressivism
1909-1917
23

In 1908 William Howard Taft, proclaiming his devotion to Roosevelt's progressive policies, was an easy winner over the perennial William Jennings Bryan. Pointing to Taft's experience in government—as a judge, as first civil governor of the Philippines, as Secretary of War and presidential troubleshooter—Roosevelt and others predicted an outstanding administration. Actually Taft had experience in every relevant area but that which proved most important: democratic politics.

TAFT AND THE PROGRESSIVES

Later, seeking reasons for the administration's relative failure, critics were to caricature Taft as a fat and lazy reactionary. Actually, Taft was handicapped not so much by his three hundred pounds as by his conception of the presidency. His devotion to the Roosevelt policies was genuine, and for causes he believed in he could work hard. But he was convinced that the president should stay within his constitutional role and not stretch it as had every successful president since Jackson. And in showdowns, he could not help preferring decent and polite conservatives to most progressives with their radical rhetoric and their disregard of constitutional niceties.

Perhaps no Republican president coming to power in 1909 could have been successful. Since the Panic of 1907 times had been a little less prosperous and the growing progressive movement demanded more drastic action about the major unsolved problems: trust control, taxes, tariffs. Roosevelt, sometimes by sidestepping these issues, had managed to avoid an outright split between Republican reformers and Republican conservatives. Yet even his political magic could not have prevented a clash much longer. Standpat conservatives still controlled the party machinery while ambitious, aggressive Republican progressives, mostly from the Midwest, were increasing their strength in both Houses of Congress with every election.

Blaming the rising cost of living on the sky-high Dingley Tariff, many western progressives demanded a tariff cut. Once more a moderate tariff reduction bill sailed through the House only to be modified sharply upward in the Senate. Taft, who was squarely on record for tariff reduction and had succeeded in toning down the bill's worst excesses, believed that the resultant compromise was the best that could be secured. Stung by progressive charges of betrayal, he went so far as to say, in September, 1909, that the new Payne-Aldrich Tariff was the best the Republican party had ever passed. At the same time he failed to support the progressives in their successful attack against the near-dictatorial power of Speaker Joseph G. Cannon. (Taft disliked Cannon but wanted his support for the tariff bill.) Again, because Taft and his Secretary of the Interior Richard A. Ballinger were slower-going and more legal minded in their attitude toward conservation of natural resources, many progressives feared that they were betraying the national domain to private interests. By the spring of 1910, Taft was seen in some progressive circles as a reactionary and a traitor to the Roosevelt heritage.

Despite the President's political ineptitude, it can be argued that his administration brought more solid progressive accomplishments than Roosevelt's. The Taft years saw the introduction of two progressive amendments to the Constitution, the Sixteenth (income tax) and the Seventeenth (direct election of senators). With the latter Taft had little to do, but he played an important part in starting on its way the income tax amendment, potentially the period's most revolutionary change in government.

Progressive legislation passed during Taft's presidency, much of it with his support, included the Mann-Elkins Act strengthening the Interstate Commerce Commission, the Postal Savings and Parcel Post acts, the establishment of a federal Bureau of Mines and a Children's Bureau, and the separation of the Labor from the Commerce Department. Still more impressive is the fact that Taft's administration brought more than twice as many antitrust suits as that of his spectacularly trust-busting predecessor. Actually Roosevelt had lost confidence early in the possibility of halting consolidation and believed instead in federal regulation to prevent unfair competition and deliberate moves toward actual monopoly. This was approximately the doctrine that the Supreme Court, in the Standard Oil and American Tobacco Company decisions of 1912, enunciated in distinguishing between unreasonable and reasonable restraint of trade. Precisely because Taft was more conservative than Roosevelt, he believed more strongly in enforcing the Sherman Act on the assumption that it meant what it said.

In the fall of 1911, for instance, Taft infuriated Roosevelt by moving against United States Steel. J. P. Morgan, who controlled the giant steel corporation, had cooperated with Roosevelt in trying to control the Panic of 1907. Roosevelt had promised that the steel company would not be sued for acquiring Tennessee Coal and Iron in that crisis. Now the Taft administration, apparently repudiating his promise, named the purchase as part of the grounds for the suit.

Like Taft's domestic policy, his foreign policy amounted to a shift of emphasis which seemed to his critics a betrayal of principle. Roosevelt had believed in American political—and, when necessary, military—intervention abroad to protect political stability and the balance of power. Within the limits of these objectives, he favored American capital export. Taft and his Secretary of State, Philander Knox, believed frankly in using American foreign investment as an instrument of policy. Positive efforts to further private foreign ventures would lead both to peace and to the welfare of the recipient countries.

The administration's ventures in what its critics called "Dollar Diplomacy" did not seem to work out that way. In the Caribbean, Taft's program involved him in unpopular military ventures, while in the Far East it led to a startling departure from realism. Roosevelt, after trying various tacks in Far Eastern policy, had finally come to recognize some of the limitations of American power in the area, especially with reference to the rising might of Japan. Taft and Knox insisted on trying to force American participation in Chinese railway development and made a further effort to internationalize Japan's economic ventures in Manchuria. This policy angered Japan and other foreign powers, failed to sustain Chinese integrity, won only grudging and temporary support from American capital, and was reversed by Taft's successor.

Even the most benign aspects of Taft's foreign policy turned out badly in political terms. His long and vigorous negotiations for tariff reciprocity with Canada were regarded by many midwesterners as an effort to sell out western agriculture for the benefit of eastern industry. When he finally pushed a Canadian reciprocity treaty through the Senate, the Canadians, alarmed by loose American talk of eventual annexation, rejected it. Earnestly devoted to peace, the President negotiated treaties with Great Britain and France promising to arbitrate all differences, even those involving vital interests and national honor. Ardent nationalists were alarmed and the treaties were amended into meaninglessness in the Senate.

REPUBLICANS AND PROGRESSIVES, 1910–1912

From early in 1910 Taft, stung by progressive criticism, threw the administration's powers, including patronage, against the progressive wing of his own party in the primary elections. In turn, progressives denounced "Dollar Diplomacy," tariff betrayal, and conservation setbacks. The result of the congressional elections was a bad beating for the Republican party as a whole and particularly severe losses for the Taft-backed eastern conservatives. From this point on Democrats controlled the House of Representatives and a Democratic-insurgent Republican coalition the Senate. Needless to say, the rest of Taft's term was a torment to him, and it became increasingly clear that he could not count on renomination, let alone reelection.

In January, 1911, the insurgents formed the Progressive Republican League, apparently backing Senator La Follette for the nomination. La Follette, showing signs of nervous collapse at an important public function, gave progressive Republicans an excuse to switch their allegiance to their real leader. For all but a few, this was the most popular living American, Theodore Roosevelt.

When he had first emerged from the African jungle in the spring of 1910, Roosevelt had heard from Pinchot and others about the administration's misdeeds. Yet when he arrived back in America after a triumphal tour of Europe, he refrained from directly criticizing his successor and former close friend. At the same time he expressed far more radical sentiments than he had ever uttered before. In a famous speech at Osawatomie, Kansas in August, 1910, Roosevelt announced that all property should henceforth be held subject to the right of the community to regulate it to whatever degree the public interest might require. This sort of language deeply alarmed the increasingly conservative President.

After the congressional debacle and the steel suit, Roosevelt began openly attacking Taft, and the President, hurt beyond bearing, referred to "political emotionalists or neurotics" with unmistakable reference. Nobody was surprised when in February, 1912, Roosevelt, at the urging of seven progressive Republican governors, announced that his hat was in the presidential ring.

Waging a vigorous primary campaign for the Republican nomination, Roosevelt roundly defeated Taft in those states which had adopted the new direct primary system. Taft, however, controlled the southern Republicans and the party machinery. Using much the same tactics that Roosevelt had used to nominate Taft in 1908, the Taft forces controlled the Republican convention, decided disputes in the President's favor, and secured Taft's renomination. Amid scenes of weeping, singing, and fighting, Roosevelt's furious followers withdrew to form their own organization and nominate their hero.

The founders of the new Progressive Party included social reformers like Jane Addams, a few of the more daring western progressive politicians, and some spokesmen of the New Business who were urging on businessmen an increase of social responsibility and self-regulation.

Some of the most fervent admirers of the new party were young intellectuals who had been influenced by Herbert Croly's *The Promise of American Life*. This book, published in 1909 and warmly praised by Roosevelt himself, called for a frank abandonment of Jeffersonian individualism and traditional *laissez faire*. The new American progressivism, it urged, should harness and not destroy the creative powers of giant industry. Government, making use of a new, highly trained elite, should aim at something like a renaissance, at once political and intellectual.

The Progressive platform showed the influence of all these elements. It called for a long list of social legislation, including prohibition of child labor, minimum wages for women, and social insurance. It repeatedly advocated "scientific" and "efficient" government, particularly with reference to conservation and the regulation of business. While it favored international peace, its foreign policy sections were distinctly nationalistic. Showing the influence of western progressives, it backed initiative, referendum, and recall; direct election of senators; preferential primaries for the presidency; woman suffrage; and even (to the horror of Taft and his friends) popular recall of some judicial decisions.

Surprisingly radical on many matters, the Progressive Party was distinctly moderate on two. A strong antitrust plank was sidetracked in favor of an appeal for "constructive regulation." Not only was the platform silent on Negro rights, but Roosevelt acquiesced in the exclusion of Negroes from progressive organizations in the South.

The Progressive Party of 1912 was more than a group of Roosevelt-worshippers. It was also an attempt to adapt traditional American liberalism to fit new conditions and combine new and old ideas. Its uneasy mixture of practicality and moral uplift foreshadowed the business reform ideology of the 1920s (see p. 338), and many of its proposals were to find their echoes in the New Deal.

Immediately, however, the campaign centered not upon the progressive program but upon the combative ex-president himself. Despite the cheers and tears, Roosevelt's exciting venture turned out badly for his supporters and himself. It deepened the Republican split and for the time handed over the party to the old guard. Destroying

Roosevelt's own very important role in American politics, it set back the necessary job of adapting traditional liberalism to twentieth-century realities. From Roosevelt's own point of view (or Taft's), it had one further bad result: it brought the Democrats to power.

WILSON AND THE PRESIDENCY

Woodrow Wilson, the Democratic candidate in 1912, was born and brought up in the South. The son of a Presbyterian preacher, he became a political scientist and historian. In 1902 he was chosen president of Princeton. In this position he was at first a distinguished success, but he became entangled in some fierce and complicated battles over university policy. To Wilson, at least, these were fights for moral principle, and he became discouraged when he was fought to a stalemate in 1910. In that year the Democratic politicians of New Jersey invited him to run for the governorship.

Up to this time Wilson's expressed opinions on public issues had been moderately conservative, and he had been tagged by some rich and influential Democrats as a possible savior of the party from "Bryanism." To the surprise and dismay of the New Jersey bosses, Wilson took the campaign and state party away from them, revealing himself as an ardent and idealistic progressive. As governor he equipped New Jersey, the "mother of trusts," with a full set of up-to-date regulatory legislation. An obvious presidential hopeful by now, Wilson carefully conciliated Bryan and other progressives while retaining the support of some conservative elements in the party. In a fierce convention battle, he took the party's nomination at a time when the Republican split made election probable.

Wilson's campaign speeches were as progressive as Roosevelt's but different both in style and content. Where Roosevelt was emotional and combative, Wilson was controlled. Where Roosevelt called for frank recognition of big business and governmental regulation, Wilson insisted on the restoration of opportunity and open-market competition. This too, of course, would mean immediately an increase in government intervention, but only for the purpose of assisting the underdog, the "man on the make." In a series of glowing orations, Wilson insisted that his program would usher in a New Freedom instead of Roosevelt's New Nationalism.

With the support of an undivided party Wilson was an easy winner, but a winner backed by only 42 percent of the popular vote. Moreover, his party, long out of power, was a curious combination of city immigrants, western followers of Bryan, eastern banking and business interests, and the more than ever Solid South. Some Republicans honestly doubted whether such a group, led by an impractical professor, could govern.

These doubters misjudged both party and President. Able leadership could, up to a point, overcome Democratic divisions as Roosevelt had once overcome Republican divisions, and Wilson was not only an experienced politician but a daring student of American political institutions. The president, he thought, could become an equivalent of the British prime minister, using both party organization and personal popular support to force his own program through the legislative branch.

From their initial doubts, many progressives turned in Wilson's first months in office to amazed enthusiasm. Yet in his career thus far Wilson had shown weaknesses as well as strong points. He demanded and needed complete support from his friends and in showdowns was likely to find his opponents wicked and perverse. Wanting to believe his own program and point of view completely right, he could become bitter and reckless when menaced with defeat. In times of adversity, his intensity and devotion could become handicaps. In his first administration, however, they were superb assets.

In office, Wilson moved immediately against the most formidable redoubts, the tariff and banking. With the help of Republican progressives, he forced through *both* Houses of Congress the Underwood Tariff, reducing the rates to about the level of pre-Civil War days and extending the free list. The tariff bill included a moderate income tax, at last clearly constitutional.

The country's banking and currency system, dating from 1863 and earlier, was unsatisfactory to different groups for opposite reasons. Many lamented the absence of a central bank able to control interest and rediscount rates, to mobilize reserves in a crisis, and thus to mitigate America's all too frequent financial panics. On the other hand, according to a widespread progressive belief currently reinforced by congressional investigation, the "Money Trust," dominated by certain private bankers and especially by J. P. Morgan, had far too much power over American credit and therefore over American economic development. Moreover, for fifty years a large section of American opinion had believed that the ups and downs of the American economy were partly caused by the inadequacy and inflexibility of the national currency.

Steering with great adroitness between advocates and enemies of a central bank, between believers in public and private control, Wilson with the help of Bryan and others secured the passage of the Federal Reserve Act of 1913. This measure divided the country into Federal Reserve Districts. In each there was to be a Federal Reserve Association which national banks must join and other banks might. A district Federal Reserve Bank was to be owned by the member banks and governed by a mixed public-private board. Each Federal Reserve Bank would receive the cash reserves of its member banks, grant loans to them, and rediscount their business and some agricultural paper. On the basis of the rediscounted business obligations, the Federal Reserve Banks would issue a new kind of currency, Federal Reserve Notes, which in addition would be partly covered by a gold reserve of 40 percent. These notes were expected to fluctuate with the needs of business since they were based mostly on business transactions. Federal Reserve Banks would pool resources in time of threatened panic. The whole system was to be supervised by a presidentially appointed Federal Reserve Board which could raise or lower rediscount rates and thus exert some control over the availability of credit. While the new system by no means solved all America's long-standing banking and currency problems, it was the most satisfactory compromise between efficiency and decentralization which had been developed thus far. After some initial hostility, it was accepted by banking and business.

The third major accomplishment of Wilson's first years, the new trust legislation, was a more doubtful success. It was a compromise between the programs of the New Freedom and the New Nationalism, with a surprisingly large element of the latter. The Federal Trade Commission Act established a presidentially appointed five person board with power to investigate corporate practice and issue cease-and-desist orders against unfair methods of competition. While its findings of fact were conclusive, its orders could be appealed to the courts.

The Clayton Anti-Trust Act prohibited specific practices such as discriminatory prices, tying agreements, interlocking directorates, or purchase by one firm of stock in another. Such actions were, however, to be illegal only when they tended toward substantially lessening competition, which meant when the courts said they did.

According to the Clayton Act's labor clauses (hailed by Samuel Gompers of the A.F. of L. as "Labor's Magna Carta"), labor was not to be considered a commodity, labor and farm organizations were not to come under the antitrust law's definition of restraint of trade, and the power of courts to issue labor injunctions was (rather cautiously) restricted. Like the Act's other clauses, these were somewhat imprecise and their meaning was whittled down in the courts. Yet the Wilson trust legislation looked formidable, and some business leaders began to consult the government before making moves toward consolidation.

With these major bills passed, the President made it clear that he believed he had accomplished his principal reform objectives. In 1914 and 1915 he seemed to go out of his way to conciliate business and conservative opinion. He refused support for either woman suffrage or child labor legislation, opposed federal loans for farmers, and sanctioned racially segregated facilities in federal departments. Many progressives in both parties were disheartened by Wilson's "conservative progressivism," especially when reform candidates lost heavily in the congressional elections of 1914.

In 1916, however, perhaps partly because a new election was pending and the Democrats had to attract some Roosevelt voters, the administration turned much more toward progressive reform. Louis J. Brandeis, the prominent antitrust lawyer and progressive intellectual, was appointed to the Supreme Court amid a storm of conservative criticism. Wilson reversed his earlier position and backed a Federal Farm Loan Act providing long-term rural credits and an act prohibiting interstate shipment of goods made by child labor (later held unconstitutional). The dollar-matching principle (federal appropriations to match state expenditures) was extended from agricultural experiment stations to an automobile highway program and (after the election) to vocational education. Finally, forgetting his *laissez faire* principles under the pressure of foreign crisis and the threat of a serious railroad strike, Wilson supported the Adamson Act establishing by law an eight-hour day on the railroads. Thus the Wilson administration, enacting a program not altogether unlike that sponsored by Roosevelt in 1912, represented the culmination of the whole movement of reform which had begun in the nineties.

WILSONIAN FOREIGN POLICY

Despite the skepticism and amusement of much world opinion, Wilson really meant his idealistic pronouncements about foreign policy. He was determined to support and increase American power and prestige, but only for the benefit of all mankind and only according to the most scrupulous methods. Some have seen in this intention a standard for foreign policy never equaled; others have found in it a misunderstanding of the nature and limits of power. To some extent, Wilson's purposes were supported by the new Secretary of State, William Jennings Bryan, perhaps the first pacifist to serve as foreign minister of a great power.

Much of Wilson's early foreign policy involved a startling abnegation of immediate national interest and was carried out amid loud outcries of nationalist indignation. Economic intervention in China was abandoned, the Philippines and Puerto Rico were given more self-government, and the United States, acknowledging treaty obligations previously denied, stopped discriminating against foreign shipping in the Panama Canal tolls.

In apparent contradiction to this policy of abstention, interventions in the Caribbean were more frequent and bloody than ever before and the United States became involved in what looked like aggression in Mexico. The contradiction was deeply ironic: the Caribbean interventions were aimed at political reform of the area and the Mexican involvement was the result of an altruistic effort to support Mexican democracy.

In 1910 one of the major revolutions of the twentieth century overthrew Porfirio Diaz, the bloody but efficient dictator of Mexico. American investors, who had $2 billion at stake and had gotten along very well with Diaz, were alarmed. When Diaz's liberal successor was murdered, the Taft administration seemed ready to support the new conservative president, Victoriano Huerta. Wilson, however, committed the United States to oppose Huerta without regard to material interests on the ground that he had come to power by violence.

Instead of making Huerta's opponents grateful, Wilson's attempt at intervention in favor of Mexican democracy came close to uniting all Mexican factions against the United States. Always concerned to back American prestige, Wilson supported an admiral who demanded abject apology over a minor incident involving American seamen at Tampico in 1915. In the same year the United States Navy, in order to prevent delivery of German munitions for Huerta, bombarded and occupied the port of Vera Cruz. Wilson was rescued from his increasingly untenable position when the major Latin American powers agreed to mediate. An international conference at Niagara Falls resulted in the coming to power of Huerta's main opponent, Venustiano Carranza, who was by this time no friend of the Wilson administration.

Even then Wilson's Mexican troubles were not finished. Francisco Villa, a picturesque bandit who might be described as a cross between Robin Hood and Jesse James, shot up American border towns, killing American citizens. In 1916 Wilson sent General John J. Pershing into Mexico in pursuit of Villa. Though Villa was a rebel against the Carranza government, the American action was bitterly resented throughout Mexico and war between the two countries seemed close. When entry into a larger war became imminent in 1917, the United States had to withdraw the expeditionary force. To Mexicans, America had become the enemy of the very revolution Wilson wanted to assist and guide.

THE MEANING OF PROGRESSIVISM

The progressive movement had not solved the problems of foreign policy. It had not produced, or tried to produce, any new social system.

It had made only the barest beginning toward the redistribution of wealth or the control of private accumulations of power. While ultraconservatives lamented the end of free enterprise, the million or so Americans who wanted to move toward socialism were impatient with progressive caution. Despite the efforts of Southern white progressives, the South still lagged far behind the rest of the country in health and wealth. The deepest rooted American form of inequality was almost untouched, North or South. In the face of massive discrimination, many Negroes accepted the program of Booker T. Washington, who counseled the temporary acceptance of social discrimination and the adoption of modest economic goals. Only a few Negro intellectuals, led by W. E. B. Du Bois, demanded complete equality. In 1909, after a peculiarly savage race riot in Springfield, Illinois, a group of white progressives joined Du Bois to form the National Association for the Advancement of Colored People and press this neglected cause.

Even some of the things progressives had accomplished proved impermanent. It was plain to close observers even before 1917 that the fervor was declining and the opposition gathering strength. Soon, in wartime, much of the progressive program was to take on a different meaning, and in the postwar decade many progressive enactments were to be emasculated or abandoned.

Yet some permanent gains had been made. Big business, neither destroyed nor much weakened, was never again as defiant of public opinion as it had been. Immensely valuable national resources had been saved for the future. New paths for possible later government action were made possible by the income tax and other measures. Outside the arena of politics, dedicated reformers, now little remembered, left countless monuments in the shape of playgrounds, schools, clinics, and parks. In architecture, poetry, social science, and psychology, innovation had characterized the Progressive Era. In some fields, indeed, intellectual experiment begun in the Progressive Era was eventually to lead in disturbing directions, pointing far beyond the optimistic reform spirit of the prewar years.

More important than any concrete accomplishment of the progressive movement was its general reassertion of the will to adapt. Like other countries, America had been confronted by the huge problems of industrial civilization. In the face of this challenge, the country had not failed to find resources of courage and vitality. More than anyone yet realized, these resources were to prove indispensable in the coming decades.

FOR FURTHER READING:

H. F. Pringle, *William Howard Taft* (2 vols., 1939) and Paolo E. Coletta, *The Presidency of William Howard Taft* (1973) are both interesting and sympathetic. W. V. and Marie V. Scholes examine *The Foreign Policies of the Taft Administration* (1970). Russell B. Nye describes the rise and character of *Midwestern Progressive Politics* (1951)*. The best account of the Bull Moose movement is G. E. Mowry, *Theodore Roosevelt and the Progressive Movement* (1946)*. Of the immense literature on Wilson, the most valuable long biography is that being written in several volumes by Arthur Link. Link summarizes Wilson's first administration admirably in his *Woodrow Wilson and the Progressive Era, 1910–1917* (1954)*. John A. Garraty, *Woodrow Wilson* (1965), is an excellent brief biography, and John M. Blum, *Woodrow Wilson and the Politics of Morality* (1956), is a sprightly interpretation. There are good biographies of nearly all major figures. H. F. May, *The End of American Innocence* (1959)*, discusses the period's intellectual history; and both Aileen S. Kraditor, *The Ideas of the Woman Suffrage Movement, 1890–1920* (1965), and William O'Neill, *Everyone Was Brave* (1969), focus on one of its most important social issues.

---

* Available in paperback edition.

The First Overseas War

24

The war which began in August, 1914, brought to an end a century of relative peace, apparent democratic progress, and European domination of the world. It helped to bring about the first Communist revolution. For the United States it ushered in a period of economic world power and political isolation. It brought far greater steps toward governmental direction of the economy than most progressives had dreamed of. All this drastic innovation produced intense emotional confusion: Americans moved in a rapid zigzag from neutrality to crusading excitement to disillusion and revulsion.

THE WAR AND AMERICA

In 1914 most Americans found it hard to understand why all Europe went to war over the murder of the heir to the throne of Austria-Hungary by a Serb. Actually, the European great powers, all heavily armed, had long been engaged in a struggle for empire and prestige. They were organized in two huge, approximately equal alliances, each fearful of the other. One consisted of the two Central European empires of Germany and Austria-Hungary (with the doubtful adherence of Italy), the other of Britain, France, and Russia. When Austria-Hungary, afraid of the disintegration of her multinational empire, demanded severe punishment of Serbia, Germany backed her ally's demands. Russia felt it necessary to assist Serbia, and France was linked to Russia. When Germany invaded France through Belgium (whose neutrality had been internationally guaranteed), England came somewhat reluctantly into the war. Later the Central Powers were joined by Turkey and Bulgaria; the Western Allies by Italy, Japan, Greece, Rumania, and other countries.

When war broke out, most Americans believed their country could and should stay out of it. Many quoted, or misquoted, the founding fathers on the subject of foreign entanglements. To many progressives, war was associated with reaction, and to the socialist minority it was a product of dying capitalism.

Yet few managed to follow completely President Wilson's advice to remain neutral in thought. Most of the eastern, Anglo-Saxon elite of the nation, including a great many editors and publicists, deeply valued British law and literature and identified their own values with Western European civilization. Still larger groups felt a vague traditional sympathy with France and a genuine moral outrage over the invasion of Belgium. Some influential individuals argued, on less emotional grounds, that American safety depended on British control of the Atlantic Ocean. The drift of American foreign policy for two decades had been toward cooperation with Britain. Thus much Allied war propaganda fell on already friendly ears.

Not all Americans, however, favored the Allies. Many, including most Irish-Americans and many Midwesterners, continued to associate Britain with empire, aristocracy, and oligarchy. To the well-organized and articulate German-American minority, the Fatherland was an innocent victim of Allied encirclement.

Even more clearly than in Jefferson's day, real neutrality was made difficult by America's economic importance and geographic position. In 1914 the country was entering a depression, and war orders promised recovery. From the beginning, America took the traditional and legally correct position that all belligerents were free to buy supplies. British naval power meant that in practice only the Allies could tap American resources, which they desperately needed. Originally inclined to insist on cash sales in the interests of neutrality, Wilson and Secretary Bryan early withdrew their opposition to loans and bank credits. By 1915 American industry was booming, and American prosperity was bound up in Allied success. A German victory, an embargo on munitions, a prohibition of loans, or a sudden peace would have meant financial crisis.

Undoubtedly this economic involvement influenced some American opinion. Yet business, and particularly big business, was by no means dominant in the formation of American foreign policy. Some progressives were against whatever business leaders supported. And the President, who bore the responsibility for foreign-policy decisions, had demonstrated in the Mexican crisis a deep hostility to "selfish interests." While Wilson loved British culture and disliked German militarism, he was determined to maintain peace. He was also determined, as always, to defend America's national honor and her power. Both were essential to the overriding goal: the promotion of worldwide democratic progress. The President's most influential advisers, including his close friend Edward M. House, tended strongly in a pro-Allied direction.

Thus the forces affecting American policy were fairly evenly balanced. Most Americans wanted to stay out, and most hoped for Allied victory. Neither economic interest nor Allied sympathy was strong enough to counter the traditional dislike of becoming involved in Europe's troubles. Perplexed by conflicting emotions, many Americans responded most clearly to surging nationalism. Only a direct challenge to American rights and feelings could tip the balance toward war. This challenge arose out of a familiar problem: neutral rights at sea.

Once again, as in the time of Napoleon, a great land power and a great sea power were fighting an all-out war. Each would prefer to remain on good terms with America, the world's most powerful neutral. Yet neither, in the long run, could afford to give up any weapon necessary to victory. The British, as expected, used their navy to blockade Germany and deny her essential supplies. The Germans, to cut off British supplies, turned to a new weapon, the submarine.

Enormously effective, the submarine was also vulnerable. Traditionally, a blockading warship was supposed to warn an enemy merchant vessel and remove passengers and crew before sinking her. If, however, a submarine surfaced to warn its victim it could fairly easily be sunk by an armed merchant ship. In at least one famous case, a German submarine which had surfaced for this purpose was sunk by a British decoy ship, disguised as an American merchant vessel. Thus the Germans, throughout the war, faced a difficult choice. They could not use their only effective sea weapon in the only effective manner without killing civilians. Yet killing civilians, in 1914, was still regarded by world opinion as illegal and brutal. Submarine warfare, which might bring German victory, could at the same time add to Germany's enemies and thereby bring defeat.

In dealing with blockade and counterblockade, the Wilson administration had three possible choices, and none of these was without its advocates. The first was strict neutrality, favored by Bryan, by many congressional Democrats, and by much midwestern opinion. Of the many methods proposed to implement such a policy, the most plausible was to prohibit American citizens from traveling on armed ships and thus to prevent the most dangerous kind of incidents. Under this plan, protests against both German and British blockade excesses would be filed for postwar negotiation. This policy, or any policy of abandoning or diminishing American neutral rights, was rejected by Wilson on grounds of national honor.

The opposite extreme would have been to intervene, early and frankly, on the Allied side. This would not only have ended the dilemma about neutral rights, it would have shortened the war and given America a more decisive voice in the peace. It was advocated by Theodore Roosevelt, which hardly recommended it to Wilson. Such a choice was completely contrary to tradition and would have divided the country disastrously.

The third choice, and one which attracted Wilson from time to time, was American mediation, either to moderate the war or to end it. Mediation efforts took two forms. The first was an effort to induce Britain to modify her blockade or cease from arming merchant vessels in return for German abandonment or modification of submarine warfare. The second was the attempt to persuade both belligerents to state negotiable war aims.

Both kinds of effort at mediation, sporadically pursued and probably illusory, had clearly failed by 1916. Neither side was willing permanently to abandon weapons it considered essential and neither would abandon the prospect of victory. As the bloodshed mounted, so did fear and hatred, until compromise became impossible even to imagine.

For America to force peace before this process had gone too far, she would have had to threaten both sides with loss of the war. Only a threat to cut off munitions could have compelled Britain to abandon her own war aims. To make such a threat and carry it out might have resulted in German victory. It was clear that the Wilson administration, in a showdown, was unlikely to take such action against the side most Americans preferred. To force Germany to make peace, on the other hand, it would have been necessary to threaten actual intervention on the Allied side. Only a heavily armed America, with a united or docile public opinion, could have made such a policy work. Really effective mediation was made impossible by the whole nature of the American political system. Thus the policy actually adopted was, and perhaps had to be, a constantly shifting compromise among the three alternatives: neutrality, intervention, and mediation.

NEUTRALITY TO WAR IN FOUR ACTS

The first stage of American policy, from the outbreak of war to February, 1915, was characterized by benevolent neutrality toward England. After the shocking invasion of Belgium, the Germans gave little direct offense, while the British blockade became increasingly rigid. Contraband of war was gradually extended to cover most commodities, neutral ships were stopped at sea and taken to port for search, and trade with other neutrals who might transship to Germany was severely rationed. Yet American protests were moderate in tone,

British concessions considerable, and, above all, no American was killed. The United States accepted without much ill-feeling even the British proclamation of a mined war zone in the North Sea, where few American ships went.

The second stage, running from February, 1915, until May, 1916, was dominated by German submarine warfare. In February, Germany proclaimed a submarine war zone around the British Isles, cutting the main Atlantic sea lanes. From this point on the administration refused to accept the legality of submarine warfare and announced that Germany would be held to "strict accountability" for American losses.

On May 7, 1915, the liner *Lusitania*, unarmed but carrying some war cargo, was sunk off the Irish coast. Of the 1198 passengers drowned, 128 were Americans. In a series of very strong notes, Wilson demanded that Germany accept responsibility for these losses and abandon her methods of submarine war. After repeated warnings, partial or temporary German concessions, and further sinkings, Wilson, in March, 1916, made it clear that a continuation of unrestricted submarine warfare would mean a break in German-American relations. This clearly implied war, and Germany, somewhat grudgingly, promised that henceforth her raiders would warn before sinking. This seemed a major American victory. The nation was, however, practically committed to go to war whenever Germany changed her mind. To give some meaning to his implied threats of force, Wilson gave his backing, in late 1915, to a preparedness program including increased army and navy appropriations and heavy new taxes.

The third stage, from May, 1916, to February, 1917, brought somewhat less tense relations with Germany, increased irritation against England, and the peak of Wilson's efforts for a negotiated peace. In this period Britain, hard pressed in war and confident of American tolerance, stepped up her enforcement of the blockade. American mail was searched, and American firms believed to have dealt with Germany were black-listed and barred from British trade. Wilson found these actions almost intolerable, and Congress made gestures of retaliation.

In November, Wilson narrowly won reelection against Charles Evans Hughes, a moderate Republican progressive running with the support of a reunited (and largely conservative) party. In the campaign Wilson was attacked by both isolationists and interventionists. His own partisans, however, pointed to his success in keeping America out of war, as well as to his recently increased domestic progressivism.

Once reelected, Wilson made his most ambitious effort at mediation, a public request to both sides for a statement of war aims. When this effort failed, and it became clear that neither side was interested in compromise, Wilson became increasingly disillusioned with the Allied cause. On January 22, in an eloquent speech he declared that the world's only hope lay in a "Peace without Victory" for either side.

The fourth and final phase started a week later when Germany, where military pressures had finally defeated civilian resistance, announced the resumption of unrestricted submarine warfare against neutral and belligerent vessels alike. Wilson had no alternative but to break relations, yet he still refused to ask for war. On March 1, the administration released to the press an intercepted German note proposing, in the event of war with the United States, an alliance with Mexico to recover lost territories and an effort to persuade Japan to switch sides. Meantime Wilson, despite a filibuster by Robert M. La Follette and other antiwar progressives, started arming American ships. Only at the beginning of April, after a series of new sinkings, did Wilson finally ask for and get from Congress a declaration of war against Germany.

AMERICA AT WAR: PATRIOTISM AND DISCONTENT

Though many Americans had expected limited, almost painless participation in the war, the state of the Allied war effort in 1917 made this impossible. Germany was sinking British ships faster than they could be built, the French army was exhausted and mutinous, and Russia was convulsed by revolution.

The first Russian Revolution in March, 1917, had caused America to welcome Russia joyfully into the ranks of democratic and constitutional states. In November, however, the Bolsheviks with their slogan of "land, bread, and peace" had overthrown the moderate Kerensky government and embarked Russia on the Soviet road. In March they signed a treaty with Germany, surrendering large territories and freeing German troops for a one-front war. Germany thus began a series of immense offensives which threatened to defeat the Allies before American help could become effective.

Faced with this desperate necessity, the United States built a conscript army of more than 3,500,000 and by November, 1918, had shipped 2,000,000 men overseas without losses. American naval forces greatly reduced the submarine menace. American ground forces in France played a distinguished and probably decisive part in the bloody operations of 1918 in which the German offensives were finally met and the German armies rolled back.

To do all this, it was necessary to regiment to a new degree the vast economic power of an essentially civilian country. Money for huge loans to the Allies as well as for America's war effort was raised by a fairly democratic system of war finance. About one-third of the total needed was raised by taxes as against about one-fifth in the Civil War. For this purpose, incomes and corporate profits were taxed at unheard of rates. For 1918, incomes of over $1 million were assessed a total tax of 77 percent. (In 1913, a top rate of 7 percent had seemed high.) Federal war bonds were sold to sixty-five million customers in four great drives. Even so, the war was financed partly by inflation and mostly through expansion of bank credit by action of the new Federal Reserve System.

After fumbling with various regulatory devices in the first war winter, Congress in the spring of 1918 gave the President almost dictatorial powers over the war economy. Under him five hundred war agencies policed the productive effort. The War Industries Board allocated raw materials, determined priorities, and standardized products. The War Labor Board opposed strikes and lockouts, but promoted union recognition, the eight-hour day, and uniform wages. The Food Administration under Herbert Hoover guaranteed the purchase and set the prices for major farm commodities, thereby greatly increasing food production. The Fuel Board and the Shipping Administration similarly increased production in their spheres. The railroads were taken over and efficiently run by the Railway Administration.

By 1918 the United States had a fairly efficient regulated economy. Some advanced progressives talked cheerfully of war socialism and prophesied that these gains for collectivism would not be lost. Most citizens, however, were probably restive under this new system and were held in line only by wartime patriotism. Businessmen objected to high taxes, resented labor's gains, and in general disliked being told what to do. Farmers, faring well, resented the fixing of prices which had never been set in periods of depression. Yet despite its widespread unpopularity, governmental direction of the war economy marked a momentous step in a generally continuing direction. There was no return to *laissez faire,* if indeed *laissez faire* had ever existed. After the war, the government was to act as a partner to business, and later under the New Deal wartime precedents were to be invoked for other kinds of intervention.

Equally great steps, with equally momentous consequences, were taken in the field of manipulating public opinion. Despite evidence of public enthusiasm, the government was apparently disquieted about national unity. The Committee on Public Information blanketed the country with pamphlets and speeches about the goals of the war. Cracking down on opposition, the Post Office barred antiwar publications from the mails. A Sedition Act passed in 1918 forbade abusive language about the American form of government, flag, or uniform or acts bringing into contempt the form of government or the Constitution. About 1,500 persons, including most of the leadership of the

Socialist party, were imprisoned for sedition. States and private organizations went much further than the federal government on the road to war hysteria. The German language was driven from the schools, German music was eliminated from concerts, and religious pacifists were physically abused. In some places, the slightest criticism of the administration or the Allies was considered punishable disloyalty. To all this emotion, a reaction was inevitable. For the future, both the possibilities and the dangers of mobilizing emotion had been demonstrated.

Far outrunning measures of compulsion, popular support of the war was extraordinarily general. Yet beneath this unity lay discontent. This was indicated in the congressional elections of 1918 when Wilson, calling for the election of a Democratic Congress as an endorsement of his war leadership, received instead a Republican majority in both Houses.

THE FAILURE OF A WILSONIAN PEACE

On her entry into the war America, democratic and free from either war guilt or aggressive ambitions, was recognized as the most effective Allied spokesman, and Wilson became the worldwide prophet of a democratic peace. On January 8, 1918, he outlined to Congress his famous Fourteen Points.

The first five of these were general liberal formulae: open treaty-making, freedom of the seas, removal of trade barriers, and impartial adjustment of colonial claims in the interest of the natives. Most of the rest of the Points were concerned with the readjustment of boundaries in the interest of the Wilsonian principle of national self-determination even for small nations. The final Point, the most important to Wilson, provided for an association of nations to maintain the peace. A number of the Fourteen Points were contrary to provisions in the secret treaties already negotiated among the Allies. Wilson knew of these treaties but ignored them, doubtless believing that he could force the Allies to abandon them.

On October 6, Germany, her military situation hopeless, asked Wilson for an armistice based on his announced program. Despite Allied objections, the Fourteen Points were accepted as the basis for peace, with some reservations. On November 11, military authorities finished negotiating an armistice which disarmed Germany and made further resistance impossible.

In January, 1919, at Paris, the victorious Allies started negotiating among themselves the peace terms to be imposed on Germany. Accompanied by an undistinguished peace delegation and a large corps of experts, Wilson left for Paris. Frantic ovations throughout Europe apparently convinced him that it was his mission, alone, to force a just peace on the world. Actually, his power was limited by that of two powerful groups of opponents, the Allies and the Senate Republicans. Like Germany, Wilson had to fight a two-front war. Insisting from the outset that the Covenant of the League of Nations be part of the Treaty, Wilson made a quick trip to Washington and found more than a third of the Senate lined up against the Covenant in its negotiated form. Returning to Paris, he had to face the Allied leaders with weakened bargaining powers. These statesmen, bound by the secret treaties, were also understandably determined to secure their nations against further attack and to make Germany pay for the long struggle. Despite a courageous fight, Wilson had to make many concessions. To Italy he had to concede sizable German-speaking border areas. Japan secured not only Germany's island colonies (which were to play a crucial part in World War II), but also, against Chinese opposition, German interests in the Shantung Peninsula. To France, who desired the actual dismemberment of Germany, Wilson had to concede very severe terms regarding the defeated nation. Germany was stripped of colonies and merchant marine, disarmed, and forced to surrender border areas. Perhaps more important, she was required to admit her guilt for the war as a basis for reparations, whose sum would be fixed later by the Allies.

With hindsight it is easy to see the inadequacies of the Versailles settlement. Too harsh to be a peace of reconciliation, it was illusory as a restoration of Anglo-French world hegemony. Japan was thwarted, China chaotic, the colonial world restive, and all nonwhites irritated by the failure of a clause affirming racial equality. Bolshevik Russia was proclaiming world revolution, and Communist revolutions seemed to threaten both Asia and Central Europe. With somewhat confused aims and limited American participation, Allied forces invaded Russian territory during her years of upheaval and civil war.

To Wilson, exhausted and implacable, all the faults of the Versailles settlement were made up for by the gains for self-determination and above all by the establishment of the League. This would, he hoped, supervise the administration of former German colonies by their new masters under the mandate system. It would secure the reduction of armaments, preserve the independence and integrity of all nations, mediate disputes, and even use force against those resorting to war. For this great hope, Wilson came home to fight.

At first, the Treaty's chances looked good. Wilson's prestige was still great, and the idea of a League of Nations had long attracted American support. Yet the Treaty aroused many kinds of opposition. Among its enemies were the disappointed minorities of German, Italian, and Irish descent, isolationists who feared that the League would involve America in European affairs, liberals who objected to the compromises of democratic principle, and, vaguer but crucially important, many Americans already reacting against wartime enthusiasm and sacrifice.

The Senate, where the struggle centered, was divided into three groups: (1) Loyal Wilsonian Democrats, in favor of the Treaty and the League; (2) A group of only about a dozen Senators including La Follette, Borah, and Johnson of California, who were "Irreconcilable," all-out foes of both; and (3) "Reservationists" who were inclined to accept the Treaty with certain changes defining and restricting the authority of the League.

In the long struggle, opposition to the Treaty was marshaled by Henry Cabot Lodge, an enemy of Wilson and a master tactician. In order to attract the crucial Reservationists, Lodge proposed not the rejection of the Treaty but its passage with a number of changes. These were carefully calculated to sound plausible, but to be unacceptable to Wilson. Lodge knew his opponent. Wilson forbade Democrats to accept the reservations, thus making impossible a two-thirds majority. Without reservations, the Treaty was opposed by Irreconcilables and Reservationists; with reservations, by Irreconcilables and loyal Democrats.

Refusing to accept defeat, Wilson embarked on a nationwide speaking tour. The people, he said, must not allow the Senate to "break the heart of the world" by rejecting the Treaty. Prematurely aged and emotionally exhausted, Wilson broke down in the midst of his tour and had to be taken back to Washington. There he suffered a severe stroke and was partly incapacitated for the rest of his presidency. Sick, isolated, but grimly determined, he continued to forbid his followers to compromise. Though the Allies were by now willing to accept the reservations, Wilson's loyal followers rejected them, and the Treaty failed to get ratification.

Once more Wilson appealed to the final authority, announcing in the spring of 1920 that the coming presidential election would constitute a "solemn referendum" on the Treaty. In the campaign the Democratic candidate, Governor James. M. Cox of Ohio, did support the Treaty and the League. The Republican candidate, Senator Warren G. Harding of the same state, opposed it only ambiguously, and some of his supporters favored it equally vaguely.

Harding won by the most sweeping majority since Monroe. It is impossible to prove that the election constituted a real referendum on foreign policy. It was certainly affected by many domestic issues, including the breakdown of the President and, to a considerable extent, of his administration. In another sense, however, the election of 1920 was a major decision: the campaign and much press comment as well as the results indicated that the American people wanted a president as little like Woodrow Wilson as possible, and this is what they got.

The United States, a country with a long isolationist tradition, had been moving for a generation toward world leadership. Now her efforts had decided a world war, and her leader had dominated a world settlement. In 1920 the people, exhausted by this break with the past and disillusioned by its results, determined to do their best to return to familiar, cherished ways.

CONFLICTING HISTORICAL VIEWPOINTS

Why Did America Enter World War I?

Contemporary accounts of United States intervention in World War I were generally favorable to Wilsonian policies. The war was a noble and necessary war, many first-hand observers agreed, and Americans could take pride and satisfaction in their role in it. Reinforcing this initial view were two semi-autobiographical publications: Burton Hendrick, ed., The Life and Letters of Walter H. Page *(3 vols., 1922–26) and Charles Seymour,* The Intimate Papers of Colonel House *(4 vols., 1926–28). Both House and Page had helped shape American policy and neither questioned the wisdom of U.S. intervention.*

A revisionist interpretation, however, was not long in developing. Disillusioned by the failures of Wilson's peace and threatened by the gathering clouds of war in Europe and Asia, many Americans in the 1920s and 1930s traced the nation's involvement not to idealism or self-interest, but to folly, sentimentalism, and greed. Scholarly advocates of this view included Harry E. Barnes (Genesis of the World War [1926]), C. Hartley Grattan (Why We Fought [1929]), and C. C. Tansill (America Goes to War [1938]), all of whom argued that Wilson's policies were neither wise, necessary, nor beneficial to the United States. In their accounts, United States intervention was attributed to the pernicious influences of misguided Wilsonian Anglophiles, skillful British propagandists, and grasping American munitions makers and international bankers.

Although the revisionist view was in many ways an accurate reflection of popular, or a least congressional, sentiment during the postwar and depression years, it has not been widely accepted by historians. A more satisfactory argument was offered by Charles Seymour, whose American Diplomacy during World War I *(1934) has been called "the first historian's history of intervention." Treating American involvement as an historical problem rather than a moral issue, this Yale professor asserted that Wilson, although pro-ally, struggled valiantly to remain neutral. Anticipating such relatively recent interpretations as Arthur Link's* Wilson the Diplomatist *(1957) and Ernest May's* The World War and American Isolation *(1959), Seymour concluded that Wilson had little choice but to lead the nation into war. In the final analysis, he believed, the German submarine was the cause of American intervention. In close agreement, Link and May have stressed the tragedy of Wilson's dilemma and the limited range of his alternatives. While they, too, endeavored to avoid judgment, their studies stress the essential correctness of presidential policy.*

Also critical of revisionism were such "realist" historians as George Kennan (American Diplomacy *[1950]) and Robert Osgood* (Idealism and Self-Interest in America's Foreign Policy *[1953]) who argued that in 1917 the United States entered the right war for the wrong reasons. Having experienced the Second World War, realists doubted that the United States could have avoided the First. Their primary complaint, then, was not that Wilson carried the nation into war, but that he did so in the name of morality and legality, not national security and self-interest.*

Radical historians, on the other hand, denied that American intervention could be attributed to altruism and idealism. In their view, the war was waged not to make the world safe for democracy, but to make the world's markets safe for American economic expansion. Although perhaps best argued in William A. Williams's The Tragedy of American Foreign Policy *(1962), a subtle and challenging variation on this theme is presented in N. Gordon Levine's* Woodrow Wilson and World Politics *(1968). According to this young scholar, it was Wilson's aim to build "a new rational international-capitalist order, safe from war and revolution and open to [American] commercial and moral expansion."*

FOR FURTHER READING:

The social history of the home front can be found in P. W. Slosson, *The Great Crusade and After, 1914–1928* (1937). The wartime state of civil liberties is described in Zachariah Chafee, Jr., *Free Speech in the United States* (1941) and wartime repression is put in a wider context in William Preston, Jr., *Aliens and Dissenters* (1963)*. George T. Blakey,

---

* Available in paperback edition.

Historians on the Homefront (1971) is a brief, detached examination of the scholars who helped sell the war effort. The rejection of the treaty is examined in T. A. Bailey, *Wilson and the Peacemakers* (1947)*; and Ralph Stone has written an able account of *The Irreconcilables* (1971)*. The beginnings of Soviet-American relations are described in G. F. Kennan, *Russia Leaves the War* (1956)*, and *The Decision To Intervene* (1958)*. Jean-Baptiste Duroselle, *From Wilson to Roosevelt* (1960, translated 1963)* is an excellent French account of American foreign policy.

Ernest R. May, *The Coming of War, 1917* (Berkeley Readings in American History, 1963)*, is a documentary study of American intervention.

THE WAR AND THE TWENTIES

	President	Political Events	Economic Conditions	Foreign Policy	Miscellaneous
1916	Wilson D		1914 Depression. 1915–1916 Recovery: war orders.		1915 Movie, "Birth of a Nation."
1918		Republicans win Senate.	1917–1918 War prosperity.	1917 (April) War declared. (January) Fourteen Points. (November) Armistice.	
		1919 (September) Wilson's collapse.	1919 Inflationary boom strikes.	1919 (June) Versailles Treaty signed.	1919 Red Scare. First regular radio station. Sinclair Lewis, Main Street.
1920	Harding R	Prohibition and woman's suffrage in effect.	Deflation and depression.	(March) Treaty finally defeated in Senate.	
1922		1921 Immigration quotas established. Fordney-McCumber Tariff. Progressive gains in Congress.	1921 Depression. Recovery.	1921–1922 Washington Conference.	

1923 (August) Death of Harding

Coolidge *R*

1924

1923–1924 Exposure of "Harding Scandals."

La Follette Third Party Movement.

Dawes Plan for Germany. **1924**

1925 Scopes Trial; Dreiser, *American Tragedy*; Fitzgerald, *Great Gatsby*.

PROSPERITY

→

1926

1926

1927 President vetoes McNary-Haugen farm bill.

1927 Decline in construction and auto industries.

1927 United States–Mexican differences compromised. **1926**

1927 Lindbergh flight.

1928

Hoover *R*

United States renounces right of intervention in Latin America under "Roosevelt Corollary." **1928**

1929 Young Plan for Germany.

1929 (September–October) Wall Street crash.

1929 Hemingway, *Farewell to Arms*; Faulkner, *The Sound and the Fury*.

The Twenties: Prosperity and Social Change

25

The postwar decade is thought of today in at least three ways. It was the Jazz Age, the roaring twenties, the romantic heyday of flappers and flivvers. It was also the period of Republican prosperity, conservatism, and isolation. Further, it was the period of Hemingway, Fitzgerald, and T. S. Eliot, a time of literary experiment and creation.

These paradoxes are not invented by historians; even at the time America looked different to different kinds of people. Businessmen and farmers, Freudians and fundamentalists were all reacting at different rates and in different ways to a series of changes so rapid as to be deeply disturbing. Some of these changes, like industrialization and urbanization, had been going on a long time and were now accelerated. Others, like the importation of challenging new ideas (among them psychoanalysis and relativity) had begun before the war. Still others were direct results of the war, which was itself a traumatic break with national tradition.

Some Americans accepted change willingly; others fought every departure from the good old ways. Still others accepted innovation in some areas, like technology and transportation, and fought it in others, like manners and morals. Even for the most conservative, however, tradition seemed hard to define or find, let alone restore.

Fortunately, change was cushioned by good fortune. For many Americans the 1920s were a time of peace and prosperity—the last for a long time.

THE FAILURE OF WILSONISM, 1918–1920

The first postwar years were by no means placid. The fight over the Treaty was only one aspect of a frustrating struggle to liquidate the war. In 1919, many advanced progressives and labor leaders were talking about planned and masterful reconstruction and even predicting the nationalization of basic industries. Actually, nothing was farther from popular demand or administration intent. From the Armistice on, government contracts were canceled, employees dismissed, and regulatory powers abandoned. Soldiers were rapidly discharged with only minimum provisions for reemployment.

Congress abandoned regulation and reform less rapidly than the administration. Immediately after the war two progressive causes reached nationwide victory. The Eighteenth (prohibition) Amendment, pushed hard by the Methodist Church and the Anti-Saloon League, was put over the top by a combination of moral zeal, desire to conserve resources, and dislike of German-American brewers. In October, 1919, the Volstead Act, passed over Wilson's veto, ended forever (most of its friends and enemies thought) the manufacture, sale, transportation, or possession of intoxicating beverages. In the same year the Nineteenth Amendment made woman suffrage a nationwide reality.

In dismantling controls the postwar Congress had a mixed record. The railroads, returned to private hands by the administration, were placed under stringent regulation by the Esch-Cummins Act of 1920. This law's purpose, however, was partly to promote rather than prevent consolidation into fewer systems. From now on the railroad industry, threatened with truck and bus competition and in places overbuilt, was to be treated more as an invalid and less as a tyrannical giant. The government-built merchant marine was returned to private interests, and here too subsidy was more needed than control. In one vital area, that of water power, Congress, in 1920, established a new regulatory agency, the Federal Power Commission, with power to license development and operation.

For the most part, however, the wartime directed economy was dismantled without planning and without disaster. In the spring of 1919, after a very brief postwar slump, business began to pick up. At the time the upturn was credited to unsatisfied consumer demand, but today economists point to government spending, temporarily continued in the form of loans to the Allies and European relief operations. Rapidly, recovery turned into speculative boom, as wholesale prices rose by about 30 percent.

Instead of Imperial Germany, the main public enemy in 1919 seemed to be the high cost of living. Salaried people were badly pinched, and labor was restive about the possibility of maintaining wartime gains in organization and real wages. Four million workers, more than ever before, took part in strikes. In most of these, including a coal strike and a bitterly fought steel strike, the unions were beaten.

Government and articulate public opinion sided strongly with employers.

Many citizens blamed strikes, the high cost of living, and foreign crises on one simple cause: radical conspiracy. The Third International, calling from Moscow for world revolution, was echoed by the two new tiny American Communist parties. A few bombings, believed to be of anarchist origin, roused public emotions. Many conservative citizens feared, and a few ardent radicals hoped that revolution was at hand.

In the fall of 1919 Attorney General A. Mitchell Palmer, until now regarded as a Wilsonian progressive, organized his famous series of raids on alleged foreign radical organizations. In the worst of these, thousands of people were arrested with little regard for legal procedure and sometimes treated with considerable brutality. Practically no evidence of dangerous revolutionary activity was uncovered, but many zealous individuals, organizations, and governmental units turned their hostility from Germans to radicals. The New York Legislature expelled five duly-elected Socialist assemblymen, and a drastic sedition bill, carrying the death penalty in certain cases, was introduced (but never passed) in Congress. In one of the last episodes of the Red Scare, two philosophical anarchists named Nicola Sacco and Bartolomeo Vanzetti were arrested for a robbery and murder which few liberals believed they had committed. Despite impassioned agitation for their release, the two men were finally executed in 1927.

Well before this, in fact before the end of 1920, the Red Scare had begun to ebb. For several years, however, fear of the alien, the dissenter, and the nonconformist showed itself in other ways: in race riots and lynchings, in anti-Semitic whisperings, in crusades against alarming ideas, and above all in suspicion of foreigners. All these tendencies played a part in the growth of the Ku Klux Klan, a new organization founded in 1915 in imitation of its Reconstruction namesake. The Klan, a secret organization stronger in the West than the South, was militantly anti-Catholic, antiforeign, and antiliberal. At its height in the early 1920s, thousands joined its sheeted parades, perhaps five million enrolled as members, and at least two states came under its political control. Only in the mid-1920s, when most kinds of hysteria gave way to complacency, did the Klan lose strength.

In 1919–1920 many Americans came to associate Wilsonian idealism with frustrated hopes and divisive emotions, with the unsolved problems of Europe, with war propaganda and foreign entanglements, and with the high cost of living and the Red Menace. Even the most devoted Wilsonians had to admit a shattering contrast between the vigorous leader of 1913 or the inspired prophet of 1917 and the sick, stubborn, old man of 1919, presiding over an administration zealous in hounding radicals but helpless in dealing with social or economic problems. It is not surprising that the country turned with relief toward a leadership as different as possible.

READJUSTMENT AND NEW DIRECTIONS, 1920–1924

Warren G. Harding was a small-town editor, a regular McKinley and Taft Republican, and a handsome, genial man with undemanding moral standards and a third-rate mind. Not unaware of his own shortcomings, he announced a plan to staff his administration with his party's "best minds." A few of these were secured, including Charles Evans Hughes, the new Secretary of State; Herbert Hoover, Secretary of Commerce; and possibly Andrew Mellon, the Pittsburgh aluminum king who became Secretary of the Treasury. In too many cases, though, the administration was staffed with party hacks and presidential cronies in a manner reminiscent of the Grant Era. A major center of power was the famous "little house on K Street" where members of the Ohio Gang played poker and forgot Prohibition. Yet this sleazy regime made decisions of great importance, most of them highly popular in their time.

In the campaign Harding, who had a gift for meaningless oratorical pronouncements, understandably avoided defining his foreign policy. Much of the Republican party was bitterly isolationist, yet an important faction, including ex-President Taft, insisted that the new administration would work out a less offensive substitute for the League of Nations. Whatever the election really meant, Harding drew from it the conclusion that American entry into the League was a dead issue. Even United States membership in the World Court, which Harding and his Republican successors favored, was blocked by ultraisolationist forces in the press and the Senate.

Despite the strength of isolationist feelings, real isolation was impossible. In the Far East, the original home of the Open Door Policy and the traditional center of Republican foreign interest, a new settlement was urgently necessary. During the war Japan had taken large steps toward the domination of China and military hegemony in East Asia. Traditional American commitments to Chinese territorial integrity and the Open Door ran well beyond America's military power. In the winter of 1921, an international conference in Washington, sometimes referred to as a Republican Versailles, struggled with the related problems of disarmament and the Far East.

In a series of interlocking treaties the United States attained the following objectives: (1) Japanese expansion was rolled back; (2) the embarrassing Anglo-Japanese Alliance was terminated; (3) the *status quo* in the Far East and the integrity of China were guaranteed by all major powers concerned except Russia; (4) the major naval powers agreed to curtail construction of capital ships, with Japan limited to three-fifths of the naval power of each of the Big Two (Britain and the United States). In return for these advantages the United States surrendered the possibility of naval superiority and agreed not to fortify her possessions in the Western Pacific. Much later, in an age of renewed Japanese aggression, these concessions were to be denounced. At the time, however, the United States was in no mood either for an arms race or for contesting Japan's control of the Western Pacific area. The Washington Settlement seemed a great success, and Japanese-American relations relaxed.

Even from Europe, it proved impossible to remain aloof. The United States had made huge loans to the Allied nations both during and right after the war. These were viewed by Europeans as American contributions to the common struggle and by most Americans as legitimate business obligations. Not without recrimination, the United States negotiated a series of funding agreements extending payment over twenty-five years with rates of interest scaled down according to ability to pay.

Payment by any scheme turned out to present almost insoluble problems. Sufficient gold was not available, and large imports of European goods were promptly rendered impossible. True to Republican traditions, formed during a period of infant American industry and devoutly upheld long after, Congress, in 1922, enacted the steeply protective Fordney-McCumber Tariff.

To many Europeans, debt payments to the United States seemed inseparably connected with German reparation payments to the former Allies. But in 1923 the Germans, racked by inflation and resentful of the sole-war-guilt principle on which reparations were based, defaulted. France promptly occupied the industrial Ruhr and was challenged by passive resistance from the German population. This situation, clearly threatening prosperity and peace, was a major test for the new foreign policy, and the test was passed. An international commission of experts, headed by an American banker, negotiated the Dawes Plan in 1923, and six years later a like group worked out the similar Young Plan. The basis of these plans was (1) successively scaled-down German payments, (2) stabilization of the German currency, and (3) an international loan to Germany to make these steps possible.

The greatest industrial nation in the world, now also the greatest creditor, could not stay aloof from world affairs. Instead, private investment was substituted for other forms of intervention. American investors, acting more or less in response to State Department suggestions, sustained the German Republic, helped the relatively moderate banker and industrialist regime in Japan, contested Near Eastern oil areas with the British and French, and supported congenial government in Latin America. Because this was done in the name of profit rather than politics and, above all, because military force was invoked only in minor Caribbean instances, the administration could quote with satisfaction the antientanglement advice of the founding fathers.

Antiforeign emotions were appeased by a drastic change in immigration policy. Well before the war, fear and dislike of "The New Immigration" from southern and eastern Europe had been spread by alarmist propaganda, and pseudoscientists continued to demonstrate the criminal tendencies of Slavs and Latins by their head measurements. Unions had long opposed the admission of cheap labor, and the advance of technology had made a mass of unskilled workers less important to industrialists. The war and the Red Scare had spread suspicion of aliens, and Congress in 1921–1924 took a series of actions designed both to decrease the number of immigrants sharply and to swing the balance back to the north European peoples. In its 1924 version the new legislation established a quota system limiting immigration from each country to 2 percent of its proportion of resident aliens according to the census of 1890. To the anger of the Japanese, a special provision totally excluded Orientals as "aliens ineligible to citizenship."

This decision, which reduced immigration from a flood to a trickle, broke decisively with a major American tradition and wounded the feelings of important minorities. In the long run, however, its results were far different from those intended by some of its supporters. The end of free immigration, like the disappearance of the frontier, lessened the wide-open, competitive, mobile tendencies of American life. It also speeded assimilation. Without the familiar flood of desperate, exploitable new arrivals, the foreign-born and their children were to insist with increasing force on a full place in American life and politics.

The economic policies of the Harding administration were developed in a time of instability. Late in 1920 the postwar boom turned into depression as government supports of basic commodity prices ended and European demand temporarily fell off. In the face of plummeting prices and mounting unemployment, government policy was simple: to do everything possible to encourage business leadership. Secretary Mellon called for strict economy and proposed sharp cuts in taxes on profits and high incomes. (Interestingly, Congress gave him only part of what he asked.) The administration continued the Wilson policy of withdrawal from all forms of government economic enterprise and cooperated still more fully with industry's drive to "discipline" organized labor. Hoover's Department of Commerce strove to further foreign investment and encouraged the formation of trade associations to prevent price cutting and other "unfair" competition. Pro-business appointments to the courts and the new regulatory commissions ended any threat of unsympathetic regulation.

Whether or not because of government policy, recovery began in 1922 and became well-established in 1923. The fact that this depression ended quickly, without government action except to encourage business, was to affect the thinking of many people at the outset of a greater depression a few years later.

One major exception to the encouraging economic tendency was the plight of the farmer. Once more production was far outrunning effective demand, and prices were falling disastrously. During the war, with demand unlimited and prices regulated by the government, farmers had prospered. Right after the war, a land boom had sustained at least the more fortunate. Now, with bumper crops to sell, mechanization putting a premium on efficiency, and European and world competition increasing sharply most farmers were in trouble. Large sections of the country were again confronted with the familiar problems of unpayable mortgages and rapidly increasing tenancy.

A series of farm organizations, from the semisocialist Non-Partisan League of North Dakota to the more conservative Farm Bureau Federation, once more voiced demands for relief. In Congress the powerful Farm Bloc secured considerable relief legislation of familiar kinds such as encouragement of cooperatives, facilitation of credit, and regulation of packers and speculators.

Farmers were not the only people to show their discontent with the Harding policies. Prewar progressivism, with its underdog sympathies and anti-big-business emotions, lived on in the hearts of millions of teachers, preachers, social workers, unionists, and others. In the new postwar circumstances, however, both high morale and unity seemed hard for progressives to attain.

In 1922 the most promising of a series of progressive coalitions took shape in the form of the Conference for Progressive Political Action, a federation of farm organizations, discontented labor groups, moderate Socialists, and assorted Bull Moosers and other progressives. In the congressional elections of 1922 the C.P.P.A. scored some startling successes. Harding Republicans lost many seats both to Democrats and progressive Republicans.

In the new Congress, investigations disclosed a series of scandals equaled only in the Grant administration. Harding cronies in the Veterans' Bureau and a number of other agencies had been dispensing favors for financial inducements. The worst revelation was that government oil lands, held for naval needs, had been transferred in a series of maneuvers to a group of private speculators. Still popular but increasingly conscious of his own inadequacy and of betrayal by his friends, the President fell ill in the course of returning from an Alaskan junket. On August 2, 1923, he died of a stroke in San Francisco. To his party's good fortune, he was replaced by Vice President Calvin Coolidge, a taciturn and parsimonious Yankee who seemed the perfect incarnation of conventional Republican morality.

In 1922–1924 many people thought that the Harding scandals and the progressive gains foreshadowed a political upheaval. The C.P.P.A. backed the redoubtable Robert M. La Follette as a "Progressive" presidential candidate. The La Follette platform had, to be sure, a rather old-fashioned ring for 1924: antimonopoly, public ownership of railroads, conservation, farm relief, and curbing of the Supreme Court. Yet the Wisconsin Senator, whose antiwar record was now an asset in his own section, looked formidable enough to frighten conservatives. The Republicans, renominating Coolidge on a *status quo* platform, denounced La Follette and his supporters as extreme radicals. Meanwhile the Democrats, deeply divided by their old agrarian-urban split, bogged down in a deadlocked convention and emerged with an unpromising conservative candidate, John W. Davis.

The result of the election was a Coolidge landslide. La Follette, without adequate organization or large funds, had scored 16.5 percent of the popular vote and ran ahead of Davis in many western states. Yet right after the election his disparate coalition fell apart. Progressivism, for the moment, seemed negative and old-fashioned. The election seemed a green light for business prosperity and its political friends.

THE NEW ERA AND ITS CRITICS

For the rest of the decade, American prosperity was the center of attention both for complacent natives and jealous or admiring foreigners. The principal basis for the good times was an increase in productivity based on advances in technology and management. Between 1923 and 1929, the output per man-hour in manufacturing rose 32 percent. The basic industrial plant and transportation systems were now largely adequate; this time much of the expansion could go into the kind of production that people notice most easily. The most spectacular advances took place in production of electric power and light and of durable consumers goods, and in construction, both of suburban houses and urban skyscrapers. By 1929 one American in five had an automobile. Radios, household appliances, and prepared foods were almost equally part of the new way of life.

Changing patterns of consumption, stimulated by mass advertising and assisted by time payments, seemed to render obsolete the old "Puritan virtues" of hard work, abstinence, and saving. Leisure and enjoyment became not only permissible but almost obligatory. From perplexing foreign problems and dull domestic politics, public attention turned to the lives of movie stars, the exploits of athletes, or the heroism of aviators like Charles Lindbergh who flew the Atlantic alone in 1927 and immediately became the most popular American.

The new prosperity brought with it a new ideology. Business, according to its spokesmen, had accomplished the dreams of past radicals without coercion or hatred. Poverty and war were both overcome and cutthroat competition had been replaced by cooperation and service. The new businessman was committed to high wages and deeply interested in employee welfare. Thus there was no further use for divisive labor unions or impractical political radicalism.

Actually the results of the new prosperity were less than Utopian. Farm prices rose a little from the postwar depression level, yet farmers as a whole failed to regain their prewar purchasing power. Real wages rose sharply, but not in proportion either to productivity or profits. In 1929, the average factory worker made less than $1,500 a year, and more than 45 percent of all families got less than $2,000. Even if these figures are doubled to represent post-World War II purchasing power, they fall far short of universal well-being. Large groups, like coal or textile workers, southern small farmers, and Negroes, remained in real poverty.

Later, many critics were to point out that the New Era's prosperity was as unsound as it was uneven. Business consolidation, though it did not usually attain the outright monopoly which had alarmed people earlier, often led to dangerous practices. Prices were often inflexible, and insider groups sometimes built crazy pyramids of holding companies. In the late 1920s, too much money was going into outright speculation in land or stocks and not enough into genuinely productive investment.

Even at the time, important minorities refused to join in the chorus of complacency. Surviving congressional progressives, led by Senator George Norris of Nebraska, were able to prevent the administration from turning over to private interests the government-built nitrate plants on the Tennessee River. (In turn Coolidge and his successor were able to block Norris's own plan for a government-run Tennessee dam and power system.) Prodded by the Farm Bloc, Congress passed ambitious farm relief laws. Of these the most discussed was the McNary-Haugen bill, vetoed in 1927. This was a complex scheme providing for government purchase and sale abroad of surplus farm commodities.

Perhaps the most important dissenters in the Coolidge era expressed themselves in ways which had nothing to do with politics. Many people of rural and small town upbringing were uneasy about the new free and easy ways of living and appalled by the alleged wildness of the younger generation. Some called for a return to sobriety, simplicity, and tradition; some swelled the ranks of Protestant religious fundamentalism. Two generations after the Darwinian controversy, the state of Tennessee passed a law against teaching in the schools that man descended from "lower animals." In 1925, when this law was challenged by shocked liberals, no less a public figure than William Jennings Bryan appeared to champion a literal interpretation of Genesis.

At the opposite extreme from the Fundamentalists but equally hostile to the dominant business ideology, were the literary intellectuals and their followers. With the war, their exuberant rebellion against moral and esthetic conventions had turned to a far deeper kind of alienation. Repelled by postwar intolerance and equally disgusted by what seemed to them the materialism and conformity of the Coolidge era, many of the most literate Americans worried out loud about the fate of American civilization. Some roundly denounced the country and withdrew to the sophistication of Paris or the primitivism of Mexico or Spain.

The most intelligent of the discontented realized that more was at stake than any set of national mores. Old questions, put in new forms, were raising doubts about human nature itself. Americans were confronting problems common to all men, but particularly distressing to those who inherited a tradition of individual freedom. To some popular behaviorist psychologists, man was a bundle of predictable and controllable responses to physical stimuli. To Freudians he was ruled by emotional drives far below the level of consciousness. Neither view seemed to offer much hope to those who cared most for individual freedom. Squarely confronting these and other intellectual challenges, some Americans produced excellent and profoundly serious novels or poems. Others laid the foundation for a deeper and richer criticism of contemporary civilization than had yet been possible.

Perhaps no group indulged more fully in this spirit of national self-criticism and personal reevaluation, and no group more fully explored the failures of American society, than Afro-Americans. The black literati of the Harlem Renaissance shared the discontented white intellectuals' distaste for bourgeois values and joined their insurrection against traditional literary forms. But the alienation of the Negro artists seemed more firmly rooted in the day-to-day realities of American life. In a rich outpouring of poems and novels, they celebrated the emergence of a "New Negro"—race-proud and militant, impatient with white injustice, determined to fight for basic human dignity. Joined by a confident new generation of black musicians, dancers, painters, and actors, they struggled to work out a new attitude toward blackness and the cultural heritage of their African past. In a parallel development, the inarticulate black denizens of the nation's industrial slums found a symbol of race pride in the exotic figure of Marcus Garvey and his Universal Negro Improvement Association. Unlike either Booker T. Washington or W. E. B. Du Bois, Garvey stirred the imagination of the impoverished black masses. His back-to-Africa movement, like his dream of an African Empire, died in embryo. But his immense popularity (estimates of his following range from one to four million) exposed as perhaps never before the depths of Afro-American despair.

But the discontent of the nation's intellectuals and the dissatisfaction of its black minority was not widely shared by other segments of the population. Everybody was not happy or rich in the mid-1920s, but prosperity was still a substantial fact, and those who were the most satisfied were also the most influential. More people than ever before moved to the suburbs, drove to the beach, or dreamed of a summer in Europe. Prosperity could be measured not only in baseball gate receipts but in such substantial terms as houses, schools, and hospitals. What civilization, complacent citizens could legitimately ask, had ever done so much for so many?

Ignoring his critics, President Coolidge could continue to issue his laconic and reassuring statements, take his two-hour afternoon naps, continue the probusiness policies of his predecessor without the corruption, and remain generally popular. The federal government could persist in trimming its costs (especially since states were spending more and more on highways). In 1926 Secretary Mellon was finally able to put over his full program of tax relief for the wealthy.

In foreign affairs, success seemed equally conclusive. In Europe, the mid-1920s were an era of apparent economic stabilization, of Franco-German rapprochement, and of increased prestige for the League of Nations. Despite congressional suspicion, the administration was able to develop a habit of unofficial cooperation with the League for many purposes. In Mexico, where conflict between the forces of social revolution and American business interests dragged on, the Coolidge administration managed to compromise serious differences over sub-soil oil rights.

Americans of the New Era believed that they could attain not only permanent prosperity, but lasting international peace. Barred by Congress from toying with collective security, the Coolidge administration made further but generally unsuccessful efforts to negotiate disarmament in 1927, an effort carried on by Hoover with somewhat more success in 1930. In August, 1928, largely through American efforts, fifteen nations signed the Kellogg Briand Pact renouncing war as an instrument of national policy. Like Prohibition, this innocuous measure was widely popular among the hopeful. Nearly all nations adhered to it during the remaining interval before World War II.

SMITH AND HOOVER

Neither foreign policy nor domestic economic argument played a major part in the presidential campaign of 1928. On the surface the issues of this contest were personal; at a deeper level it involved the most divisive group loyalties. Herbert Hoover, the Republican nominee, was presented as a self-made engineer, a nonpolitical expert administrator, and a major spokesman of the new business outlook. The Democratic candidate, Alfred E. Smith of New York, though no radical, was known as a friend of the underprivileged, and a champion, during the Red Scare, of civil liberties. The only major issue on which the two sharply differed was Prohibition.

This issue symbolized the real division between supporters of the two men. In many rural and Protestant areas, Prohibition was still regarded as at least a hopeful attack on a great evil, demanding the support of all respectable people. To many city dwellers, on the other hand, it was associated with lawlessness, gangsterism, and puritanical prejudice. Hoover had the conventional presidential background of Protestantism and rural poverty. Smith was a Catholic, a wet, and a city product with a New York accent. Without concrete issues, the campaign was fought to a large extent in terms of stereotypes and prejudices.

On the surface, the result was another Republican landslide. Hoover carried several states of the Democratic, but Protestant and rural South. Yet later students have noticed that the big cities voted far more heavily Democratic than in previous twentieth-century elections. Despite his religion and his origins, Smith also scored significant Democratic gains in a number of discontented western farm regions. One can glimpse, in the Smith vote, the beginnings of the unbeatable Democratic coalition of the New Deal years.

In 1929, to most people, the new administration seemed to promise increased efficiency and broader humanitarianism within the framework of the Harding-Coolidge policies. Yet Hoover, the ablest of the three postwar presidents, encountered disaster at home and menace abroad. Whether one looked back at the 1920s, with nostalgia or distaste, they were soon to seem a strange interlude in the tragic and turbulent history of the twentieth century. It was perhaps just as well that the United States had enjoyed an interlude of peace and prosperity, however illusory, between two times of appalling and challenging crisis.

FOR FURTHER READING:

William E. Leuchtenberg, *The Perils of Prosperity* (1958)* is a readable and intelligent interpretation. John D. Hicks, *The Republican Ascendancy* (1960)*, is a solid factual survey, political in emphasis. Robert K. Murray's *The Harding Era* (1969) and *The Politics of Normalcy* (1973), valiantly struggle to rehabilitate the Ohio president's tarnished image. The best biography of *Calvin Coolidge* (1967) is the one by Donald McCoy. Economic history is excellently summarized in George Soule, *Prosperity Decade* (1947)*. Irving Bernstein, *The Lean Years* (1960)*, is a revealing history of labor from 1921 to 1933. Foreign policy is illuminated by Selig Adler, *The Isolationist Impulse* (1957)*. Robert K. Murray examines the *Red Scare* (1955)*. F. L. Allen, *Only Yesterday* (1931)* is an informal and very perceptive reminiscence of social change. Preston W. Slosson, *The Great Crusade and After* (1930), is a more academic and comprehensive social history. Roderick Nash, *The Nervous Generation* (1970)*, is a superb revisionist history of popular culture. Garvey's career is the subject of E. David Cronon's *Black Moses* (1955)*; and Nathan Huggins has surveyed the *Harlem Renaissance* (1971). An influential contemporary sample of American society is R. S. and H. M. Lynd, *Middletown* (1929)*. President Hoover's Research Committee on Social Trends summarizes a great mass of interesting material in *Recent Social Trends* (2 vols., 1933). Andrew Sinclair, *Prohibition* (1962)*, is a fascinating interpretation. For literary history the best source is contemporary writing, and the best introduction Alfred Kazin, *On Native Grounds* (1942)*.

Henry F. May, *The Discontent of the Intellectuals: A Problem of the Twenties* (Berkeley Readings in American History, 1963)*, is a documentary study of a familiar but puzzling aspect of the period.

---

* Available in paperback edition.

THE NEW DEAL

	Labor	Agriculture	Business and Industrial Recovery	Relief	Reform	Miscellaneous
1932			R.F.C. established.	Relief and Construction Act. Federal Home Loan Bank Act.		Bonus March. Election of Roosevelt.
1933	Section 7A of NIRA.	Agricultural Adjustment Act. Farm Credit Act.	Thomas Amendment to AAA (inflation). Emergency Banking Act. Beer and Wine Revenue Act. Banking Act of 1933 (guaranteed deposits). National Industrial Recovery Act.	Civilian Conservation Corps. Federal Emergency Relief Act. Home Owners Refinancing Act. Farm Credit Act. Public Works Administration. Civil Works Administration.	TVA. Federal Securities Act.	Economy Act. Twenty-first Amendment (Repeal of Prohibition).
1934		Cotton Control Act. Federal Farm Bankruptcy Act.	Gold Reserve Act. Silver Purchase Act. Trade Agreement Act (reciprocal trade treaties).	Civil Works Emergency Relief Act.	Home Owners Loan Act. Securities Exchange Act. National Housing Act.	

THE NEW DEAL (continued)

Year	Labor	Agriculture	Business and Industrial Recovery	Relief	Reform	Miscellaneous
1935	National Labor Relations (Wagner) Act.	Resettlement Administration. Relief Electrification Administration.		Works Progress Administration and National Youth Administration.	Banking Act of 1935. Social Security Act. Public Utilities Holding Company Act. Revenue Act (wealth tax).	First Neutrality Act.
1936		Soil Conservation and Domestic Allotment Act.				Neutrality Act extended. Soldier's Bonus. Roosevelt reelected.
1937		Farm Security Administration.			Court Reorganization Act (not passed). United States Housing Authority.	Neutrality Act revised. Depression (fall).
1938	Fair Labor Standards Act.	Agricultural Adjustment Act of 1938.				Billion dollar naval expansion. Republican gains in Congress.

Depression and Social Experiment
1929-1938

26

In the summer of 1929, while stock prices rose beyond all relation to earnings or dividends, most industrial and financial experts predicted nothing but permanent prosperity. Signs of trouble, including declines in both construction and automobiles, the two key industries of the New Era, were generally ignored. In September the market hesitated nervously, and then, in late October, a devastating series of crashes canceled 40 percent of the paper values of common stocks.

Despite the continuing optimism of government and business leaders, the crash of 1929 was not a mere correction of inflated values. Like the panics of 1873 and 1893, it turned into severe and prolonged depression. In the years from 1929 to 1933, as stock prices fell ever lower and confidence evaporated, manufacturing production was halved and building nearly stopped. Banks and businesses failed, farm income, already low, was cut in half, and, worst of all, unemployment grew steadily. By 1932 it was variously estimated at from thirteen to seventeen million. American prosperity, and with it the spirit of the New Era, had disappeared.

The impact of the great depression on those who lived through it is hard to exaggerate. At the lowest economic level, the unemployed faced the threat of actual starvation when charities, cities, and states ran out of relief funds. Apple selling and breadlines became common sights, shanty towns sprang up on the edge of cities, men and women were sometimes seen pawing through restaurant garbage. At the opposite end of the scale, some respected financiers were caught misusing investors' funds. Only a few killed themselves or fled to Europe, but both bankers and big businessmen in general rapidly lost public prestige. In the large, previously contented middle class, people unused to disaster lost savings, houses, jobs, and hope. Even those who suffered no personal privation found it hard to dispel fear. Anyone might be the next victim of a disaster nobody understood.

Why did catastrophe paralyze the richest and most productive country in the world? At the time, many blamed some of the more obvious weak spots in the economy: the loose and ill-coordinated banking structure and the irresponsible financial manipulation that had piled one holding company on another. Later, New Dealers insisted that Republican policies had crippled foreign trade, encouraged inequality and concentration, fostered the boom and then clung doggedly to financial conservatism after the crash. On the other hand, President Hoover was always to believe that the depression was almost beaten when the election of a Democrat destroyed business confidence. In the long run, many historians have concluded that the fault lay in the unsoundness and inadequacy of the previous decade's prosperity. In the 1920s prosperity depended as never before on mass consumption. Yet inequality and a too rigid price structure limited consumption. By 1929 effective demand for automobiles and some other products was apparently about filled. Attractive outlets seemed to be lacking for really large scale investment. In other words, prosperity could not continue as the prosperity of part of one country in a poor world. The New Era picture of liberal and progressive American capitalism, while not without much truth, was not true enough.

HOOVER AND THE DEPRESSION

On coming to office in 1929, President Hoover found himself confronted by two familiar problems of the twenties, farm relief and the tariff. Each of these grew more difficult with the coming of depression.

Like Coolidge, Hoover fought off Farm Bloc proposals which seemed to involve subsidy and price fixing. In their place Hoover secured the passage of a complex measure establishing a Federal Farm Board empowered to promote such time-honored remedies as cooperative marketing. By 1930 the "Stabilization Corporations" also created by this law were buying and storing surplus wheat and cotton. Already the government was up to its neck in undisposable surpluses, and prices were still going down.

As part of his farm program, Hoover proposed another old panacea, tariffs, on agricultural products. This led, in Congress, to further demands for industrial protection and the enactment of the Smoot-Hawley Tariff, signed by Hoover despite the protest of more than a thousand economists. The high rates of this measure ended all prospects of reviving foreign trade.

In his measures specifically designed to fight the depression, President Hoover, the elected representative of New Era know-how, broke sharply with the past. When Secretary Mellon recommended that the government allow prices and wages to fall until recovery set in, according to traditional *laissez faire* formulae, Hoover decided that such a drastic purge might kill the delicate patient. His first action, following New Era doctrine rather than nineteenth-century economic theory, was to call conferences of leading businessmen, which urged employers to maintain wages and production. When this proved ineffective, Hoover used available government machinery to cut taxes, liberalize credit, and prop farm prices.

By 1930, the administration turned to more drastic remedies. In that year, however, the long-brewing revolt against the Republicans was speeded by depression and Hoover lost the support of Congress. Many administration measures failed, but the President managed to secure large public works appropriations and measures to refinance home mortgages and further stimulate credit. A new agency, the Reconstruction Finance Corporation, lent large sums to banks, railroads, and businesses and also eventually to states, cities, and agricultural credit corporations. To stem international financial disaster, Hoover called successfully in 1931 for a one-year moratorium on German reparations and Allied debt payments.

Thus, in a major break with the past, the Hoover administration assumed governmental responsibility for fighting an economic crisis. Yet the Hoover measures, sweeping and large scale as some of them seemed by the standards of the twenties, were not on a scale adequate to the dimensions of the crisis. Moreover, the President flatly refused to meet two widespread demands. First, he declined to countenance currency inflation. Second, he fought all measures designed to provide direct federal responsibility for unemployment relief. Either of these actions, he sincerely believed, would have grave effects on American tradition and character.

As the plight of the unemployed became desperate, Hoover was wrongly seen as heartless. By 1932 dejection, apathy, and bad luck seemed to have destroyed the administration's earlier vigor. In that year a "Bonus Army" of unemployed servicemen assembled in Washington to demand immediate cash payoff of twenty-year insurance policies provided for World War veterans by legislation in 1924. Panicking at a minor threat to order, the administration had the Army destroy the veterans' camp with tanks and tear gas. This episode helped to make Hoover, a sensitive man, the worst-hated president since Cleveland. His reelection was obviously unlikely.

The leading Democratic candidate to succeed him, Governor Franklin D. Roosevelt of New York, was little known to most of the public. A Hudson River aristocrat from the Democratic branch of his family, he had yet been influenced by his cousin Theodore as well as by Wilson, whom he had served as Assistant Secretary of the Navy. After his sacrifice campaign for the vice presidency in the Republican year 1920, Roosevelt had been crippled by poliomyelitis. Nonetheless, he had remained active in Democratic politics and in 1928, bucking a Republican trend, had succeeded Smith as governor of New York, where he had tackled depression problems with considerable energy.

The trait the public immediately saw in the new Roosevelt was a gay, jaunty confidence which seemed a welcome opposite to Hoover's dogged gloom. What lay beneath the confidence is a question on which observers never agreed. To Roosevelt's critics, his cheerful nonchalance, his willingness to try anything, his tolerance of contradictions and his impatience of theory meant superficiality and arrogance. To some of his admirers, his flexibility seemed to rest on a bedrock of courage and to be complemented by a genuine humanitarian and religious concern for the underdog.

Nominated by adroit maneuvers in a close convention, Roosevelt in his campaign pledged drastic action to end the depression. What sort of action was not clear; while Roosevelt called for public power development and other progressive reforms, he also pledged a 25 percent cut in spending and evaded the tariff question. Hoover, meanwhile, asked the people to sustain his own battle with the depression and grimly predicted disaster if his opponent won. The result was hardly in doubt; the Roosevelt landslide approximately equaled the Hoover victory of 1928.

During the interregnum before the new administration could take over in March, Hoover tried hard to persuade the president-elect to commit himself to a balanced budget, maintenance of the gold standard, and other central Republican policies. Roosevelt committed himself to nothing and was blamed by Republicans for a further economic downturn. In February the Governor of Michigan announced a bank holiday to prevent financial collapse, and other states followed suit. By Inauguration Day all banks were shut and some cities had turned to scrip. In the Midwest, farmers had resorted to old methods of semiviolent protest against a hopeless situation; milk trucks had been overturned and mortgage sales forcibly halted. Unemployed vagrants, many of them boys, were roaming the country. As never before, the stage was set for masterful presidential action.

THE FIRST NEW DEAL

In his arresting inaugural, Roosevelt promised that he would, if necessary, ask for powers to fight the depression equal to those given presidents in wartime. America's resources were adequate for the task ahead: the only thing she had to fear was "fear itself." Resounding with confidence and vigor, the speech committed the administration to no single course. For a while nearly all Americans, from bankers to tenant farmers and the unemployed, counted on Roosevelt to help them. The New Deal, taking various forms through the next years, can best be understood as a continuing experimental response to these demands. Back of each measure demanded by the President lay group pressures, party needs, conflicts among presidential advisers, and the balance of congressional blocs. Fully to understand the New Deal, one would have to understand two profound mysteries: American society and Franklin D. Roosevelt.

In the spring of 1933 Congress, with unheard-of speed, passed a series of administration measures. Roosevelt later summarized his objectives as "Relief, Recovery, and Reform," and this First New Deal can be described in terms of these "Three R's."

Relief for the country's most urgent needs started with legislation to open and sustain the sounder banks, leaving the weaker ones shut. Direct federal help for the unemployed began with the Civilian Conservation Corps, which set young men to work on reforestation and other conservation projects. Larger unemployment relief programs included federal grants to states and plans for vast public works. Relief for home and farm owners was the main purpose of further legislation to refinance mortgages.

Recovery of the economy called forth the most spectacular measures of the First New Deal, measures which demonstrated its lack of consistent economic theory. Approaches to recovery included the Economy Act, which reflected the traditional belief that government spending somehow caused economic decline; the Trade Agreements Act, which gave the President power to negotiate low-tariff agreements in order to revive foreign trade; and even the Beer Act, which legalized one promising industry. (By the end of the year, the Twenty-first Amendment swept away Prohibition completely.) The most important recovery programs of the First New Deal, however, relied on two main methods; first, raising prices by restricting output and controlling competition; and second, inflation, now irresistibly demanded by western Democrats.

During the campaign Roosevelt and some of his advisers had declared that the expansion of the American economy, like that of the frontier, was finished. In the future better distribution and planned production would replace violent competition. This theory owed something to Herbert Croly and the Bull Moose movement and something to Herbert Hoover and the trade associations of the twenties. Now the ambitious National Industrial Recovery Act gave industry the legal right to agree on binding codes of common practice. These codes would, it was hoped, end sharp practice, unfair treatment of labor, and unjust, below-cost cuts in prices. How much they would permit prices to *rise* was never clearly settled. To make such agreements possible, the antitrust laws were suspended. To compensate for this favor to industry, workers were promised in the famous Section 7A of the NIRA the right "to organize and bargain collectively through representatives of their own choosing . . . free from the interference, restraint or coercion of employers. . . ."

Reflecting a somewhat similar purpose, the Agricultural Adjustment Act of 1933 sought primarily to raise farm prices by many and complex methods. Its most striking feature was a system of subsidies to be given farmers who agreed to decrease production. Such payments were to be financed by taxes on the industries which processed agricultural products.

Inflation, the other principal recovery device, was provided for in an amendment to the AAA, sponsored by Senator Elmer Thomas of Oklahoma, who remembered Bryan's crusade against gold. The Thomas amendment gave the President power to inflate the currency in many ways. Moving reluctantly at first, Roosevelt took the dollar off gold, sanctioned special measures to support the price of silver, and eventually stabilized the currency at about 60 percent of its former value.

Reform, that is deliberate effort to render the social system more just or humane, could be seen in the new programs to regulate stock exchanges and investment banking, in the labor clause of the NIRA, and, mostly clearly of all, in the Tennessee Valley Authority. This daring project, bringing to fruition the long frustrated dreams of Senator Norris and other progressives, was designed to remodel a whole river system by building a series of dams. Among its objectives were cheap power and fertilizer, flood control, soil and forest conservation, the improvement of inland waterways, and new recreation areas. Reform and recovery were both objectives of the National Housing Act of 1934, which provided insurance of loans to promote repair and modernization of homes, farms, and small plants.

NEW DEMANDS AND
A SECOND NEW DEAL, 1934–1936

Through these and other laws, the First New Deal seemed to have scored a qualified success. Its first actions brought a sharp rise in production and prices. Then the rate of recovery slowed, and people realized that the depression had not disappeared. The elections of

1934, increasing the already large Democratic majorities, showed clearly that a majority approved the administration's efforts. Yet more was needed; the First New Deal had brought to light a whole series of new demands.

Farmers had benefited from price rises, but were still distressed. Some of them had been disturbed by the destruction of crops and animals undertaken as an emergency measure in time of surplus. Then in 1934 the worst drought in the nation's history threatened to change surplus to shortage. Thousands of tenants and sharecroppers were driven from the land and left destitute. This seemed to be caused in part by the drought, but also in part by the AAA, which encouraged landlords to mechanize and cut acreage. So far, it seemed to many angry small farmers, the New Deal farm program had helped the richest most.

The unemployed demanded faster relief than was provided by the cautious handling, so far, of public works. Organized labor, which had reached a low point in 1933, took new courage from clause 7A with its guarantees of freedom to organize. But as new millions rushed into the ill-prepared unions, hard problems arose. Employers, many of them still hostile to "outside" organizations, thought that Section 7A had authorized them to form more or less docile company unions. Workers insisted that only national organizations could be effective. The National Labor Board, formed by the President to arbitrate multiplying controversies, lacked both authority and consistent policy.

Business and industry, at first eager for New Deal help and willing to promise drastic reform, had become restless with partial recovery. Despite gains made through NIRA codes, many businessmen resented excessive government interference in the details of their operations. Some hoped to exclude the government altogether and make the program into one of simple business self-regulation on the Hoover pattern. On the other hand, progressives were charging that big business already dominated the codes and gouged consumers. Worried liberals, looking both at NIRA and AAA, doubted increasingly whether raising prices and cutting production was the best answer to widespread scarcity.

Thus the administration, which had tried to please everybody, found itself attacked from right and left. Conservatives looked back with nostalgia at the probusiness policies of the Republican years or lamented the end of *laissez faire* and traditional individualism. Just below the surface of some of the most fervent complaints ran an undercurrent of fear that the balance of power in the country was shifting away from those who ought to be in charge, in the direction of the shiftless, the irresponsible, and the foreign born. Not a few outraged citizens concluded that the whole New Deal was a conspiracy against free enterprise, sound money, and American tradition and even that it was secretly aiming at ushering in socialism or communism.

At the other extreme, it was true that the tiny Communist party of the United States had made some progress. It was aided in 1935 by a sharp change in the international Communist line. Instead of denouncing all non-Communist efforts at reform as insipid and useless, Communists were now to call for a "United Front" and to make every effort to work with "progressives" and "anti-Fascists." During the period from 1935 to 1939, while this line endured, the Communist movement achieved some influence among American intellectuals and among some elements of labor. More important than actual Communist gains, which remained numerically small, was the conviction, or half-conviction, fairly widespread among intellectuals, that capitalism could not recover.

Still more important in practical politics was the rapid spread of economic panaceas. Most of these appealed, as in the past, to disgruntled rural and small town people, and most involved a combination of currency tinkering and old-fashioned anti-big-business rhetoric. Among them were the Townsend Plan for liberal old-age pensions; the inflationary suggestions of Father Coughlin, the radio priest who denounced international bankers in speeches with anti-Semitic overtones; the sweeping production-for-use plan of Upton Sinclair in California; and the glittering, enticing, "Every Man a King" proposal of Huey P. Long, a talented, ruthless spokesman of the dispossessed who made himself governor and near-dictator of Louisiana. All these plans, however illusory, gained their strength from two undeniable truths. First, the richest country in the world had too many poor people. Second, the New Deal had not yet produced a convincing remedy.

In response to all these pressures the President, supported by new advisers, backed a new set of measures. This Second New Deal, often seen as more radical than the first, was not really aimed at systematic alteration of the economic or social system. Indeed, one important group of young men who prepared it were under the influence of Louis D. Brandeis, who had helped to prepare Woodrow Wilson's "New Freedom" program, and imbued his followers with a dislike of bigness and a fervent belief in competition and diversity. The Second New Deal contained no measures aimed at direct regulation of business on the scale of the NIRA and none whose objectives were as sweeping as those of the TVA. Its main object, like that of its predecessor, was to get the economy going and correct in the process some obvious injustices. Some of its measures had the further purpose, a highly traditional one, of breaking up concentrations of power.

The new measures were sometimes proclaimed, however, in combative tones. Often they were carried through with hard-boiled political efficiency. Quite obviously, some of them reflected the demands of newly articulate groups. It is not surprising that some businessmen, remembering the placid 1920s, were both resentful and alarmed. To many young people and to believers in social experiment, on the other hand, the Second New Deal brought a time of heady excitement, when almost any goal seemed possible, and almost any method worth a try.

In the sphere of unemployment relief, the administration committed itself to the principle of providing work rather than handouts. A special agency, the National Youth Administration, provided employment for unemployed youths and assisted students to stay in college. The Second New Deal's principal relief agency was the gigantic Works Progress Administration administered by the former social worker Harry Hopkins, a devoted, self-sacrificing, and sometimes ruthless New Dealer. The WPA built roads, schools, parks, and countless other projects. In addition to construction workers it employed actors, painters, musicians, and writers. Astounded conservatives and delighted liberals found the federal government sponsoring symphony concerts, excellent guidebooks, colossal murals of varying quality, and the production of plays, some of them experimental and some left-wing.

Existing farm programs were supplemented by efforts to help the neglected poorest farmers. The Resettlement Administration tried to move families from submarginal land, and the Rural Electrification Administration brought power lines to areas not served by private utilities.

In the Social Security Act, the United States, entering the field much later than other leading industrial countries, laid the foundations for a system of old-age, unemployment, and disability insurance financed largely by employer and employee contributions. The Revenue Act of 1935, though whittled down in Congress, sharply increased taxes on high incomes, corporations, and estates. The Banking Act of 1935 increased the power of the Federal Reserve Board to buy and sell government securities in the open market for stabilization purposes, and the Public Utility Holding Company Act restricted the practice of piling one company on another in the fashion popular in the late 1920s.

Finally, as the new labor problems became more and more pressing, the President, in 1935, gave his backing to a bill long advocated by Senator Robert F. Wagner of New York. The Wagner Act outlawed employer coercion and support of company unions. Henceforth an employer was required to bargain with the union chosen by a majority of his employees in government-supervised, secret-ballot elections.

Sweeping changes in the size and shape of organized labor were partly a cause and partly an effect of new government policies. Since NIRA days, organizers had turned their attention to the long-unorganized millions in such great industries as steel, automobiles, rubber, and textiles. Inevitably, swelling numbers and this change of direction strained the traditional craft organization of the American Federation of Labor. Led by John L. Lewis, the colorful and domineering head of the United Mine Workers, a group of rebels formed within the A.F. of L. a Committee for Industrial Organization. This group, expelled in November, 1935, became in 1938 the independent Congress for Industrial Organizations.

In a series of hard-fought, sometimes bloody, strikes, the C.I.O. attacked the long-defended bastions of American heavy industry. This time the outcome of labor warfare was a sweeping union victory. Beginning with the surrender of United States Steel and General Motors in 1937, America's most powerful corporations were to make agreements with C.I.O. unions. Already, by that year, organized labor had grown from a depression low of under three million to more than seven million, and it was still growing fast.

Not only the size but the nature of the American labor movement was changed. Most of it, unlike the labor movements of other industrial countries, continued to accept the capitalist system of production. (An important faction of the C.I.O., later to be expelled, was under Communist influence.) But American labor by the mid-1930s was far more deeply committed to political action to further its social objectives than it had been before.

In 1936 the Republicans, sharply denouncing the New Deal, nominated Alfred M. Landon, the moderately liberal governor of Kansas, to oppose Roosevelt. In a victory which surpassed all but Harding's, Roosevelt got more than 60 percent of the popular vote and carried all states but Maine and Vermont. In this election the Democrats were supported for the first time by an emerging, powerful, but unstable coalition consisting of labor, most farmers, recent immigrants, Negroes, and the South; while the Republicans had the support of most businessmen. Though this pattern was to vary from election to election with changing circumstances, it would affect American politics for a generation.

DEADLOCK AND A THIRD NEW DEAL, 1937–1938

Despite this resounding election victory in 1936, the New Deal in 1937 and 1938 ran into a series of partial defeats. The first was in its conflict with the Supreme Court. In its sessions of 1935 and 1936 the Court had overturned a number of important New Deal statutes, sometimes in five-to-four decisions. These included the National Industrial Recovery Act and the processing tax of the Agricultural Adjustment Act. According to a majority of the Court, Congress during the New Deal had unconstitutionally delegated detailed legislative power to administrative agencies (as in the NIRA) and had gravely misinterpreted the taxing power, the interstate commerce clause, and other parts of the Constitution.

To the President and many New Dealers, the Court majority seemed to be interpreting the Constitution in a rigid and reactionary manner. Concluding that it would be impossibly slow and difficult to amend the Constitution, Roosevelt in February, 1937, unveiled a drastic proposal for changing the Court's personnel. One justice was to be added for every member who failed to retire after seventy. Some people were shocked by this attack on the Court, and many disliked the President's unsuccessful attempt to present his plan as part of an innocuous program for judicial efficiency. While the argument raged fiercely, the Court itself took a hand in the struggle. A number of important New Deal statutes were suddenly sustained, and one conservative justice voluntarily retired. This made Court reform seem less urgent, and despite the President's refusal to compromise, the bill was defeated in Senate committee.

In the long run, the change in the Court's attitude constituted a major New Deal victory and ushered in a long period of increase in the government's power for social and economic legislation. Yet the prestige of the Court as an institution survived; that of the President was sharply damaged.

It was further injured by the onset of a new depression. In the summer of 1936, production, profits, and wages (though not employment) had been edging toward the levels of 1929. Apparently this was partly because of large government spending for New Deal purposes and for payment of the veterans' bonus (finally provided by Congress over Roosevelt's veto in 1936). The President, worried about deficits and mounting debt, acted to tighten credit and cut the budget, particularly WPA funds. In the fall a sudden collapse seemed to bring back conditions of 1932. Farm prices headed down again, unemployment grew, and some critics concluded that the administration had failed to find a solution for the depression.

Whether this was true or not, the New Deal proved in 1937–1938 that it had not lost its energy. Expenditures were sharply increased for relief, public works, and, under the Wagner-Steagall bill, for public housing. Whereas earlier governmental expenditures had usually been defended only as humanitarian necessities, now spending was advocated partly as a means of inducing recovery. This reflected the increasing influence among economists, in and out of the administration, of the theories of the English economist J. M. Keynes. Keynes argued impressively that in time of depression, deficit spending by government was necessary in order to induce recovery and "prime the pump" of private investment.

Partly to further recovery by breaking up price fixing (a direct reversal of the First New Deal's objective), antitrust prosecutions were vigorously increased. A new Farm Security Administration tried hard to help the tenant farmers and migratory workers who were still America's most poverty-stricken people. A new AAA sought to raise all farm income by many devices, including new measures for crop restriction and government loans on stored surplus crops. Finally, the Fair Labor Standards Act of June, 1938, made possible by the Supreme Court's new attitude, established modest minimum wages and maximum hours for most employees and killed that old and tough enemy of American progressives, child labor. Some of the innovations of this last New Deal, including compensatory spending and wage regulation, proved to be among the most permanent and substantial changes brought about in the whole period.

THE MEANING OF THE NEW DEAL

The 1938 congressional elections ended the New Deal period. Not only did conservative Republicans gain sharply in the West, but conservative Democrats in the South beat off the President's daring attempt to defeat them, and thereby turn the Democratic party into a clear-cut New Deal organization. Though Roosevelt remained popular and existing New Deal measures remained in effect, further concerted or rapid reform action was impossible. For the next quarter-century, the same conservative coalition was normally to control Congress.

Why did the New Deal lose momentum in 1938? Most obviously because foreign crisis began to draw the country's attention away from domestic reform. Yet many have blamed the slowdown partly on the program's own shortcomings, particularly its shifting approach to economic problems, its effort to combine incompatible groups of supporters, and its dependence on Roosevelt's personal leadership. It had, certainly, failed to solve one of the country's most serious problems: in 1938 there were still ten million unemployed. Government spending seemed to be the only really successful way of stimulating recovery, and agriculture still depended on heavy subsidies.

Yet when Americans looked abroad, they could feel more reason for pride. No country had solved the problems of modern industrial society with complete success and several, struggling with those problems, had lost political freedom. Without revolution, without even major constitutional change, the American republic had taken on a big new responsibility. So far, its function had been at most to provide a favorable environment for private economic action and to regulate when necessary. Now, in the face of economic collapse, first Hoover and then Roosevelt had made the government responsible for reaching and maintaining adequate prosperity.

Some of the most important changes brought about by the New Deal were social rather than economic and incidental rather than programmatic. Domination of American society by an elite made up of the native, urban upper-middle class, a domination never secure and never official but long partially effective, had become impossible.

To many who remember these years, however, the most important fact was neither the big accomplishments, the big failures, nor the hidden social changes. It was rather the revival of creativity, daring, and hope, qualities that were to be badly needed in the decades just ahead.

CONFLICTING HISTORICAL VIEWPOINTS

How New Was the New Deal?

To many conservative observers the New Deal was a destructive experiment in socialism. Al Smith angrily denounced the "Brain-Trusters" as Marxists in Jeffersonian clothing, and Herbert Hoover shuddered when he contemplated the horrors of "New Deal collectivism." Yet, with the exception of Edgar Robinson—whose deprecatory The Roosevelt Leadership *(1955) is read largely for its novelty—this contemporary judgment has found no support among historians. Whatever else it was, scholars generally agreed, the New Deal was not socialism. Richard Hofstadter (*Age of Reform *[1955]), it is true, called it the "New Departure" and Carl Degler (*Out of Our Past *[1959]) termed it the "Third American Revolution." They both agreed that the New Deal departed in fundamental ways from the American reform tradition, but neither viewed it as particularly radical or dangerous. The New Deal was something of a break with the past, these liberal scholars argued, but it was also an essentially constructive and healthy response to the challenge of the Great Depression.*

The argument for benign discontinuity was widely, although not universally, accepted. Many distinguished historians, including Arthur Link, Henry Steele Commager, and Eric Goldman, believed that Roosevelt's programs evolved naturally from traditional American reform impulses. In Rendezvous with Destiny *(1952), Goldman discovered the New Deal's antecedents in the ideas and policies of Theodore Roosevelt, Woodrow Wilson, and even Herbert Hoover. The roots of the New Deal, then, were firmly fixed in the soil of traditional American values.*

Although once heatedly debated, the revolution-evolution controversy is no longer an issue dividing the scholarly community. In recent years historians have worried less about the origins of the New Deal and more about its effectiveness. Liberal sympathizers, most notably Arthur M. Schlesinger, Jr., have cast the Roosevelt administration in the most favorable light. Sharply contrasting New Deal dynamism with the static "Old Order," Schlesinger's brilliant Age of Roosevelt *(3 vols., 1957–60) portrayed FDR as a common-sense democrat who spurned "dogmatic absolutes" and sought a middle way between the extremes of "chaos and tyranny," laissez faire and collectivism. Other liberal scholars, including James MacGregor Burns (Roosevelt: The Lion and the Fox [1956]) and William E. Leuchtenburg (Franklin D. Roosevelt and the New Deal [1963]), however, were less laudatory. Although generally favorable, Leuchtenburg focused on the limited effects of New Deal recovery and reform measures; and Burns, though not without sympathy for Roosevelt, faulted the Democratic president for failing to embrace Keynesian economics and to recast his party as the party of reform.*

More recently radical scholars offered vastly more damning analyses. Such New Left scholars as Howard Zinn (ed., New Deal Thought [1966]) and Barton J. Bernstein (ed., Towards a New Past [1967]) attempted to expose the poverty of the New Deal imagination and the essential conservatism of its leadership. In their view, Roosevelt was the creature of corporate capitalism; he failed to solve the problems of the depression and he made no effort to create an equitable society.

The radical interpretation has won much support among younger historians who find little that was bold or innovative in the New Deal record. Many older scholars, however, have attacked the New Left for measuring the past with the yardstick of the present.

FOR FURTHER READING:

President Hoover's revealing *Memoirs* (3 vols., 1951–1952) describe his own administration well and comment without admiration on the policies of his successor. Conflicting assessments of Hoover's presidency are offered in Harris G. Warren, *Herbert Hoover and the Great Depression* (1959), and Arthur M. Schlesinger, Jr., *The Crisis of the Old Order* (1957). The 1929 debacle is illuminated by J. K. Galbraith, *The Great Crash* (1954)*; and *The Bonus March* (1971) is analyzed by Roger Daniels. Hoover's long lame-duck period is the subject of Jordan A. Schwarz, *The Interregnum of Despair* (1970). The Roosevelt literature is exceptionally full. In addition to the works not included in the preceding essay, some of the most interesting and contradictory works are those by FDR's contemporaries. Compare, for example, Francis Perkins, *The Roosevelt I Knew* (1948), and Raymond Moley, *After Seven Years* (1939). Dixon Wecter, *The Age of the Great Depression* (1948), is an introduction to the period's fascinating social history. Samuel Lubell, *The Future of American Politics* (1952)* points out underlying political change. Of an enormous literature on American Marxism in the thirties, one of the most readable and understanding accounts is Murray Kempton, *Part of Our Time* (1955)*. In *Turbulent Years* (1970) Irving Bernstein writes brilliantly of the labor movement; and in *Cry from the Cotton* (1971) Donald Grubbs focuses sympathetically on southern tenant farmers. Aspects of the era's intellectual history are detailed in C. C. Alexander, *Nationalism in American Thought, 1930–1945* (1969)*, and Arthur A. Ekirch, Jr., *Ideologies and Utopias* (1969). Otis L. Graham, Jr., *An Encore for Reform* (1967)*, is a sensitive examination of the relation between the New Deal and the Progressive Era.

---

* Available in paperback edition.

The Reversal of Foreign Policy
1931-1941

27

During most of the 1930s, American attention was centered on domestic problems. Yet foreign events, occurring in the same period, were to affect the United States even more profoundly than the New Deal. The fragile international order established at Versailles and propped by prosperity broke down. Aggressive military states threatened to dominate Europe and Asia. To meet this challenge, America moved from relative disarmament to colossal military power, and American opinion swung from an extreme of isolationism to unprecedented acceptance of worldwide commitment. This commitment was to prove permanent, and under its stress American tradition and society were to be profoundly altered.

THE BREAKDOWN OF ORDER, 1931–1933

When Hoover took office, he intended to carry on, with only slight revision, the foreign policies of the New Era. More internationalist in outlook than Coolidge, he carried much further the policy begun under Coolidge of substituting conciliation for intervention in Latin America. Cautiously, the Hoover administration moved closer to cooperation with the League of Nations. In any efforts to preserve world peace, however, he was determined to stick to noncoercive political or economic methods. At the London Conference of 1930 the administration worked hard, with some success, to reduce naval armament further according to the pattern set by the Washington Conference of 1921. This was the last victory for disarmament. The effort to limit land armies at Geneva in 1932–1933 resulted in complete failure. By that time, the very idea of arms limitation was rejected by several powerful states.

The Versailles order in Europe had always been unstable. With American power withdrawn, France and England confronted Fascist Italy, Communist Russia, and defeated, unstable Germany. If these discontented powers were united and armed, their strength might outweigh that of the defenders of the *status quo*.

In the late 1920s, the Central European order was upheld to some extent by American investment. In 1931, partly because of the withdrawal of American funds, a major Austrian bank failed, and panic threatened to spread to Germany. To prevent further collapse, Hoover suggested a one-year suspension of payments of both German war reparations and Allied debts to the United States. After a damaging delay caused by French suspicions this "Hoover moratorium" was accepted. Frightened by the growing power of the aggressive Hitler movement in Germany, the Western Allies finally, in 1932, agreed to cancel almost all reparations—too late to save the German Republic. The United States refused to cancel war debts in a parallel manner, and most countries paid the first installments due after the end of the moratorium. These were, in most cases, the last payments made.

In 1931 Britain, the home of *laissez faire* economics, found it necessary to abandon the gold standard for a managed currency, and many other countries promptly followed suit. Hoping to restore currency stability, the United States helped plan a World Economic Conference which would give first priority to exchange stabilization.

The most dramatic collapse of international order occurred in the Far East. Since the Washington Conference, Japan had been ruled by conservative cabinets, and American-Japanese relations had been relatively good. Now, however, the Japanese military were becoming increasingly angry at arms limitation and civilian control. Since Theodore Roosevelt's Treaty of Portsmouth, Japan had possessed railroad and port rights in Manchuria where many Japanese saw an opportunity to acquire raw materials and living space. In 1931, taking advantage of incidents in Manchuria produced by rising Chinese nationalism, the Japanese army embarked on a program of conquest in this vast, nominally Chinese region. This action, carried out apparently against the will of the civilian government in Tokyo, violated not only the League Covenant but also the Republican security structure, consisting of the Washington Nine-Power Treaty and the Kellogg Peace Pact. The Open Door and Chinese integrity, moreover, were part of Republican tradition.

Thus Hoover had to act, but once more American commitments in the Far East outran American power. Furthermore, the deepest beliefs of the Quaker President ruled out either military reprisal or cooperation with the League in economic sanctions. In addition, England, whose collaboration would have been necessary for effective action, had no wish to provoke Japanese threats to her own huge Asian holdings. Resorting to purely moral force, Secretary of State Stimson announced that the United States would not recognize any situation brought about by force in violation of the Open Door or Chinese integrity. After much hesitation, the League took a somewhat similar stand, advising its members not to recognize the Japanese puppet state of Manchukuo. Neither the so-called Stimson Non-Recognition Doctrine nor world disapproval deterred Japan in Manchuria, although she did withdraw from a brief military occupation of Shanghai undertaken in 1932 in retaliation for a Chinese boycott. At the same time, despite Hoover's abhorrence of coercive international action, the United States had become further involved in the defense of the crumbling international order.

THE NEW DEAL AND THE WORLD, 1933–1937

In the first years of the New Deal, American isolationism reached its peak. To the disillusion of the 1920s was added the new disillusion of the depression. A host of plays, movies, and novels depicted the horrors of war, and in 1935 a Senate investigation seemed to show that munition makers caused most wars for the sake of sordid profits. Many Americans believed that European propagandists had made a sucker of the United States in 1917 and were trying to do it again. At the same time, our former Allies were defaulting on their obligations and even failing to sustain their own League. (Throughout the decade, European appeasement and American isolationism were to be called on to justify each other.)

Traditional suspicion of Europe was only one of a number of components, all powerful and some mutually contradictory, in the isolationist frame of mind. Many young people were deeply affected by pacifism, and some liberals wanted to concentrate on building a good society at home. On the other hand, conservatives were suspicious of foreign threats to American tradition. Many Midwesterners and most Irish-Americans maintained their historic suspicion of British imperialism.

In the early years of the New Deal, Roosevelt failed to challenge the dominant isolationist creed, though as an old follower of Wilson and his cousin Theodore he could hardly accept it. He was primarily concerned with getting his program of national economic reform through Congress and into action and he badly needed the support of midwestern isolationist progressives. Thus he refrained from opposing such measures as the Johnson Act of 1934, which forbade loans to nations in default.

As Japanese expansion slowed down to assimilate its gains, American-Japanese relations seemed to improve. Though nearly all Americans disliked the brutal Hitler regime which took power in Germany in 1933, few proposed to do anything about it.

In cooperation with some kinds of isolationists or continentalists, Roosevelt backed a modest program of naval building and continued the program of cementing good relations with Latin America. The nonintervention policy was not only restated, but backed in practice by abandonment of the right of intervention in Panama and Cuba. Expropriation by Mexico of the property of United States oil companies was accepted and compensation agreed on. At the Inter-American Conference of 1936, intervention by one state in the affairs of another was condemned, and mutual consultation provided for in case of threats to the peace of the hemisphere. This Good Neighbor policy, though it by no means ended all Latin American suspicion of the United States, was to produce good results in wartime when most of the Latin American countries were to be first friendly neutrals and then allies.

In economic matters, the main drive of the early New Deal was nationalistic. In order to save his own program of raising prices through currency inflation, Roosevelt abruptly reversed his early approval of exchange stabilization and in so doing broke up the World Economic Conference in London. On the other hand Cordell Hull, the new Secretary of State, had a deep southern-Democratic belief in lower tariffs, and Roosevelt succeeded in getting congressional backing for the Hull program. From 1934 on, the administration had and used authority to negotiate mutual tariff reductions through reciprocal trade treaties. Hope for a revival of international trade was also involved in Roosevelt's decision in 1933 to recognize Soviet Russia. This action, long prevented by ideological hostility, was supported by political realists and by some businessmen who prophesied (mistakenly) a major expansion of Russian-American trade.

American isolationist policies were little changed by the new challenges to world order which occurred in the mid-1930s. In 1935 Mussolini's Italy invaded Ethiopia, and in the same year Adolf Hitler felt strong enough to remilitarize Germany in defiance of the Versailles Treaty. In the next year German troops marched into the Rhineland where the same Treaty prohibited their presence. In July, 1936, Francisco Franco opened a Fascist rebellion against the republican government of Spain, and in 1936–1937 the Berlin-Rome-Tokyo axis united the major dissatisfied, essentially aggressive states. All these actions were dealt with ineffectually by the Western European powers. In the Ethiopian affair the League invoked only half-hearted sanctions, England condoned German rearmament in a naval treaty, and Western countries, through a policy of "nonintervention," denied munitions to the Spanish government. Turning increasingly to the left, that government got some aid from Russia while the Spanish rebels were more effectively supported by Germany and Italy.

American policy toward these crises was dominated by a determination to keep out of war rather than to keep war from occurring. The neutrality legislation of 1935–1937 was designed to prevent the particular kinds of mistakes which were believed to have drawn America into World War I. The first neutrality law, passed in 1935, forbade arms shipments to all belligerents, rejecting an administration wish to discriminate between aggressor and victim. In the Ethiopian crisis this was supplemented by a "moral embargo" on oil, the commodity most needed by Mussolini. American refusal to take stronger action gave an excuse for the League also to refuse an outright oil embargo. The second neutrality law (1936) forbade loans to belligerents. In 1937 a congressional resolution, requested by the President, extended the application of the neutrality system from international war to the Civil War in Spain, thus shutting off American arms from the Loyalist government and helping to ensure Franco's success. Finally, the neutrality law of 1937 made the existing prohibitions permanent and, in addition, forbade American travel on belligerent ships. It also gave the President power, for two years, to list commodities other than munitions which belligerents would be required to pay for and transport in their own ships (the cash-and-carry provision). Thus the United States had reversed the policies of Woodrow Wilson and returned to something like those of Jefferson. Neutral rights were waived in order to stay out of war. It seemed clear to the aggressive nations that they had little to fear from American counter action, as long as America herself was not attacked.

DEEPENING CRISIS AND
CAUTIOUS CHANGE IN POLICY, 1937–1939

Once more, a shift in American policy was brought on by events in Asia, not Europe. Japan, which had continued to press from Manchuria into North China until 1933, made a truce in that year. In 1937 fighting broke out again near the Peiping-Tientsin railway in relation to which Japan had certain treaty privileges. Since the ensuing war, though full scale, was undeclared, the American neutrality legislation was not automatically applied. Partly in order not to cut off arms to China, and partly to keep some anti-Japanese action in reserve, Roosevelt refrained from invoking the neutrality laws, and America shipped some war materials to each belligerent. However, in October, 1937, Roosevelt expressed his feelings about Japanese action with new vigor. Referring to a "spreading epidemic of world lawlessness," he suggested that aggressors be "quarantined."

Alarmed isolationist reaction made it plain to the President that he had moved beyond public opinion. The United States joined in League of Nations condemnation of Japanese action but opposed sanctions. In December, when Japanese planes sank an American gunboat on the Yangtze, apologies were accepted without much excitement. Once more, world disapproval without action failed to deter Japan, and her forces proceeded to bomb and occupy the principal Chinese cities. By 1938 she had set up a puppet government in China and committed herself fatefully to the establishment of a New Order in East Asia.

Lacking a clear European policy, the United States played only a minor role in the major European events of this period, periodically and fruitlessly appealing for moderation and conciliation. In 1938 Hitler absorbed Austria and began threatening Czechoslovakia. This led to the Munich Agreement among Britain, France, Italy, and Germany, which forced Czechoslovakia to surrender certain strategic frontier districts inhabited by German-speaking people. This settlement was brutally nullified in March, 1939, when Hitler took over the rest of Czechoslovakia. During the same spring Italy invaded Albania, while Hitler seized the Lithuanian town of Memel and unmistakably began threatening Poland. This time, however, Britain and France guaranteed the prospective victim, and it became evident to nearly everybody that major war was imminent.

Roosevelt, who shared this opinion, believed also that Britain and France could win with American material help. He therefore called for a cautious and moderate program of rearmament mainly on the basis of continental naval and air defense. He also asked Congress to repeal the arms embargo in order to make it possible for belligerents to buy American munitions on a cash and carry basis. Though most press opinion favored this action, it was defeated by isolationists in Congress. This was to be their last major victory.

In the summer of 1939, while Britain and France were making a half-hearted effort to make a defensive alliance with Russia, Stalin instead suddenly concluded pacts of trade and nonaggression with Hitler. This apparently left Germany free to attack Poland without becoming involved in a major two-front war, and on September 1, Hitler's troops crossed the Polish frontier. France and England, this time, declared war as they had promised. Poland, destined to be the most tragic victim of World War II, was quickly overrun. As German troops advanced through western Poland, Russian troops occupied the eastern part of the country.

Now that war was a fact, Roosevelt was able (in November, 1939) to prevail on Congress to repeal the arms embargo and place shipments of both munitions and other commodities on a cash-and-carry basis. Once more, as in 1914, the Western Allies were free to come and get American arms, provided that they could pay cash and provide shipping. This seemed enough to assure Western victory without further American commitment. Most observers predicted that the major belligerents would settle into a long stalemate, confronting each other in the "impregnable" Maginot and Siegfried lines.

CATASTROPHE AND THE END OF NEUTRALITY, 1940–1941

In the spring of 1940 the stalemate war came to a sudden end as the Germans conquered first Denmark and Norway and then the Low Countries. In a lightning assault from Belgium, mobile German units poured into France and in a month had crushed and demoralized the French army, supposed by many to be the world's strongest. It seemed as if there was no possible resistance to the new German combination of parachutists, divebombers, and tanks. On June 22 France surrendered. The Germans occupied half the country, leaving the collaborationist government at Vichy in charge of the rest.

Thinking he had won his war, Hitler hoped that England would make a compromise peace. Instead, though isolated and almost without land armament, the British replaced their ineffective premier with Winston Churchill, who announced his determination not only to resist but ultimately to destroy the Nazi regime. In the ensuing battle of Britain, though British cities were heavily bombed, the Royal Air Force defeated the German effort to clear the way for invasion. It began to seem once more possible that American support might sustain England, and many Americans wanted to do this at all costs. Others, however, insisted that the most important objective still was to keep America out of war.

In the ensuing foreign policy argument, one of the most important in American history, both sides were made up of diverse elements. On the antiinterventionist side with the traditional midwestern isolationists, were Anglophobes, including many Irish-Americans; people who thought Britain's cause hopeless; pacifists; young people who had heard with horror about the intolerance and hate generated by World War I and middle-aged people who had shared the postwar disillusionment; progressive reformers reluctant to give up domestic objectives; and some, but not by any means all, of those who disliked Roosevelt because of his domestic policies. This diverse coalition was supported by the small group influenced by the Communist party, which had supported collective security until 1939 and was to support war after 1941, but which was isolationist during the two years of the German-Soviet alliance. Those who favored drastic action in support of Britain included, as in 1914, many influential Americans conscious of deep ties to British culture. These were joined by those who were outraged by atrocity stories, this time true, about Nazi barbarism. Most important, perhaps, was the increasing group which felt that American security would be seriously threatened by Nazi control of the Atlantic.

Most Americans, probably, were neither isolationists nor outright interventionists. Most wanted to help Britain and also to stay out of the war. The decisive question was which of these last objectives was the more important. Before the fall of France, opinion polls seemed to show that most Americans wanted first of all to keep out of war. After it, the majority gradually shifted; most concluded that British survival came first. This decision, however, was neither universal nor clear-cut, and the administration did not help to clarify the choice.

Insofar as one can understand Roosevelt's policy, the President was by no means neutral in his sympathies and clearly wanted to contribute as much material aid as possible to Britain. This policy, he said, would keep America out of war. At first he doubtless believed that this *would* be so, and until very late he hoped that it *might* be the case. Always conscious of the dangers of hostile public reaction, and once more desperately anxious to put over his program, he continued to say that America would stay out of war when he must have known that this was no longer certain. Whether a franker policy would have had better results, either at the time or in the long run, will long be debated.

The steps taken by the administration, and approved by a majority of Congress and public opinion, were drastic enough. In May, Roosevelt called for a billion-dollar defense appropriation and for airplane production of fifty thousand a year. At Charlottesville on June 10, he promised continued material help to "opponents of force." In September, by executive agreement, he traded fifty over-age destroyers, desperately needed by Britain, for defense bases in British Western Hemisphere possessions. In the same month, Congress adopted the first peacetime conscription law in American history.

In the fall of 1940, foreign policy argument was channeled into an election campaign. Because of the national emergency, the Democrats broke the anti-third-term tradition to renominate Roosevelt. His opponent Wendell Willkie, though a utility company president who had fought TVA, was a representative of the liberal wing of the Republican party. Accepting much of the New Deal, Willkie attacked mismanagement and bureaucracy. Since Willkie accepted the necessity of aiding Britain and since both candidates promised that America would stay out of actual foreign war, there was little difference on foreign policy. In the closest victory of his presidential career, Roosevelt got 55 percent of the popular vote.

Once more securely in office, Roosevelt asked for and got a still more binding commitment to British victory. In March Congress passed the lend-lease bill, giving the President authority to transfer equipment, rather than money, directly to nations whose defense was vital to that of the United States. In response to urgent appeals from the beleaguered British, munitions were furnished in enormous quantity. In the spring of 1941 British and American staff officers discussed common strategy in the event of American belligerency. In August Roosevelt and Churchill, meeting at sea, committed themselves to the liberal principles of the Atlantic Charter, promising a free and warless world "after the final destruction of the Nazi tyranny."

Committed to Hitler's defeat, America could not allow her shipments of munitions to be destroyed by the increasingly powerful German submarine offensive. In the summer of 1941, the United States entered into undeclared naval warfare with Germany. American ships reported submarine sightings to the British. American troops occupied Greenland and Iceland, and finally America began convoying British and American shipping to Iceland, halfway across the Atlantic. Sinkings occurred, and in September Roosevelt, denouncing German "piracy," ordered American naval vessels to "shoot on sight."

Meanwhile the nature of the war in Europe had profoundly changed. Unable to knock Britain out of the war before American deliveries became effective, Hitler decided to secure his continental flank. Germany already controlled Hungary, Rumania, and Bulgaria, and in April, 1941 her armies conquered Yugoslavia and Greece. Germany's moves toward the East intensified Hitler's growing difficulties with his quasi ally, Stalin. In June, 1941, the Germans invaded the Soviet Union, penetrating so deeply that it looked for some months as if they would win another major victory. Promptly both Churchill and Roosevelt announced that any enemy of Hitler was a friend of theirs, and lend-lease aid to Russia began. While Russian participation stimulated antiinterventionism in some quarters, it reduced it in others. For the first time, it seemed, a coalition existed which actually could destroy the Nazis, and the United States was a member of it in all but actual land fighting.

For some time, Roosevelt had concluded that official American participation in war would be desirable, and a majority of the public had decided, according to the polls, that war would be preferable to British defeat. Hitler, however, was by no means eager to provoke further American intervention and add another great power to his already formidable list of opponents. Once more, the crucial development came from the other side of the world.

WAR WITH JAPAN

In the Far East also the Hitler breakthrough of 1940 precipitated great changes. To Japan, it seemed to offer a last chance to consolidate her new East Asian order and thereby to end the costly and indecisive "China incident." By moving southward toward the colonies of occupied France and Holland and hard-pressed Britain, Japan could secure needed supplies of oil, rubber, and tin.

So far Roosevelt, concentrating on the European danger and not eager for involvement on another front, had continued the United States' rather ambiguous policy toward Japan with one important change. In July, 1939, the United States threatened future economic measures by giving a six-months' notice of the abrogation of her 1911 commercial treaty with Japan. In July, 1940, sensing that a Japanese forward movement was at hand, the President prohibited the export of some kinds of oil and scrap metal. Later measures tightened this embargo and increased the pressure on Japan to find alternate sources.

In September, 1940, the Japanese with Hitler's diplomatic assistance forced the Vichy government to concede ports and bases in the northern part of French Indo-China. In September Germany, Italy, and Japan signed the Tripartite Pact, obliging each to help the other in case of attack by any power not now at war. Since a special article excluded Russia, this could mean only the United States.

There were still, however, powerful Japanese who hoped to achieve Japan's goals without war with America. Through much of 1941, the attitudes of both countries were set forth in a series of negotiations. Japan was willing, at most, to refrain from armed aggression in Southeast Asia and even to "interpret" in America's favor the promises of the Tripartite Pact. To pay for peace in the Far East even in the event of war with Germany, the United States would have had to restore Japanese-American trade, help Japan to obtain oil supplies from the Netherlands East Indies, and recognize (or at least cease to obstruct) her new order in China. The United States was unwilling to accept these terms and offered instead to restore trade and help Japan gain some of her economic goals provided she gave up her military objectives both in Southeast Asia and China. Once more, the American commitment to the Open Door and Chinese integrity assumed enormous importance.

In July of 1941 Japanese forces moved into southern Indo-China and clearly headed for Malaya and the Dutch East Indies. Roosevelt promptly responded by freezing all Japanese funds in the United States. In August, still hopeful of keeping the United States neutral, Prince Konoye, the Japanese premier, requested a "Pacific Conference" with Roosevelt. Though Konoye suggested the possibility of further important concessions, Roosevelt refused to meet unless there was some preliminary agreement on basic issues. In October the Konoye government fell, and the new Tojo government prepared for war.

Well before the complex Washington discussions of November, 1941, the positions of each side had been repeatedly made clear, and the two positions had proved incompatible. The American government considered trying to gain time by presenting proposals for a temporary Pacific truce, but decided against this. Knowing that an attack was at hand, the Americans restated for the record their earlier position. On December 7, 1941, Japanese planes attacked and severely crippled the American fleet at Pearl Harbor. The next day Congress declared war, and three days later Germany and Italy declared war on the United States.

Later, Roosevelt was much criticized, first for not pursuing further the effort for peace with Japan and second for not preventing the Pearl Harbor disaster. It was to be argued bitterly that his real objective was to force Japan to attack the United States and thereby to get America into war with Hitler by the "back door."

Probably a real compromise with Japanese ambition, short of surrender of old American commitments and betrayal of American allies, would have been difficult to achieve. It is arguable, however, that a Roosevelt-Konoye meeting might have gained time and, less plausibly, that it might have strengthened the opponents of Japanese militarism. As for the second charge, it seems that by late November, 1941, the American government had decided that war was inevitable and that further stalling would be no use. Roosevelt knew before December 7 that a Japanese movement was actually under way and indeed warnings were sent to American Pacific bases to that effect. Apparently because an attack was expected farther west, the warnings to Pearl Harbor were insufficiently frequent and emphatic and defensive action was neglected. Thus a small cloud remained over the official version of the Pearl Harbor incident. At the time, however, the Japanese "sneak attack" united the American people for war as nothing else could have.

FOR FURTHER READING:

An able study of American Diplomacy in the Great Depression (1957) is offered by Robert H. Ferrell. Lloyd Gardner examines Economic Aspects of New Deal Diplomacy (1964). The most formidable attacks on the Roosevelt foreign policy are Charles A. Beard, President Roosevelt and the Coming of the War (1948) and C. C. Tansill, Back Door to War (1952). Roosevelt is defended in Basil Rauch, Roosevelt: From Munich to Pearl Harbor (1950). W. L. Langer and S. E. Gleason, The Challenge to Isolation, 1937–1940 (1952)*, and The Undeclared War, 1940–1941 (1953)*, are well-documented and informative studies, generally favorable to United States policy. Other notable accounts include Donald Drummond, The Passing of American Neutrality (1955); Robert Divine, The Illusion of Neutrality (1962); and Roberta Wohlstetter, Pearl Harbor: Warning and Decision (1962). American relations with Japan are assessed in Herbert Feis, The Road to Pearl Harbor (1950)*, and Paul Schroeder, The Axis Alliance and Japanese-American Relations, 1941 (1958). Richard Triana has studied American Diplomacy and the Spanish Civil War (1968); and in Prelude to Downfall (1967) Saul Friedlander surveys American relations with Nazi Germany on the eve of war.

---

* Available in paperback edition.

WORLD WAR II

	Diplomatic	Military — Pacific Theater	Military — European Theater	Home Front
1939—OUTBREAK	March 14 Germany annexes Czechoslovakia. March 31 Anglo-French pledge to Poland. August 23 German-Russian Pact.		September 1 Germany invades Poland. October 14 Russia invades Finland.	November 4 Neutrality Act of 1939 (cash and carry).
1940—DISASTER	September 3 United States–British "Destroyer Deal." September 27 Japan-Germany-Italy Tripartite Pact.	September 22 Japan gets bases in French Indo-China.	April 9 Germany invades Norway, Denmark. May 10 Germany invades Benelux. June 22 German-French armistice. August–September Battle of Britain.	September 16 Selective Service. November 5 Roosevelt defeats Willkie.
1941—INTERVENTION	July 26 United States freezes Japanese funds. August 14 "Atlantic Charter" statement by Roosevelt and Churchill. November United States–Japanese Washington negotiations.	July 24 Japan occupies French Indo-China. December 7 Pearl Harbor.	April Germany invades Greece, Yugoslavia. April–May United States extends protective action in Atlantic. June 22 Germany invades Russia. September 11 "Shoot on sight" order in Atlantic.	March 11 Lend-Lease Act. November 17 Neutrality Acts repealed. December 8 Declaration of War.
1942—LOW POINT	May Molotov in Washington. June Churchill in Washington. August Moscow Conference (Stalin, Churchill, Harriman).	February 15 Singapore surrenders. May 6 Corregidor surrenders. May 7–8 Coral Sea. June 3–6 Midway. August–February Guadalcanal.	January–June German offensive North Africa. Summer German offensive Russia. September–February. Stalingrad. November 4 El Alamein. November 8 United States landings in North Africa.	January 30 Office of Price Administration established. February–March Japanese–American "relocation." November Republican gains in Congress. December 2 First self-sustaining nuclear reaction (Chicago).

WORLD WAR II (continued)

Military

	Diplomatic	Pacific Theater	European Theater	Home Front
1943—ALLIED UNITY	January 14–24 Casablanca Conference (Roosevelt, Churchill). August 11–24 Quebec Conference (Roosevelt, Churchill). November 22–26 Cairo Conference (Roosevelt, Churchill, Chiang). November 28–December 1 Teheran Conference (Roosevelt, Churchill, Stalin).	Throughout year Allied gains in South Pacific (Solomons, New Guinea). November 21 United States invades Gilberts (Tarawa) (start of central Pacific offensive).	January–May Allied victory in North Africa. July–December Russian offensive. July 10 Sicily invaded. September 9 Italy invaded (Salerno).	November 5 Senate resolution for international organization.
1944—VICTORY IN SIGHT	July 1–22 U.N. Monetary and Financial Conference (Bretton Woods). August 21–October 7 Dumbarton Oaks Conference (plans U.N.). October 9–18 Second Quebec Conference.	January 31 Marshalls invaded. June 18 Marianas invaded. October 23–25 Philippine Sea. November 24 Beginning of air attack on Tokyo.	June 6 Normandy invaded. July 25 St. Lô breakthrough. September 12 United States enters Germany. December "Battle of the Bulge" (German counteroffensive).	United States reaches twice Axis war production. November 7 Roosevelt defeats Dewey.
1945—THE ATOMIC AGE	February 4–11 Yalta Conference. April 23–June 26 San Francisco U.N. Conference. July 17–August 2 Potsdam Conference (July 26, ultimatum to Japan). September 2 Japan surrenders.	February Manila recaptured. February–March Iwo Jima. April–June Okinawa. August 6 Hiroshima. August 9 Nagasaki. August 15 V-J Day.	March 7 Rhine crossed. April 25 United States and Soviet forces meet on Elbe. May 8 V-E Day.	April 12 Roosevelt dies. July 16 First atomic bomb exploded, Alamogordo, New Mexico.

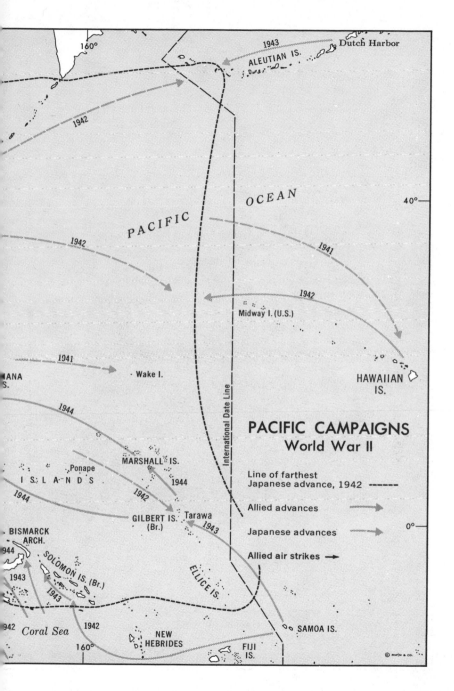

160°

1943   Dutch Harbor

ALEUTIAN IS.

1942

PACIFIC   OCEAN   40°

1942

1941

1942

Midway I. (U.S.)

1941   Wake I.

MANA
IS.

HAWAIIAN
IS.

1944

MARSHALL IS.

Ponape

I S L A N D S   1944

1942

1944

GILBERT IS.   Tarawa
(Br.)   1943

BISMARCK
ARCH.

944

SOLOMON IS. (Br.)

1943

1943

ELLICE IS.

International Date Line

PACIFIC CAMPAIGNS
World War II

Line of farthest
Japanese advance, 1942   -------

Allied advances   ➔

Japanese advances   ➔

Allied air strikes   ➔

0°

942   Coral Sea   1942

160°

NEW
HEBRIDES

FIJI
IS.

SAMOA IS.

© RAND & CO.

RECONQUEST OF EUROPE
World War II

15°

0°

NORWAY

SWEDEN
(Neutral)

55°

Atlantic Ocean

North Sea

EIRE
(Neutral)

UNITED
KINGDOM

DENMARK

55°

London

NETH.

1945

Berlin

Landings, 1944

Calais

GERMANY

Cherbourg

1944

BELG.

Brest

St. Lo

ARDENNES

1945

1944

Paris

1944

CZECH.

Nantes

1944

1944

1945

FRANCE

SWITZ.
(Neutral)

AUSTRIA

Toulouse

1944

Genoa

Venice

YUGO.

PORT.

Marseille

Cannes

1945

40°

SPAIN
(Neutral)

Landings
1944

ITALY

1944

1944

Rome

1943

1943

40°

Mediterranean Sea

15°

⟵⟵⟵ Allied advances

SICILY

⟵⟵⟵ German counter offensive

Landings
1943

0°

0   150   300

MILES

© RAND & CO.

War for the World
1941-1945
28

FROM DEFEAT TO VICTORY, 1941–1944

Through the winter and spring of 1941–1942, the United States confronted her most serious challenge since 1861. One headline after another reported successful Japanese invasions: Malaya, Guam, Wake, Hong Kong, Singapore, the Dutch East Indies, Burma, the Western Aleutians. On May 6, 1942, the last organized American forces in the Philippines surrendered at Corregidor. The New Order in Greater East Asia was almost a fact. Any counteroffensive against Japan, it seemed, would have to conquer concentric rings of islands scattered over vast ocean areas.

Hitler, meanwhile, held firmly the productive power of Western Europe. His first invasion of Russia was turned back in the winter of 1941 after reaching the outskirts of Moscow. His second, beginning in June, 1942, reached deep into the Caucasus and entered Stalingrad on the Volga. Britain was threatened with the collapse of her Atlantic supply line. Sinkings mounted after American entry, many of them occurring within sight of American coastal cities. The worst fears of Western leaders were that Russia would collapse and Britain starve long before American power became really effective.

Already Anglo-American staff conferences had decided that the main Allied offensive must be directed against Germany, the more formidable enemy, while a holding action was carried on in the Pacific. But any offensive seemed a long way away, and even a holding action was not immediately apparent.

By summer and fall of 1942 more hopeful news began to appear. Japanese naval power, checked at the Coral Sea in May, was ended as an offensive threat at Midway in June. In August American troops began a grim and bloody offensive in the Solomon Islands. In October the British stopped the German drive toward Suez at El Alamein, the next month American forces landed in North Africa and began fighting German troops. In the gigantic battle of Stalingrad, the Russians captured a German army and began the reconquest of the vast territories they had lost.

In 1943 the Allies passed decisively to the offensive. After hard fighting, German forces were cleared from Africa, and in the summer and fall Anglo-American forces invaded Sicily and Italy. Though Mussolini fell from power and Italy surrendered, the Italian dictator escaped and bitter German resistance formed in central Italy. In the Pacific War, the island-hopping strategy indicated the means of American victory. Sea and air power made it possible to isolate and bypass Japanese garrisons; it would not be necessary to reconquer the vast Japanese holdings one by one. Bitter fighting brought control of the Solomons, and in November the battle of Tarawa began the Central Pacific campaign.

By this time the technique of amphibious warfare was so highly developed that it became possible to land on any hostile shore with sufficient preparation, provided one was willing to accept immense casualties. The crucial difficulty was maintaining the beachhead after landing. This was borne out in June of 1944 in the long-awaited landing in Normandy. This attack on the heavily defended French coast, the greatest amphibious operation in history, was seriously endangered by bad weather and stubborn resistance. By the end of July, however, a breakthrough at St. Lô ended the Normandy campaign and opened that of France. American tank units were able to sweep around the defenders as German forces had in 1940. By November most of France and Belgium had been liberated by Anglo-American forces, but in December a fierce counterattack surprised Americans in the Ardennes Forest.

On the eastern front in 1944 the Russians entered Poland, Yugoslavia, Hungary, and even East Prussia. In the Pacific the island-hopping campaign continued through the Marshalls, Marianas, and Carolines. In November bombers from the Marianas began devastating raids on the Japanese home islands. In the Philippines, American reentry brought on the greatest naval battle in history at Leyte Gulf, where the remaining power of the Japanese navy was broken. By the end of the year, though much fighting remained in Europe and on the Pacific, victory was clearly in sight and so were its problems.

THE HOME FRONT

Perhaps the greatest single factor in this victory was American production of ships, tanks, planes, and the infinitely varied tools of modern war. In 1941, though the buildup had begun, there was still a long way to go. Shipments to Britain had depleted American supplies, and once more it proved difficult to organize American economy and society for war production. The gigantic task was handled with all the best and worst features of New Deal government: with imagination and vast scale, and also with a full complement of reversals, reorganizations, bureaucratic battles, bottlenecks, and waste. Yet by 1943 the huge machine was operating, and by 1944 America was producing double the combined total of the Axis countries.

This goal was won, moreover, without the extreme measures of coercion urged by some experts. There was no single production "czar," and there was no draft of labor. Adjustment of incentive seemed to work far better than totalitarian force. Industrialists received very high rewards in depreciation allowances and government construction of war plants. Yet corporation profits and high individual incomes were again taxed at confiscatory rates. Business, and especially big business, played a major part in planning and accepted a partnership with the government as it had in World War I and had not in the New Deal period. Labor strikes, much denounced in the press, were actually few in proportion to manpower. Labor kept the gains of the New Deal, including a forty-hour week with time and a half for overtime. Earnings rose rapidly, and unions expanded from ten to nearly fifteen million persons.

The biggest wartime gains of all went to the previously depressed farmers or, more accurately, to some of them. Their continued strength in Congress pushed the regulated farm prices up to 110 percent of parity, and government efforts to keep food prices down were at first only partly successful. While 17 percent of the farm population left for the cities, the income of the remainder went sharply up and so did their production.

While many people in Europe and Asia were starving, American consumers had to cut down their driving, go without new cars, and accept rationing of food and some other products. From 1943 on control of most prices was reasonably successful. Not only was there no real civilian suffering, but many people—especially people previously deprived—lived and ate better than ever before.

Not the long efforts of the New Deal, but the incidental effects of war brought prosperity, and with it, fundamental social change. Apparently the mechanism was government spending on a new scale. In 1936, the biggest New Deal spending year, a federal outlay of $8 billion had caused many citizens to worry about the foundations of the Republic. In 1945, when federal expenditures reached $98 billion, unemployment practically vanished and the country seemed to reach new levels of production and prosperity. High wages and farm prices, together with war taxes, produced a greater measure of economic equality than had ever existed. As war industry redistributed the population, the Pacific Coast gained wealth and power. With full employment, Negroes were accepted in some kinds of jobs previously closed to them, and the federal government, through the Fair Employment Practices Commission, began to concern itself with equality of employment. Negroes and southern whites both migrated in large numbers to industrial cities. Thus northern racial problems grew more intense, while southern racial mores began very slowly to shift.

Many of the changes accelerated or begun during the war were to prove permanent. Neither wages, prices, employment, government expenditure, nor taxes were to return to prewar levels. Control of inflation, as well as prevention of depression, had become a major governmental concern. In addition to strictly economic fields, government was deeply involved in race relations, public information, and the promotion of scientific endeavor. Perhaps most fateful of all, the size, political influence, and economic importance of the armed forces in this most unmilitary of nations had been expanded. Few Americans guessed that this time demilitarization was to prove elusive.

In politics, the war seemed superficially to bring unity. Since America had been attacked, overt opposition to the war was negligible. Startling worldwide commitments seemed to be accepted, and many said that isolationism had died at Pearl Harbor. In contrast to 1917, unity seemed to exist without hysteria. Civil liberties were generally preserved with one large exception: 117,000 Americans of Japanese ancestry, two-thirds of them citizens, were moved from their West Coast homes first to barbed-wire temporary camps and then to isolated relocation centers in the interior. Though most were resettled in the East or Midwest before the war was over and some eventually received financial compensation for their losses, the scars of this ruthless and unnecessary action remained.

If there was less overt opposition and less hysteria than in World War I, there was also less idealistic enthusiasm. The Four Freedoms, Henry A. Wallace's glowing picture of a "Century of the Common Man," Wendell Willkie's commitment to "One World" were highly effective in liberal circles. None of these, however, came as close to producing a nationwide response as Wilson's appeal to "make the world safe for democracy." For many Americans, this was less a crusade than (as Roosevelt called it) a "War for Survival."

American opinion, deeply divided in 1941 over both the New Deal and Roosevelt's interventionist foreign policy, was not magically reunited in wartime. But division had to manifest itself in indirect ways—in hostility to the Europe-first policy, resentment of price control, exaggeration of strikes, and (despite much countereffort) criticism of the Allies. Some liberals attacked the government for its tactical compromises with Vichy or alleged tenderness toward the British Empire. A larger group remained deeply suspicious of collaboration with Russia, and a still larger faction was determined to prevent the postwar survival of the New Deal.

In 1942 the Republicans sharply increased their strength in Congress. In 1944 Roosevelt, like Lincoln, won a wartime election, this time against the rather ineffective opposition of Thomas E. Dewey, and in the same year many archisolationists lost their seats in Congress. Thus Franklin Roosevelt, again like Lincoln, retained the decision-making power of a wartime president. But for this he paid a price. It was necessary—or so he decided—to postpone discussion not only of important unsettled domestic controversies, but also of some of the thorniest unresolved international problems. The only goal on which all could agree was military victory.

THE GREAT ALLIANCE

In international relations, as in so many fields, World War II seemed to reverse American precedents. In World War I, America had been a gingerly cobelligerent; now she was a full-fledged ally bound to refuse a separate peace. She took the lead in the efforts to make the wartime international coalition into a new international organization. Both public opinion and, this time, the Senate seemed heartily to back the proposal for a new United Nations.

President Roosevelt placed his major hopes both for victory and postwar stability on the "Four Policemen": Britain, China, Russia, and the United States. Only with Britain was real cooperation achieved. Similar national traditions plus the mutual admiration of Roosevelt and Churchill helped to make the Anglo-American war effort the most successful combined operation in history, yet even here major differences appeared.

The Americans were used to thinking of war in terms of an all-out drive for victory followed by a return to peace and normality. The British had some experience of victory's delusions and costs. Many of the American leaders were suspicious of British efforts to cling to empire. Above all, Roosevelt and Churchill differed in the later stages of the war over Russian relations.

In 1942 American political and military leaders demanded an immediate cross-channel invasion of Europe, partly to prevent collapse of the eastern front. Churchill accepted the necessity of such an operation in the future, but thought it impossible without further buildup and fought hard for diversionary operations in southern

Europe. After 1943 his reasons were partly political: Western penetration of the Balkans and Central Europe would prevent Russian domination of these areas. This argument was settled by compromise. To Stalin's chagrin, the Normandy invasion was put off until 1944, while the North African and Italian campaigns represented a partial concession to Churchill's views. A Balkan front was never opened.

Roosevelt's program for making China a great power was a complete failure. Chiang Kai-shek's Nationalist government shared control of the huge country with a well-intrenched Communist movement, and each side fought the other as well as Japan. Exhausted by long war, the Nationalist government was further weakened by corruption. Neither General Joseph Stilwell nor anybody else could bring about a major Chinese contribution to victory. Yet at Cairo in November, 1943, Roosevelt, Churchill, and Chiang agreed that after the war China would get back Manchuria as well as Formosa and the Pescadores. The first of these pledges was largely nullified by the Yalta Agreement, and the second was to be the source of endless trouble.

By far the most difficult relationship was, of course, with Russia. America began this wartime association with a recent past of deep hostility toward that nation. During the period of the Russo-German Pact, American opinion had been outraged by Russia's moves into eastern Poland and Rumania; by her absorption of the three small Baltic states, Latvia, Lithuania, and Estonia; and, above all, by her Winter War with Finland, who had refused to surrender certain border districts considered by Russia necessary to her own defense. With the German-Russian break, however, both Roosevelt and Churchill immediately saw the possible importance of Russian contributions to the war. To help keep Germany occupied in the east, America sent Russia lend-lease aid amounting to $11 billion. Temperamentally optimistic and used to thinking in terms of only one opponent at a time, many Americans managed to convince themselves that Russian society and government had fundamentally changed. Russia and America were to remain friendly after the war, and this friendship was to be the mainstay of world peace. This opinion was held by Roosevelt and by his principal advisers, liberal and conservative, civilian and military.

Through 1943 some success was achieved in shaping common military objectives. Good feeling reached its height in late November, 1943, when Roosevelt, Stalin, and Churchill met at Teheran, Persia. There the coming offensive against Hitler was roughly coordinated. It was agreed that German military power must be permanently eliminated, perhaps by division of the country. In Yugoslavia, Allied aid was to go only to Tito, the Communist leader of one branch of the underground. Both the eastern and western frontiers of Poland were to be shifted radically to the west.

From here on, as Soviet armies penetrated Eastern and Central Europe, postwar control of this area became the principal subject of inter-Allied argument. Churchill, while fully aware that Russia's losses entitled her to some security and even more conscious of her unquestioned power in the area, wanted to bargain sharply with Stalin. He was willing, for instance, to concede Russian predominance in Rumania and Bulgaria in return for British predominance in Greece and equality in Yugoslavia and Hungary. Poland presented a harder problem. Russian forces had set up a government in Poland independent of the exile government in London, which had contributed large fighting forces to the Allied side and on whose behalf Britain had gone to war. Churchill was willing to put pressure on the London Poles to accept the realities of Russian power, but he was not willing to recognize the unqualified sovereignty of the Russian-supported Polish government. He wanted to use Allied bargaining power, including troop dispositions, to secure as favorable a Polish settlement as possible.

Roosevelt was unwilling to concur completely in Churchill's policy of firmness. He too was concerned about Polish freedom, and could not ignore the strong feelings of Polish-Americans. Yet he was aware also of America's historic dislike of power politics. Eager to mediate between Russia and Britain, overconfident of his own ability to charm and persuade Stalin, he continued his effort to build a future based on genuine Russian-American collaboration.

This effort shaped the most important of the Allied conferences which took place at Yalta, in the Crimea, in February, 1945. By this time, the approach of victory made it necessary to agree on some concrete plans. Though the political future of Germany was left undecided, it was agreed that she would be divided into four zones of military occupation. Stalin here conceded that one zone, formed out of previously constituted Western zones, would be occupied by France, now back in the war under the leadership of Charles de Gaulle and jealous of equal treatment. Germany, it was further agreed, would pay heavy reparations in the form of goods and labor. At Russian insistence, the United States agreed on a figure of $20 billion, half of it for Russia, as a basis for future discussion.

The Polish boundaries agreed on at Teheran were confirmed. This meant that Russia gained large territories in the east, to some of which she had historic and ethnic claims. In the west, Poland was to be liberally compensated with German territory, though the final German-Polish boundary settlement was postponed until a German peace conference. The Communist government in Poland was to be broadened by the inclusion of new members from the exile government in London and from the underground. Free and secret elections, in which all democratic parties could take part, would be held as soon as possible. Similarly, in the rest of liberated Europe, interim governments would be formed on a basis "broadly representative of all democratic elements," and free elections would be held as early as possible.

Another section of the Yalta Agreement dealt with world organization. The nations united against the Axis were to meet in the United States to form an organization, some of whose structure had already been determined at a conference in Dumbarton Oaks in Washington. Of the two most important organs, the Assembly and the Security Council, the latter was to act by unanimity alone. This "veto" provision, much criticized later, was wanted by the United States as well as by Russia. The new organization would not, it was recognized, be in a position to coerce great powers; its effectiveness would depend on the close collaboration of the major states.

Finally, by a secret section of the agreement, Russia was obligated to enter the war against Japan within two or three months after the defeat of Germany. For this Russia was to receive liberal compensation. The *status quo* was to be recognized in Outer Mongolia, a Soviet puppet state nominally a part of China. Russia was to get back what she had lost to Japan in the Treaty of Portsmouth, including railroad and port concessions in Manchuria and possession of the southern portion of the huge island of Sakhalin. Russia would also receive the Kurile Islands north of Japan. Roosevelt was to "take measures" to secure the concurrence of Chiang Kai-shek in these terms which would, however, be "unquestionably fulfilled."

In later years, the Yalta Agreement was to be subject to bitter criticism which made two sorts of cases against it. The first of these was idealistic and humanitarian. America had conceded forced labor as part of German reparations and, despite many pious references in the text to the "principles of the Atlantic Charter," had disposed of millions of people without their consent. Moreover, important rights in Asia, which the United States had refused to concede to Japanese pressure, were handed over to Russia without consulting China.

The second case was concerned with the postwar balance of power. The complete destruction of German power and the concession of new Polish boundaries brought Russian armies into the heart of Europe and left Russia potentially dominant on that continent, while the Far Eastern terms brought her back into the crucial Manchurian region. Thus one potentially hostile great power was substituted for another in each area.

Defenders of the Yalta Agreement on the basis of power politics have answered these criticisms mainly by pointing to the current military situation. The Russians were in occupation of much of Poland and the Balkans. Anglo-American forces were not within reach of these areas and had no way of getting there. American Pacific commanders, expecting a fanatical resistance in the Japanese home islands and wrongly informed about the size of Japanese forces in Manchuria, were demanding that Russia be brought into the Far Eastern war.

The moral indictment of Yalta has been answered in several ways. First, defenders have pointed out that the hope for collaboration with Russia was a hope for world peace, noble and natural however unrealistic. The incredible Nazi atrocities, increasingly exposed by the reconquest of occupied territory, did not dispose America to be tender of German rights or to think about resurrecting German power. These disclosures served also to take American attention away from the brutality of some Russian behavior in Poland and elsewhere. Second, it has been argued that the provisions regarding free elections in Poland and other reconquered countries would have safeguarded democratic principles if they had been carried out by Russia after Yalta. Finally, the objectors have been reminded that the Far Eastern provisions were accepted by Chiang, when he learned of them, with little protest. The Soviet Union shortly concluded a treaty with Nationalist China promising to support only the Chiang regime as the central Chinese government.

Taken together, these defensive arguments explain many things. The errors of Yalta were not caused by treason, as extremists later alleged, but by optimism. Yet even the best that can be said is not entirely reassuring. Certainly the agreement did not meet the standards of idealism which America had so often invoked in the past, even when power to enforce these ideals was lacking (as in Manchuria in 1931). On the other hand, if the Yalta Agreement is to be judged in terms of hard-boiled realism, it can hardly be called an American success.

Nonetheless, when Roosevelt returned from his long journey, exhausted but triumphant, most Americans gratefully accepted his heartfelt statements that a future of democracy and peace had been assured. In the months after Yalta Russian actions in some parts of Eastern Europe made it clear that such phrases as "free elections" and "all democratic elements" had different meanings East and West. There was no possibility that Russia would allow hostile elements to hold power in the most important border countries. In some of these, notably Poland and Rumania, it was equally impossible to form governments at once democratically chosen and friendly to Russia. When American commanders discussed with German agents in Switzerland possible surrender terms for German forces in Italy, the Russians made it clear that they suspected the United States of plotting to shut them out of peace negotiations. Depressed by increasing friction, Roosevelt began to doubt the future he had planned. Before these doubts could lead to action, however, he died (of a cerebral hemorrhage on April 12).

Most Americans, and nearly all Europeans, believed that a great leader was lost. Surely they were right: Roosevelt's confidence and optimism had been as important in war as they had been earlier in depression. His mistakes flowed from the same great qualities.

FROM YALTA TO HIROSHIMA

The victory of 1945 was clouded by Allied dissent and darkened by cruelty and destruction. In the spring of that year, however, this was not apparent to the American people, and even the President's death failed to spoil the news of success on every front. In Europe, the German counteroffensive was stopped at Bastogne, Belgium, before the end of 1944. By March, 1945, American forces had crossed the Rhine. In early April, when American troops reached the Elbe, General Eisenhower decided on military grounds not to push forward toward Berlin, but to make sure first of the Southern Alpine redoubt where it was believed that the Nazis might make a last stand. This decision, communicated to Stalin, was protested by Churchill. It was, however, upheld by Truman, the new President, on the basis of prior agreements among the Allies on zones of occupation. A little later Eisenhower refused to press toward Prague, and the Russians occupied both Central European capitals. On May 1, while Soviet troops were entering Berlin, Hitler killed himself, and three days later Germany surrendered to England, Russia, and the United States.

As American forces drew closer to the Japanese home islands, they continued to meet fierce resistance. No Pacific battles were harder fought than Iwo Jima, in February, or Okinawa, in May. Off the latter island, as in the Philippines, Japan made use of a strange and effective weapon, the suicide plane. Hundreds of pilots dove deliberately at American ships. This and other fanatical behavior convinced most Americans that they were in for a desperate fight in Japan itself.

Actually, Japan's resistance was almost at an end. American submarines had cut off necessary supplies, and since November American bombers had inflicted terrible destruction. In June the Japanese war cabinet fell, and a new government began unsuccessfully to seek Russian mediation.

President Harry Truman and Winston Churchill, meeting at Potsdam, demanded on July 26, that Japan surrender. If she did, they promised, the Japanese would neither be destroyed nor enslaved; if she did not she would meet "utter destruction." Since Truman had received word of the first explosion of an atomic bomb, he was in a position to carry out this threat. It had long been decided that the new weapon would be used against the enemy for maximum effect, rather than being dropped first on uninhabited territory as a warning. Some of the President's advisers believed that use of the new weapon would greatly increase the power of the United States in the postwar settlement. On August 6 an atomic bomb was dropped on the city of Hiroshima. On the 8th Russia hurriedly entered the war in advance of the agreed time. On August 8 another atomic bomb hit Nagasaki, and on August 14 Japan agreed to the Potsdam terms. A formal surrender was signed aboard the *Missouri* in Tokyo Bay, September 2.

Even in the euphoria of victory celebrations, some Americans could not avoid asking themselves how it happened that their country, with its deeply humanitarian traditions, had been the first to use history's most terrible weapon. The Hiroshima bomb killed eighty thousand people and injured many more, some of whom died horribly in the ensuing weeks and months. Yet in 1915, the United States had been genuinely outraged by the death of 1,198 civilians on the *Lusitania*. Throughout the 1930s, and as recently as 1939, American spokesmen had denounced aerial bombing of civilian populations.

The advent of the atomic bomb typified several tendencies, good and bad, that ran through the history of the war. It was, in the first place, a typical result of the American civilian war effort. It depended on a bold decision based on immensely complex science and engineering. It was conceived by scientists from many countries, some of them refugees. Thus it was a product of a liberal society associated with some of the best American traditions.

At the same time, its use in war was the climax of a period of mounting inhumanity for which all major nations bore some responsibility. The worst atrocity of the period was the systematic German annihilation of six million Jews. In places Russian treatment of political and national minorities was almost as bad. Bombing of cities was carried out by Axis nations from Shanghai in 1932 to Rotterdam in 1940. City destruction was carried to new lengths by Britain and America in Germany, in 1943–1944, when three hundred thousand civilians were killed. The American fire bombings of Japan killed about 330,000 people. Thus the annihilation of two cities in 1945 could be taken for granted by callous people, while more sensitive ones defended the action as a means of shortening the war and thus reducing both Japanese and American losses in the long run.

Postwar examination by American experts seemed to indicate that Japanese resistance had been almost over before Hiroshima. (Somewhat similarly, precision bombing of industries and transport turned out to have been far more decisive than city destruction in Germany.) But whatever the military or other judgments on the use of the atomic bomb in 1945, its existence became henceforth a major and incalculably frightening fact.

Thus the United States came to the end of a period of great and revolutionary achievement. From a policy of isolation she had emerged to a stance of worldwide involvement. She had helped to build a great alliance, and through this and her productive and military achievements she had helped destroy perhaps the worst regime in history. All this had been accomplished without dictatorship, without the destruction of either economic or political liberty at home.

The price for these great achievements started with a million American casualties, but that was only a beginning. Millions of people in Europe and Asia were starving in their ruins. Hate and fear were rampant as never in modern history. Another totalitarian state had been brought to immense worldwide power. The peaceful, democratic world promised by Roosevelt, and by Wilson before him, seemed nowhere in sight.

FOR FURTHER READING:

For military and diplomatic history, probably the single most valuable work is Churchill's monumental though not infallible *The Second World War* (6 vols., 1948–1953)*. American involvement is traced in detail in A. R. Buchanan, *The United States and World War II* (2 vols., 1964). Walter Millis, *Arms and Men* (1956)*, is a humane and enlightened study of American military policy from the beginning and is especially valuable for this period. Robert A. Divine, *Roosevelt and World War II* (1969) is brief and sympathetic; while James MacGregor Burns, *Roosevelt: The Soldier of Freedom* (1970) is more detailed and critical. The tangle of Washington bureaus is to some extent unraveled in Eliot Janeway, *The Struggle for Survival* (1951). The tragic tale of Japanese-American internment is told in Roger Daniels, *Concentration Camps USA* (1971). Lawrence S. Wittner examines the peace movement during and after the war in *Rebels Against War* (1969). One of the most thorough accounts of inter-Allied negotiations is Herbert Feis, *Churchill, Roosevelt, Stalin* (1957)*. The same author's *The Atomic Bomb and the End of World War II* (1966), and Gar Alperovitz, *Atomic Diplomacy* (1965) disagree sharply on the motives behind a momentus decision. Robert Sherwood, *Roosevelt and Hopkins* (2 vols., 1948)*, gives a highly favorable picture of the American effort to achieve good relations with Russia. Chester Wilmot, *The Struggle for Europe* (1952)*,

---

* Available in paperback edition.

provides a stimulating and intelligent English criticism of American strategy and diplomacy. Diane Shaver Clemens, *Yalta* (1970)* offers a revisionist view. Among important memoirs are those of secretaries of state Cordell Hull, Edward R. Stettinius, and James F. Byrnes; of Admiral William D. Leahy; and of Generals Dwight D. Eisenhower* and Omar Bradley*.

THE TRUMAN YEARS

	Domestic	The Atom	Europe	Asia	
1945	April 12 Death of F.D.R. November Coal strike.	Baruch Plan. McMahon Act (AEC). Bikini atomic explosion.	July 17–August 2 Potsdam Conference. August 21 End of lend-lease. November 20–October 1 Nuremburg trial.	August 14 Sino-Soviet Treaty. December Beginning of Marshall mission to China.	**1945**
1946	June–November End of price controls. November 5 Republicans capture both Houses.		November 4–December 12 Foreign ministers complete treaties with German allies (ratified 1947).	January–April Iran incident.	**1946**
1947	March 22 Truman loyalty program. June 23 Taft-Hartley Act. July 26 National Security Act.		March 12 Truman Doctrine (aid to Greece and Turkey). June 5 Marshall Plan announced. November–December London Conference (Britain, Russia, United States) breaks up over German question.	January End of Marshall mission to China.	**1947**
1948	November 2 Truman defeats Dewey.	Eniwetok explosion.	February Communist coup, Czechoslovakia. June Yugoslav-Russian break. June 24 Berlin blockade begins.	May 15 Israel independent, recognized by United States.	**1948**

THE TRUMAN YEARS (continued)

	Domestic	The Atom	Europe	Asia
1949	October 14 Smith Act convictions.	First Russian atomic explosion	April 4 North Atlantic Treaty. May Russians agree to end Berlin blockade.	January 20 "Point Four" announced. Chinese Nationalist defeated. December 8 Chiang to Formosa.
1950	January 21 Hiss convicted. February 9 McCarthy attacks State Department. September 23 McCarran Act. November 7 Republican election gains. December Hoover attacks Truman foreign policy.	United States starts work on hydrogen bomb.		January Acheson "defense perimeter" speech. June 25 North Korean attack. November 26 Chinese attack in Korea.
1951	1951–1952 Corruption disclosures, foreign policy and communism argument.		April 2 Eisenhower Headquarters in Paris opens.	April 11 MacArthur recalled. July 10 Korean Peace talks open. September 8 Japanese Peace Treaty.
1952	April 8 Truman seizes steel mills. June 30 McCarran-Walter (immigration) Act. November 4 Eisenhower defeats Stevenson.	British atomic explosion. United States hydrogen explosion.	August 2 West German peace Contract (occupation ends).	

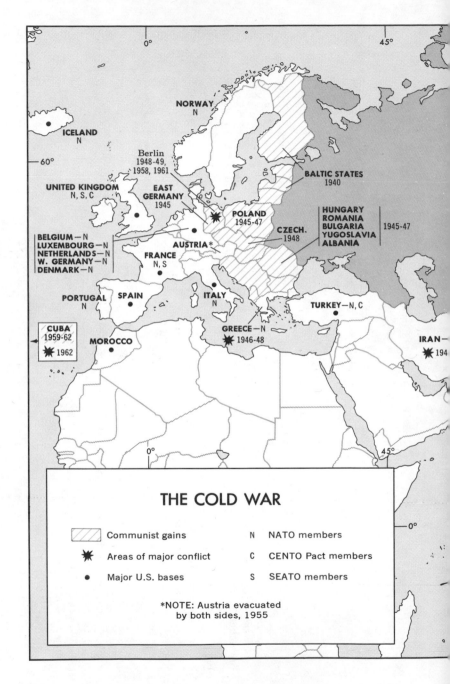

NORWAY
N

ICELAND
N

Berlin
1948-49,
1958, 1961

BALTIC STATES
1940

UNITED KINGDOM
N, S, C

EAST
GERMANY
1945

POLAND
1945-47

HUNGARY
ROMANIA
BULGARIA
YUGOSLAVIA
ALBANIA

1945-47

CZECH.
1948

BELGIUM — N
LUXEMBOURG — N
NETHERLANDS — N
W. GERMANY — N
DENMARK — N

AUSTRIA*

FRANCE
N, S

PORTUGAL
N

SPAIN

ITALY
N

TURKEY — N, C

CUBA
1959-62

✹ 1962

MOROCCO

GREECE — N

✹ 1946-48

IRAN —

✹ 194

0°

45°

60°

45°

0°

THE COLD WAR

////// Communist gains

✹ Areas of major conflict

• Major U.S. bases

N   NATO members

C   CENTO Pact members

S   SEATO members

*NOTE: Austria evacuated
by both sides, 1955

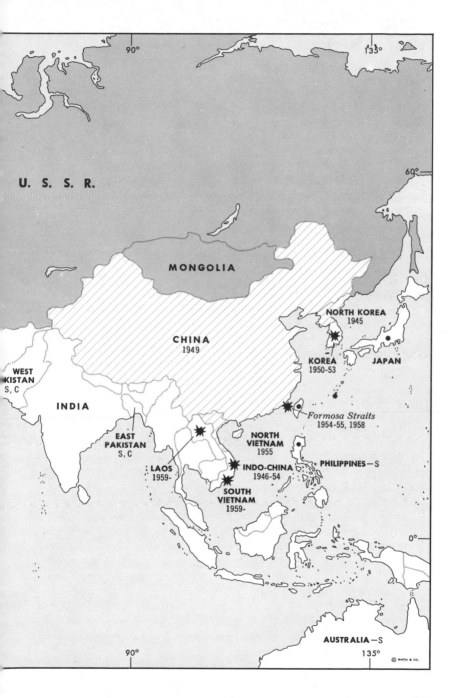

U. S. S. R.

MONGOLIA

CHINA
1949

NORTH KOREA
1945

KOREA
1950-53

JAPAN

WEST
PAKISTAN
S, C

INDIA

EAST
PAKISTAN
S, C

Formosa Straits
1954-55, 1958

NORTH
VIETNAM
1955

LAOS
1959-

INDO-CHINA
1946-54

PHILIPPINES — S

SOUTH
VIETNAM
1959-

AUSTRALIA — S

© RMcN & CO.

395

Neither Peace nor War
1946-1952
29

After World War II, American history became impossible to separate from world history. The scene grew too large for a historian to grasp, just as events were too complex for contemporaries to understand. Yet the American people, who lived through these years, had not changed overnight. Both their traditions and their leaders had been formed in a period of relative safety and isolation.

THE END OF THE GREAT ALLIANCE

The first postwar president, Harry S. Truman, seemed particularly old-fashioned. He looked to many like a small-town machine politician. He was this, but he was also much more. Truman had to make some of the most tremendous and dangerous decisions in the history of the United States. He made all with courage and some with great intelligence. Sometimes hot tempered, inclined to tolerate unreliable cronies, he possessed a deep sense of American history and a profound understanding of the responsibilities of his office.

When Truman found himself president, in April, 1945, he confronted an alarming world. The United States was the only remaining great power under constitutional government. England's might and wealth were nearing exhaustion, Western Europe was wrecked and impoverished, Germany was a disputed battleground. In the Far East, both the old colonial order and Japan's New Order were about to disappear, and almost everywhere nationalists and Communists were preparing to struggle for power.

The breakdown in Russian-American relations began in Eastern and Central Europe where Russia had military strength and was determined that her approaches should be guarded by friendly nations. At first

Soviet occupation policies varied from country to country, but it shortly became apparent that serious opposition to Russian interests would not be permitted. Russian policies were harshest in Poland and Rumania, where Russian interests were crucial and anti-Russian sympathies widespread. While Russian domination of Eastern Europe became more rigid, the Stalin dictatorship was becoming harsher in Russia. Western European economies were faltering and Communist parties, still under Moscow's control, were both active and formidable in France and Italy. Rightly or wrongly, American policy makers feared not only the consolidation but the extension westward of Russian power.

To counter this danger, American choices were limited. The Churchill policy of frank division of Europe into spheres of influence had been rejected by Roosevelt and was not revived by Truman. The Roosevelt policy of collaboration with the Russians seemed to lead only to misunderstanding and frustration. Liberals hoped to settle all disputes through the United Nations, but the veto provision made coercion of a great power impossible. At the other extreme, some wanted to use both the economic and the military power of the United States to challenge Russian gains and to push toward the illusory, traditional American goals of political democracy and the Open Door everywhere. For such purposes America had a choice of economic or military weapons. Economic pressure was applied clumsily in 1945, when the United States abruptly cut off lend-lease and lost a Russian request for a loan. With her armies being demobilized, America still had the monopoly of the atomic weapon, and there were those who wanted to threaten, at least, to use it. Yet a policy of preventive war was politically impossible and, to most Americans, morally repellent. The only remaining possibility was some policy of limited resistance. In 1945–1947, through trial and error, the American government moved gradually in the direction of this uncongenial choice.

In the first Truman years, the policy of collaboration seemed still to work in some areas. At Potsdam, in July, 1945, Truman met Stalin and Churchill (replaced during the conference by Clement Attlee of the British Labor Party). The Potsdam Conference sent an ultimatum to Japan and agreed on a complex set of principles for the government of Germany by the Allied Powers. Unable to agree on Eastern European problems, the Big Three turned them over to future meetings of foreign ministers. From 1945–1947, these managed with much difficulty to draw up treaties with the German allies, and the United States reluctantly recognized the Soviet-oriented regimes in Hungary, Rumania, and Bulgaria. An International Military Tribunal, sitting at Nuremberg in 1945–1946, condemned twelve major Nazi war criminals, military and civilian, to death. A similar international court, meeting in Tokyo in 1946–1948, resulted in the hanging of seven Japanese war leaders.

In these years, however, strained relations were more common than agreement. In March, 1946, Winston Churchill warned at Fulton, Missouri that an "Iron Curtain" had cut Europe in two and that Stalin, who did not want war, might gain his objectives without it. At first received with some hostility, Churchill's thesis seemed more plausible as tensions tightened.

The earliest and most difficult impasse took place in Germany. The agreed provisions for four-power government there had been based on an assumption of continued East-West cooperation. For a situation of East-West disagreement, they proved to be absurdly impractical. Berlin, the German capital, was to be governed by the four powers jointly. Though it lay a hundred miles inside the agreed Russian zone, no definite access routes from the west were provided.

According to the Potsdam agreement, Germany was to be denazified, demilitarized, stripped of her warmaking power, and left with a standard of living no better than that of the average for Europe (at that time very low). Though no central German government was to be set up for the present, the country was to be administered as an economic unit through the agreement of the four zonal administrations. Though the final amount of reparations was not set, removal of German industrial equipment was to commence. In addition to what it removed from its own zone, Russia, which had suffered frightful destruction at German hands, was to receive 25 percent of the equipment removed from the Western zones, part of which was to be paid for by shipments of German food and raw materials from the Russin zone. For the present, the United States went ahead with this program, including the dismantling of German industry.

It was soon clear that completely different social systems were emerging in the Eastern and Western zones. As German productive facilities were further weakened, it proved difficult to feed the West German population, swollen by twelve million refugees from the east. Food from the Russian zone was not forthcoming.

In 1946 the United States announced a change in policy, including revision upward of German production, eventual political unification of Germany on a decentralized basis, and reexamination of the German-Polish frontier. To quiet Russian fears, the United States offered to guarantee German disarmament for twenty-five or even forty years. This offer was promptly refused. In January, 1947, Britain and America agreed to join their zones. Later that spring, a foreign ministers' conference completely failed to agree about reparations, and the deadlock over Germany was complete.

A dramatic plan for international control of atomic energy, drawn up by a committee headed by Bernard Baruch, the veteran financier, was rejected by the Soviet Union on grounds that were to become familiar. The Baruch plan called for destruction of American bombs only after international inspection and control had become effective, while the Soviet Union demanded immediate destruction. Meanwhile the Russians, with the aid (perhaps unnecessary) of espionage, were working hard on their own weapon. In August, 1946, Congress created its own system for tight government control of American atomic research and development by an Atomic Energy Commission.

In 1946 and 1947, the strategic Middle East was threatened by Russian demands on Iran for oil concessions and on Turkey for border changes and joint control of the Black Sea straits. The Truman administration responded vigorously and Russia withdrew her troops from Iran in the spring of 1946. The pressure on Turkey continued intermittently while in Greece the conservative government, supported by English troops, was attacked by indigenous Communist guerrillas, assisted by Greece's Communist neighbor, Yugoslavia. In February, 1947, the British government, strained to the economic breaking point, informed the United States that it would have to withdraw from Greece. Fearing the consequences of Soviet control of the Middle East, and dreading the collapse of the Western European economy, Truman decided on a course of major and independent American action.

CONTAINMENT IN EUROPE, 1947–1949

The new policy of containment was described by George F. Kennan of the State Department in 1947. Soviet policy, Kennan said, was dominated by a belief in the inevitable triumph of communism. World Communist victory, while it might be pursued with patience, could not be abandoned as an objective without a fundamental change in the Soviet system. Such a change might eventually be induced if the United States (1) demonstrated to the world its own vitality and (2) frustrated Soviet plans by the patient application of counterforce wherever necessary.

Counterforce was first applied under the "Truman Doctrine" announced in March of 1947. Calling for economic and military help for people menaced by armed minorities or outside pressures, Truman persuaded Congress to appropriate funds for Greece and also for Turkey. The withdrawal of Yugoslav assistance to the Greek guerrillas, together with American military aid, allowed the Greek government to defeat the Communist insurgents. Threats to Turkish independence also abated.

In June the United States proposed a more general program for European economic relief. In a speech at Harvard, General George Marshall, now Secretary of State, offered to assist the recovery of all European nations including the Communist ones. Russia forced her satellites to refuse, but the Western European countries willingly presented a united recovery plan. After considerable debate, Congress established the European Cooperation Administration and, in the next three years, appropriated more than $10 billion for its purposes. This "Marshall Plan" was the greatest success of American postwar policy. It laid the basis for the startling European recovery and unprecedented European unity of the 1950s.

Naturally, these American actions produced sharp Russian reactions. The Communist parties of Western Europe, through strikes and political agitation, tried hard though unsuccessfully to make the Marshall Plan a failure. Communist control of Eastern Europe tightened, and in February, 1948, Communists in a *coup d'état* took over Czechoslovakia, a country already aligned with Russia in foreign policy but until now governed by a coalition. This event, which deeply alarmed Europeans, was partly balanced by a break between Yugoslavia (hitherto the most important European Communist satellite) and the Soviet Union. From then on Tito's realm was to be Communist but independent in foreign policy. This development might, it seemed, indicate one road toward the disintegration of Stalin's empire, and alleged Titoists were ruthlessly eliminated in all Communist-bloc states.

In the summer of 1948, Russia decided on drastic countermoves in the crucial German area. Reacting sharply to a reform of the currency in the Western zones, Russia announced that the division of Germany ended all reason for Western presence in Berlin. Russian forces cut all surface communication between West Germany and the former capital, threatening with starvation the city's Western garrisons and West Berlin's two million pro-Western inhabitants. This threat, the most dangerous so far, was resolutely met by flying supplies into Berlin in American planes. In May, 1949, the Russians suddenly decided to end the blockade, but the division of Germany was already complete. In September the (West) German Federal Republic was proclaimed at Bonn, and in the following month the (East) German Democratic Republic was created with its capital East Berlin. Thus the most difficult American-Russian problem had taken a new shape. It was obvious that most Germans wanted their country united and preferred Western alignment. It was equally obvious that the Russians would not allow a united Germany to join the Western bloc.

Alarmed by the Berlin threat and encouraged by economic revival, the European countries made gestures toward unity and asked for American commitments. In April, 1949, the United States broke with its ancient dislike of binding alliances and signed a treaty of mutual defense with thirteen nations of Western Europe. Later this North Atlantic Treaty was signed by Greece and Turkey.

Obviously, such commitments to defend vast areas demanded military means. In July, 1947, the National Security Act overhauled the defense establishment, creating the office of Secretary of Defense, the National Security Council, the Central Intelligence Agency, and other new organizations. In June, 1948, Selective Service was revived and at the same time two bomber groups, capable of delivering nuclear bombs, were sent to air bases in Britain.

Despite these steps the United States had only begun to build forces sufficient for a sustained worldwide power struggle. Congress was still reluctant to make very large appropriations, and the President was determined to make further cuts. Up to 1950 defense expenditure was limited to $15 billion, and the armed forces to little over a million men. This meant that the nation was still depending heavily on the atomic bomb. In September, 1949, a Russian nuclear explosion announced the end of American atomic monopoly. In the winter of 1949–1950 the administration decided to begin work on the hydrogen bomb which would be far more devastating than any existing weapon.

Thus by 1949 the United States had adopted, in theory and practice, the policy of containment. It was not clear whether she was bound to undertake counter action in *any* area of Communist activity or only in those areas where resistance seemed promising. This problem was to cause immense difficulty later. So far, however, the most obvious threat had been to Western Europe, and here there was no doubt of America's commitment. She was bound to support European freedom with her economic might and also, if necessary, with weapons of incredible and unknown powers of destruction. Despite vigorous debate, public opinion apparently supported this commitment more fully than it had approved resistance to the Nazis before 1940.

THE NEW AMERICAN SOCIETY, 1945–1949

In domestic as in foreign affairs, the first Truman years were a time of profound change, of conflict, and of considerable success. Remembering 1921 and 1929, many people predicted a postwar depression. Instead, it soon became apparent that the most serious economic problems were to be shortages and inflation. Price controls, fairly efficient in the last years of the war, were mostly destroyed in the summer and fall of 1946 in a long wrangle between the President, who favored them, and the Congress, which distrusted them. Between December, 1945 and December, 1947, prices rose by about a third.

As in 1919, organized labor wanted to protect its wartime gains and defend wages against inflation. This time its efforts were successful. In several rounds of strikes beginning in 1946, unions achieved compromise settlements with employers, usually providing considerable wage increases for which the consumers paid most of the bill in higher prices. For the first time in American labor history, a period of major strikes passed almost without violence. Yet both the public and the administration were concerned about the growing power of labor to bring the economy to a standstill. In 1946 the government briefly took over the coal mines, and Truman threatened to have the army run the railroads if necessary.

By no means placid, postwar American society was richer and more productive than any in history. America's gross national product, in the prosperous year 1929, had been worth a little over $100 billion and in the depression had fallen below $70 billion. By 1948 it was above $174 billion (using the same dollar value) and only beginning a spectacular upward movement.

At first prosperity was apparently stimulated by pent-up consumer demand. Undoubtedly, federal spending for European relief and other purposes helped sustain it. From the wartime peak of $98 billion, federal spending fell to $33 billion by 1948, as against the $3 billion which had seemed normal in the 1920s. In the gloomy 1930s, certain economists had said that booms were unlikely to be sustained in the future either by a rising birthrate or new industries. Now they were proved wrong by a spectacular "baby boom" and by important new developments in such fields as electronics and aviation.

Once more, as in the 1920s, spokesmen for American capitalism claimed that it had outstripped the dreams of past radicals. This was at least more nearly true than it had been in the earlier period. Continued high taxes and high wages were redistributing wealth to a significant degree. While farm income once more started downward after 1947, wages continued to rise and so did the share which workers had in the country's total net income. While some corporations were huge and powerful, all business including small business had grown. Most people did not believe that the gloomy predictions of 1900 trustbusters were about to be fulfilled. Competition did not seem to be disappearing.

Compared to the early 1920s, the new postwar period saw far less hostile reaction to national and racial minorities, partly, no doubt, because there were fewer foreign-born Americans. All too slowly, the

Negro made some important advances. Truman desegregated the armed forces and called, in 1948, for a series of civil rights measures. The "G. I. Bill of Rights" sent thousands of veterans to college who would never otherwise have gone. It was arguable that the postwar American society, with its vast new middle class, its burgeoning suburbs, and its high-paid labor, was not only the richest but the most equalitarian society the world had seen. Yet, when one looked into the pockets of poverty that lay beneath the rich surface, one found many people who did not share in the new well-being. Among these were small farmers, technologically displaced workers, the old, the mentally deficient, and, despite all advances, most Negroes.

These paradoxical facts shaped the politics of the postwar period. Most Americans, not directly affected by the new kinds of distress, wanted neither to abandon the New Deal nor to extend it. Thus both left and right were frustrated, and the political pendulum swung indecisively, almost regularly, back and forth between a moderately conservative Congress and a surprisingly liberal President.

In September, 1945, Truman called for a long list of reform measures which he called the "Fair Deal." These included higher minimum wages and broader social security, public housing and slum clearance, more regional development along TVA lines, federal assistance to education and health protection, and an attack on racial discrimination in employment. The familiar Southern-Democrat-Republican coalition frustrated most of these aims. Yet the Employment Act of 1946 marked official acceptance of federal responsibility for the maintenance of maximum employment.

In 1946, during the peak of inflation and strikes, the Republicans gained control of both Houses of Congress. Liberals predicted disaster, yet few New Deal laws were repealed. One important new measure, the Taft-Hartley Act, indicated a conservative swing in labor policy, but regulated unions much less strictly than many conservatives wanted (it outlawed the closed but not the union shop). The same Republican Eightieth Congress, denounced by Truman for frustrating his Fair Deal, cooperated remarkably with his spectacular and novel foreign policy.

As the election of 1948 approached, most people still underrated both Harry Truman and his chances. While conservatives disliked the Fair Deal, labor and liberals were tired of Truman's peppery intervention in strikes and longed for a leader of Roosevelt's inspirational gifts. Even the Democratic party itself seemed to be falling apart. The left wing threatened to follow Henry A. Wallace, who roundly denounced Truman's foreign policy for unnecessary hostility to Russia. A strong civil rights bill in the platform brought the secession of most conservative Southerners, who supported the "Dixiecrat" movement of Governor J. Strom Thurmond of South Carolina. The confident Republicans, once more fighting back their right wing, renominated Governor Dewey of New York.

Actually, the situation was less unfavorable to Truman than it seemed. The people were not yet deeply divided about foreign policy, and some had resented the tendency of a Republican Congress to frustrate reform and curb labor. The two secessions actually proved advantageous. Wallace's well-intentioned protest movement was captured by the Communists, which doomed it to insignificance and drew antiradical fire away from the Fair Deal. Thurmond carried only four Deep South states, and his candidacy helped keep northern Negroes in the Democratic camp. The Democrats regained control of Congress.

Jubilantly, the President called once more for the enactment of the Fair Deal, to which he added a new farm program, civil rights measures, and repeal of the Taft-Hartley Act. He called also for a new "Point Four" in foreign policy, providing for American technical assistance to the vast underdeveloped areas of the world. Congress passed some of the milder Fair Deal measures in such familiar fields as minimum wages, social security, and housing. But there were no new TVA's, no dramatic new farm program, and no drastic revision of the Taft-Hartley Act. Point Four operations were commenced with an appropriation of $35 million for all Asia, Africa, and Latin America.

If they looked to history, rather than to their highest hopes, for their standards of comparison, Americans had some reason to be pleased with their government's record in the first four postwar years. At home they had achieved great prosperity and retained sufficient political unity. Abroad they had assumed vast responsibilities and scored some successes. In the middle of the century, this relatively cheerful picture was shattered by unforeseen events.

CHALLENGE IN ASIA, 1949–1951

In 1949–1950, as in 1941, disaster struck not in Europe, where American policies and commitments were fairly clear, but in the Far East, where both goals and responsibilities were cloudy.

The only major success in this area was the occupation of Japan, where American power was not seriously contested by Russia. Issuing his orders through the Emperor and receiving a surprising degree of cooperation from the Japanese, General MacArthur carried through with considerable success a program of remaking Japanese government and society on democratic and pacifist lines.

In China, at the end of the war, the government of Chiang Kai-shek faced a well-entrenched, experienced, and armed Communist opposition which controlled about a fourth of the Chinese population. Russia, which occupied Manchuria as a result of her brief war with Japan, recognized the Chiang government as sovereign throughout China, including Manchuria. Stalin's forces gave limited assistance to the Chinese Communists, but turned over the Manchurian cities to Nationalist garrisons often flown in from the south by America. (It is by no means certain that Stalin, at this time, wanted a Communist success in China which would provide him with a powerful rival in the Communist world.)

In the era of high hopes and Roosevelt-Stalin accords, many American observers, not all of them left-wing, found the Chinese Communists efficient and honest and the Nationalists corrupt and hopeless. Some advocated an effort to produce a coalition government. Encouraged by a few gestures in this direction from both Chinese sides, Truman sent General Marshall to try to bring about such a union and temporarily cut off the supply of American arms. By December, 1946, Marshall concluded that the task was hopeless and asked to be recalled.

After the Marshall mission, limited aid to Chiang was resumed, with little effect. In 1949 the Nationalist armies disintegrated, the Communists captured city after city, and in December Chiang's government moved to the island of Formosa. Suddenly the American people awoke to the fact that China, whose integrity America had long upheld, was now indeed united, but under hostile control. From the Baltic to the Yellow Sea over the whole vast Eurasian mainland, Communists were in power.

Later many argued that America should have given Chiang more active support. At the time very few demanded the kind of massive commitment that would have been necessary to keep the tottering Nationalists in power. Here as elsewhere, the faults of American policy were to a large extent the result of traditional American optimism. Roosevelt's program for making Nationalist China a great power, Truman's hope for Nationalist-Communist coalition, and later suggestions that Chiang could have been sustained with a little more effort were all equally unrealistic.

Many Americans were genuinely shocked at events for which they were unprepared. Neoisolationists and Asia-firsters blamed the Roosevelt policies for the disaster, and some partisans saw in the loss of China a means of ending Republican defeat.

Accused not only of mistaken judgment but also of deliberate treason, Truman and his Secretary of State, Dean Acheson, insisted that the Chinese Nationalists were to blame for their own defeat, and the President announced that the United States would not get involved in Chinese civil war in behalf of Formosa. And in January, 1950, Secretary

Acheson made a speech defining a broad American "defense perimeter" in the Pacific—very broad, but covering neither Formosa nor Korea. This raised in a new form the most difficult problem concerning the containment policy. *Any* announced boundary for American intervention might seem to invite Communist attack in the area left outside. Was the only answer American commitment *everywhere?* Or was it possible, in a democratic country, to decide for or against action in each case without advance commitment or public preparation?

The next challenge came in Korea, where postwar zones of Russian and American military occupation had solidified into hostile political entities. On June 25, 1950, the (Communist) North Koreans crossed the South Korean border in force. Truman ordered the dispatch of supplies to South Korean troops and also directed the Seventh Fleet to move into the straits between China and Formosa, with orders to prevent attack by either side. Meanwhile the United States brought the North Korean aggression before the Security Council. Since Russia happened to be boycotting this body and could not cast its veto, the Council demanded North Korean withdrawal and urged its members to assist South Korea.

In obedience to this order, and also to sustain a regime created and fostered by the United States, President Truman first sent to Korea American air and sea forces and then ground troops under General MacArthur. Fifteen other nations sent small contingents to the UN army in Korea. Thus the situation was an ambiguous one: MacArthur was nominally in command of an international army under UN orders. Actually, his army was made up of 90 percent Americans and South Koreans. Thus this international "police action" was also an American war. It turned into a bloody and frustrating struggle with profound effects on American foreign and domestic policy.

At first the North Koreans swept the raw American troops southward. In September, holding only a small area around the port of Pusan, the UN force started a northward counterdrive. By a brilliant landing behind enemy lines at Inchon, near Seoul, MacArthur achieved a major victory. This raised the question whether the UN troops would stop at the old boundary or push on to unify the nation under the South Korean government (both Korean governments claimed to represent the whole peninsula). When the General Assembly resolved that its aim was to create a "unified, independent, and democratic Korea" MacArthur's troops crossed the thirty-eighth parallel and drove northward toward the Chinese boundary at the Yalu River, which MacArthur was forbidden to cross. Though President Nehru of India and others warned of possible Chinese intervention, General MacArthur assured President Truman that this was most unlikely. At the end of November, however, Chinese troops surprised the UN army near the Yalu, inflicted a severe defeat, and started a drive southward against stiff resistance.

Chagrined at what he called a new war, MacArthur demanded new measures to win it. These included permission to bomb the "privileged sanctuary" in China from which Chinese troops and some Russian-made planes were coming, the use of Chinese Nationalist troops from Formosa, and an all-out commitment to victory over the new enemy, with or without the support of America's European allies. When MacArthur carried his protest to the extent of press interviews and letters to members of the Republican opposition, Truman promptly recalled him from command.

This bold action, taken by Truman to protect what he considered the all-important control of the president over foreign policy, precipitated an angry debate. At first the public seemed to side with the general's eloquent demand for complete victory. Defenders of the administration, however, stuck to their position that an all-out war with China would be disastrous. In Korea the line between the two sides was stabilized at about the old border between North and South, and in July, 1950, American representatives began a long, frustrating effort to negotiate peace with the Chinese and North Koreans.

Limited but determined military resistance in Korea was part of a developing American policy, based on an increasing fear of worldwide Communist aggression, and a determination to avoid all-out war. In 1950–1951, only partly for Korean purposes, the military budget was quadrupled and the armed forces increased to 3,500,000 men. In Europe, where recovery was now well under way, American aid shifted from an economic to a military emphasis. At American suggestions, the North Atlantic Treaty Organization decided to build a Combined Western European force to deter possible Russian attack. Headquarters were established in Paris, and once more Eisenhower was placed in supreme command of an allied army.

Almost inevitably, European rearmament raised the question of contributions from West Germany, the most exposed and now the most prosperous European state. A separate German army was still an intolerable idea to the French and other victims of the Nazis. In 1952, following a French suggestion, the Western European nations formed a European Defense Community in which national components, including a German one, would be placed under a single command.

Japan had proved an important base for the Korean action, and in September the United States signed a peace treaty dropping all restrictions on Japanese economic growth or even rearmament. (Ironically, Japan insisted on remaining disarmed.) A separate security treaty gave American forces the right to remain in Japan. At about the same time the United States signed mutual defense treaties with the Philippines, Australia, and New Zealand.

Thus the Korean War, following the Berlin blockade and the Russian atomic explosion, changed the nature and degree of American commitments once more. A combination of courage and restraint had turned back Communist aggression and prevented the development of a third world war. For this achievement, a heavy price had been paid, and not all of it by Americans. The United States had lost twenty-five thousand men, Korea was devastated, and the Korean civilian population had suffered almost incredible losses. Yet it seemed that victory, or even an end of the fighting, was not in sight. Instead of guarding a limited defense perimeter, the United States seemed to have undertaken to resist Communist advances in even the most remote and difficult theaters. Europe seemed permanently divided, and the German question farther than ever from solution. War had brought its usual accompaniment of conscription, inflation (comparatively moderate), and high taxes. Military expansion seemed to threaten more than ever the traditional civilian character of American society and government. Both America and Russia were known to be developing the hydrogen bomb, potentially a thousand times more powerful than the weapon that had destroyed Hiroshima. It is not surprising that the American people, most of whom remembered years of apparent security, were very deeply disturbed.

CONFUSION, HYSTERIA, AND THE END OF THE TRUMAN ERA

Popular unrest first took the form of a new debate over foreign policy, similar in some ways to those of 1898–1900, 1914–1917, and 1939–1941, but more violent than any of them. Some extremists argued that the whole diplomacy of Roosevelt and Truman had been part of one gigantic plot, including the New Deal, Pearl Harbor, the buildup of Russia, the sellout of China, and war without victory in Korea. Less violent critics of the administration argued, as former President Hoover did in 1950, that it was a mistake for America to make any commitments on the continents of Europe or Asia. Senator Taft and others called for a reliance on air power rather than ground troops, and many urged that timid or uncooperative allies be disregarded. On the other hand the somewhat demoralized liberals maintained that the real mistake had been support of corrupt and reactionary regimes or reliance on military rather than economic methods of defense against communism.

Though none of these arguments held up very well in its extreme form, discontent was not to be dismissed lightly. Nobody knew just where, if anywhere, the limits of American commitment were, and the long-run positive goals of foreign policy were not clear. American "cold war" resistance had been improvised to meet unforeseen threats. Attempts to provide it with a theory were not altogether convincing, and its opponents offered no clearly feasible alternatives. Thus the argument centered, increasingly and disastrously, on one emotional issue: Communists in government.

Unfortunately, neither the facts nor the arguments affecting this issue were simple. Liberals usually appealed to free speech, and it was true that the United States, since its beginnings, had normally tolerated advocacy of revolution. But free speech, even revolutionary speech, did not clearly cover new forms of secret political activity. No earlier radical group had been under the control of a foreign great power. And it was not quite clear whether, during a cold war, wartime or peacetime precedents should govern.

Between 1941 and 1945, when Communists throughout the world were supporting the anti-Hitler alliance, some Communists had found employment in Washington, usually in low-echelon jobs. A few of these had been exploited by the Soviet Union for espionage. In some intellectual circles and in sections of organized labor, the Communist party had regained a portion of the strength it had held in the 1930s. These facts, exposed and greatly exaggerated at the moment Americans were dying in a frustrating war with Communists in Korea, produced an explosive reaction.

Responding to early disclosures of Communist activity, Truman established a government loyalty program in March, 1947. Employees were investigated by the F.B.I., and those found disloyal (later, also those considered "security risks") were discharged. Despite efforts for fairness, the novel and secret character of this program led to some abuses and much uneasiness. Turning from the problem of secret infiltration to a quite different area, Truman's Justice Department started in 1948 to prosecute the leaders of the American Communist party under the Smith Act of 1940, which forbade advocacy of, or conspiracy to advocate, forcible revolution.

Though these actions were disapproved by many liberals, they were not enough to pacify current fears. The demand for more drastic measures arose partly from the House of Representatives' Committee on Un-American Activities whose methods had long drawn liberal criticism. The most spectacular, though not the only or the clearest, case of communism in government arose in this Committee in 1948 when Whittaker Chambers, an ex-Communist, accused Alger Hiss of having been a Communist and, a little later, of having engaged in espionage.

Hiss, a brilliant and widely admired young man, had held a moderately influential State Department post and had attended the Yalta Conference. Nearly all liberals believed him innocent, and President Truman referred to the Committee's work as a "Red Herring." Yet Chambers' melodramatic and baffling charge proved very hard to refute. In 1950 Hiss was finally convicted in court, not of espionage but of perjury in his denial of Chambers' charges. Still more alarming to the public was the discovery that spies had been operating in wartime atomic installations. Now the threat of annihilation was added to the loss of China as a result of Communist conspiracy.

In 1950 Congress passed, over Truman's veto, the McCarran Internal Security bill which among many drastic provisions required the registration of Communist organizations and provided that subversives could be interned by presidential order in time of war. In 1952 the McCarran-Walter bill severely increased political restrictions on immigration. And in 1950, when fear of communism had reached its peak, the Communist issue was discovered by its great promotional genius, Senator Joseph McCarthy of Wisconsin.

Charging that many Communists (the number varied) were employed in the State Department and moving on to attack as traitors General Marshall and Secretary Acheson, McCarthy succeeded in creating a wide following and an unparalleled amount of public alarm and confusion. In the congressional elections of 1950, the new political technique of extreme, unsupported charges seemed to work remarkably well, as critics of McCarthy went down to defeat and clever politicians adopted his tactics. As in the anti-German hysteria of World War I, states, cities, and private organizations took up the crusade. Soon self-appointed groups were purging libraries, harassing teachers, and listing dangerous television stars. For a time, it seemed as if traditional individual freedom, decency, and common sense were to be sacrificed in the search for a complete, impossible security.

In this disturbing atmosphere the 1952 election campaign began. In April, when a threatened steel strike seemed to threaten paralysis, Truman seized the steel plants, an action held unconstitutional in June. A series of sordid political scandals in the administration, not enormous by Harding or Grant standards but still disturbing, began to be exposed. Opposition extremists spread the picture of an incompetent President, surrounded by traitors and crooks, committed to a hopeless war.

Actually, in the summer of 1952 the nation's right-wing extremists received their severest blow when the Republican convention nominated not a McCarthyite demagogue and not even the widely respected conservative Senator Taft, but General Eisenhower. The General, long identified with both the Roosevelt and the Truman foreign policies, could hardly lend himself to McCarthy's charges of "Twenty Years of Treason." Eisenhower did, however, support all Republican candidates, including McCarthy, while he confined himself to more moderate discussions of "the mess in Washington" or at most "creeping socialism." In foreign policy, the Republicans promised both peace and victory. John Foster Dulles, their leading foreign policy spokesman, promised that Republicans would roll back communism instead of merely containing it. Near the end of the campaign, Eisenhower promised that if elected he would fly to Korea and bring the war to an end.

The Democrats nominated the eloquent Governor of Illinois, Adlai Stevenson, who aroused immense liberal enthusiasm but proved unable to stem the Republican tide. Surprisingly, the overwhelming Eisenhower victory failed to produce much change in Congress, where Republicans barely gained a two-house majority. Ironically, the first election of a Republican president since Hoover guaranteed that there would be no sharp change in American foreign policy.

CONFLICTING HISTORICAL VIEWPOINTS

Who Started the Cold War?

The governments of the Soviet Union and the United States have offered remarkably similar explanations for the origins of the Cold War. Each side has characterized the conflict as a morality play in which the other is cast as the villain. Both have presumed to act in the name of the world's "peace-loving" peoples, and each portrayed the other as an imperialist power bent on global conquest.

Articulated initially by top spokesmen for the Truman administration, including George F. Kennan (Foreign Affairs Quarterly [July, 1947]), head of the State Department Policy Planning Staff, the official American interpretation of Cold War origins was not seriously questioned by most historians in the United States until the 1960s. Although scholarly accounts were often less hysterical than those by journalists and other popular writers, historians generally agreed that Russia's aggressive designs threatened the stability of the postwar world. Indeed, one of the most methodical and authoritative apologists for American diplomacy was Herbert Feis, a State Department adviser-turned-historian. In a series of books (Roosevelt-Churchill-Stalin

[*1953*], Between War and Peace [*1960*], The Atomic Bomb and the End of World War II [*1966*], *and* From Trust to Terror [*1970*]), *Feis argued that in its Cold War policies the United States was merely responding to a Russian challenge. Fomenting revolution and seeking conquest, the Soviet state, he believed, shattered the Grand Alliance, violated its Yalta Agreements, and forced a reluctant and war-weary United States to assume the leadership of a threatened "free world."*

Although the orthodox view dominated popular and scholarly writing throughout the 1950s, there were from the beginning of the Cold War a few precocious dissenters who raised disturbing questions about American policy. Years before popular disenchantment with the war in Vietnam found reflection in a multitude of revisionist attacks on American postwar policy, the philosopher-journalist Walter Lippmann (The Cold War [1947]) *questioned the rationale for containment. And such "realist" historians as Hans Morgenthau* (In Defense of the National Interest [*1951*]) *and William McNeill* (America, Britain, and Russia [*1953*]) *offered early challenges to prevailing assumptions of exclusive Russian guilt. But the first systematic revision of the traditional interpretation was probably William A. Williams's* American-Russian Relations, 1871–1947 (*1952*). *In this volume and in such later works as* The Tragedy of American Policy (*1959*) *and* The Contours of American History (*1961*), *Williams attributed the onset of the Cold War to the dollar diplomacy of the United States. Linking American foreign policy to the "needs" of American capitalism, he viewed containment as the latest manifestation of a traditional American diplomacy of economic expansionism dating at least from the days of the Open Door. American counterrevolutionary activities, then, were designed not to contain Communist aggression but to promote commercial penetration of Eastern Europe.*

In recent years Williams's thesis has been documented and extended by a number of New Left scholars. In The Politics of War (*1968*) *and* The Roots of American Foreign Policy (*1969*), *Gabriel Kolko, for example, has offered the most extreme indictment of American policy yet available. Although typical of much New Left scholarship on the period, Kolko's work is more extreme than studies by such thoughtful radicals as Walter LaFeber and Lloyd Gardner. In his balanced* America, Russia, and the Cold War (*1967*) *LaFeber surveyed the entire era and concluded that both powers must share the blame for the war of nerves. In* Architects of Illusion (*1970*), *Gardner was also highly critical of American policy shapers, but he too conceded that "neither side could fully control events, or even freely respond to them in many instances."*

The critics of revisionism are numerous, and many historians reject the economic determinism of the New Left. But recent scholars have shown little willingness to defend the simple pieties of the orthodox interpretation. Thus in The United States and the Origin of the Cold War *(1972), the most persuasive antirevisionist counterattack now available, John L. Gaddis concluded that "leaders of both super-powers sought peace" and that "neither side can bear sole responsibility for the onset of the Cold War." Clearly, although the question of Cold War origins remains open, there is now widespread scholarly belief that the orthodox answer is no longer satisfactory.*

FOR FURTHER READING:

Among general histories of the period, Herbert Agar, *The Price of Power* (1957)*, is thoughtful and very brief; Eric F. Goldman, *The Crucial Decade* (1956)*, is colorful and anecdotal. F. L. Allen, *The Big Change* (1952)*, points out some of the differences between this period and the previous postwar era. The origin of the Cold War is the subject of several of the books included in the essay above. Two able but differing interpretations of American involvement in the struggle are: John W. Spanier, *American Foreign Policy Since World War II* (1960)*, and Louis J. Halle, *The Cold War As History* (1967). Good, brief overviews include John Lukacs, *A History of the Cold War* (1961)*, and Norman Graebner, *Cold War Diplomacy, 1945–1960* (1962)*. Robert James Maddox's *The New Left and the Origins of the Cold War* (1973) is harshly critical of revisionist scholarship. The memoirs of Truman and Kennan are indispensable and Dean Acheson, *Present at the Creation* (1969) is outstanding. Robert Griffith, *The Politics of Fear* (1970) is an excellent study of the McCarthy phenomenon; and William F. Buckley and L. Brent Bozell, *McCarthy and His Enemies* (1959) is a spirited defense of the Wisconsin senator. Alistair Cooke, *A Generation on Trial* (1950) conveys the atmosphere surrounding the Hiss Case. Perhaps the best introduction to the Truman administration is the Missouri president's own *Memoirs* (2 vols., 1955–1956)*, but these volumes should be supplemented by Barton J. Bernstein, ed., *Politics and Policies of the Truman Administration* (1970), Alonzo Hamby, *Beyond the New Deal: Harry S. Truman and American Liberalism* (1973), and Cabell Phillips, *The Truman Presidency* (1966)*. William C. Berman has written *The Politics of Civil Rights in the Truman Administration* (1970).

Richard Lowitt, *The Truman-MacArthur Controversy* (Berkeley Series in American History, 1967), deals with this period.

---

* Available in paperback edition.

MODERN REPUBLICANISM

	Domestic	Space and the Atom	Europe	Asia, Latin America, and Africa
1952	November Eisenhower elected.	November 1 Eniwetok hydrogen explosion (United States).		December Eisenhower visits Korea.
1953	1953–1954 McCarthyism. Recession.	August 20 Russian H-bomb.	March 5 Stalin's death. June Riots in East Berlin. August 30 France rejects EDC.	July 27 Korean armistice.
1954	April–June Army-McCarthy hearings. May 17 Court outlaws school segregation. November Democrats capture Congress.	March 1 Bikini H-bomb (United States).		May–June Guatemala Crisis. July 21 Geneva Agreement. September 8 SEATO Pact.
1955	July 11 Dixon-Yates contract cancelled.		May 15 Austrian Peace Treaty. July 18–23 Geneva meeting (Eisenhower, Bulganin).	
1956	November Eisenhower elected with Democratic Congress.	Stevenson proposes H-bomb ban.	February Khrushchev denounces Stalin crimes. October–November Hungarian insurrection. March 28 European Common Market.	October Suez Crisis.
1957	Recession. September 24 Troops to Little Rock.	May 15 British H-bomb. October 4 Sputnik.		January 5 "Eisenhower Doctrine" in Middle East.
1958	November Democratic gains in Congress.	January 31 United States satellite. March 31 Russia suspends tests (United States follows).		May Lebanon Crisis.
1959	July Steel strike.	September 13 Soviet "Lunik" hits moon.	September Khrushchev visits United States.	February 16 Castro premier of Cuba. June Tokyo riots.
1960	Recession. November Kennedy elected.	February 11 French atomic explosion. July 20 Polaris sub launches missile.	May U2 incident. November West Berlin threatened.	June 30 Congo independent; civil war. August Laos Crisis.

Modern Republicanism
1953-1960

30

Some Americans had hoped, and others had feared, that the Eisenhower administration would sharply change American foreign policy and reshape post-New Deal American society. It did neither. In nearly every sphere, the history of the administration seemed to go through three stages: first, announcement of sweeping change; second, reversion, with overwhelming public approval, to a slightly modified version of earlier policies; finally, frustration and renewed crisis. One explanation of this cycle is not hard to find. In the circumstances confronting American policy-makers of this period, real alternatives were few, and completely satisfactory solutions impossible. Yet the American people did not give up easily their search for security and contentment. In 1953 many wanted a change; in the middle 1950s most believed that they had found security; by the end of the decade it was apparent that they had not.

Dwight D. Eisenhower had been trained all his life for war, yet nobody questioned his devotion to peace. Far from bringing to the White House a habit of command, he was devoted to consultation and consensus. A moderate conservative, he was thwarted more by the right wing of his own party than by the opposition. Unwilling to use fully his political power, he remained, despite overwhelming personal popularity, an ineffective party leader.

FROM REACTION TO COMPLACENCY

In 1953, fear of domestic subversion reached panic proportions. The federal security program was drastically tightened, while congressional committees searched for disloyalty in education, entertainment, and private foundations. For a while Senator McCarthy, now chairman of

the Committee on Government Operations, seemed the most powerful individual in Washington. Far from admitting that Republican
victory had ended the danger of Communist infiltration, he intensified
his accusations. The State Department, long his principal victim,
seemed to have surrendered. Officials who criticized the Senator were
suspended, and books which offended him were removed from
American information libraries and destroyed (sometimes their authors
were called to Washington and harshly grilled). Two junior members of
McCarthy's staff junketed through Europe issuing portentous reports
on the loyalty of senior American officials after talking briefly with
shady foreign informants. Civil servants and even army officers were
encouraged to disobey their superiors and disclose confidential
information. The morale of federal employees sank dangerously, and
some of America's staunchest friends abroad were dismayed.

In 1954, the Senator fell from power as rapidly as he had risen. The
President had shown signs of disquiet, and, perhaps more important,
the public was beginning to be bored. A prolonged and complicated
controversy with the Department of the Army resulted in a series of
television hearings in which McCarthy's manners and methods
shocked the public. Finally a select committee of the Senate condemned his conduct as contradictory to senatorial traditions. Discredited and comparatively ignored, McCarthy died in May, 1957.

Later in the decade the Supreme Court, now presided over by Earl
Warren, a liberal Republican, delivered a number of decisions which
restricted the scope of congressional committees and in other ways
reaffirmed the importance of traditional individual freedoms. At the
polls, the congressional elections of 1954 demonstrated that the "Red
issue" had lost its potency, and in 1956 it was hardly used. In the
prosperity and complacency of the middle Eisenhower years, hysteria
died down more quickly than it might have under more vigorous
counterattack. Yet the costs of tolerating McCarthyism were high. An
ugly image had been presented to the world, sections of the government service had been demoralized, and some important issues of
foreign policy seemed to have been placed beyond the range of
effective discussion. As McCarthyism waned, a shrill minority on the
Far Right added Eisenhower and Warren to their list of worldwide
conspirators.

In the same period the administration's economic and social
policies shifted from right to center. At the outset, many cabinet
members were wealthy businessmen, the conservative Senator Taft
apparently wielded great power in Congress, and the President's own
pronouncements on domestic matters were highly conservative. Senator Taft died in July, 1953. In the winter of 1953–1954 a recession set in
causing the Treasury Department to modify its conservative, antiinfla-

tion policies. Without drastic government action, recovery came swiftly, and in the mid-1950s an unparalleled prosperity prevailed. Despite this fact and despite the President's great and continuing popularity, Democrats recovered control of Congress and kept it throughout the Eisenhower administrations. With the Korean War over and the McCarthy hysteria abated, it became clear that the country's dominant mood had not changed greatly since the Truman years. Few Americans wanted to dismantle the New Deal, and few wanted radical new departures. Under these circumstances, the Eisenhower instinct for compromise and conciliation had free rein.

In the prosperous mid-1950s, the political pattern seemed to consist of (1) administration friendliness to business, (2) administration efforts, seldom strikingly successful, to promote economy and decentralization, and (3) compromises between President and Congress in support of moderate, familiar kinds of reform programs. Efforts to win business confidence included tax concessions, increased "partnership" of government and private enterprise in the development of public power and even nonmilitary atomic energy, and support for state, rather than federal, control of tideland oil resources. On the other hand, Eisenhower's first Republican Congress created the Department of Health, Education, and Welfare, extended social security, and gave moderate support to public housing. Even after the Democrats recovered control, few measures more startling than these were passed. Such controversial programs as health insurance or federal support of education were regularly defeated or heavily amended.

A major effort to change the direction of New Deal and Fair Deal farm policies was made by Ezra Taft Benson, Eisenhower's conservative Secretary of Agriculture. Amid loud outcries from farm spokesmen, price supports were made "flexible" rather than rigid; that is, lowered. Yet, since farm income was declining, many New Dealish measures, including a "Soil Bank" scheme to reduce acreage, received administration support. Neither farm subsidies nor the farm problem seemed at all likely to disappear.

A surprisingly vigorous program of antitrust prosecutions and various efforts to help small business failed to achieve a significant movement in the direction of *laissez faire*. Government spending, so long denounced as the road to socialism, was cut back only moderately after the Korean War. It remained higher than the 1950 post-World War II low of $45 billion and by 1957 was to reach a new peacetime high of $82 billion. Government decisions of many kinds continued to affect every part of the economy. To the President's obvious distress, it became clear that this fact placed vast temptations in the way of competing interests. In 1955 the Dixon-Yates contract, an effort to provide for private construction of a huge power plant for Memphis, proved to be improperly negotiated and was canceled by Eisenhower. The next year disclosures of attempted bribery of a senator forced the President to veto a bill to exempt natural gas producers from federal rate control.

The most important advance of the period, that made by Negroes, was not a product of executive action. Despite some recent gains, in 1952 Negroes were still generally subject to enforced segregation in the South, and throughout the nation they were far behind whites in jobs, income, housing, education, and health. In 1954 the Supreme Court reversed its 1896 position on segregation. Until now, "separate but [nominally] equal" treatment of Negroes in transportation, recreation, and education had been legal. Now segregation, specifically in education, was pronounced inherently unequal. The decision produced fierce defiance in the South, where massive resistance campaigns were led by highly influential private Citizens' Councils. Only in the border states did effective school desegregation begin. Despite his personal misgivings about the Court's decision, Eisenhower supported it in the name of constitutional duty. In 1957 he sent federal troops to Little Rock, Arkansas, where Governor Orval Faubus, alleging fear of mob action, was using state guards to obstruct court-ordered integration of the high school. In 1957 Congress passed the first Civil Rights Act since 1875. It created a Civil Rights Commission with power to investigate denial of voting rights or equal protection of the law. Under this and later legislation, the federal government began a cautious effort to protect Negro voting in the South.

More important than any government action was the new determination of Southern Negroes to achieve equality for themselves. In 1955 the Negroes of Montgomery, Alabama, under the leadership of Martin Luther King, Jr., an eloquent young minister, achieved the desegregation of the bus system by a determined boycott. Similar efforts, carried on with remarkable discipline in a spirit of passive resistance, made further gains in desegregating transportation, restaurants, and housing. More progress was made by the Southern Negro than in any decade since Reconstruction. Yet violent resistance continued and frustrations were many. By the end of the decade it was clear that the hardest problems lay in the swelling Negro slums of northern cities, islands of poverty in a sea of wealth.

In its social effects, Eisenhower prosperity had something in common with Coolidge prosperity. Like the 1920s, the 1940s and 1950s added large numbers of citizens to the complacent, suburban, moderately conservative ranks of the middle class. As in the 1920s, however, the culture of prosperity excluded some people and was repudiated by others.

Until nearly the end of the decade, few middle-class citizens noticed that a large minority remained poor. Esthetic blight and moral sluggishness were the main targets of criticism. Perhaps the most obvious failure of America—here the critics were repeating strictures made since the 1880s and 1890s—was her cities. Traffic choked them, old slums disgraced them, and new jerrybuilt housing spread from their edges into the countryside. In the slums and, more shockingly, in some wealthy suburbs juvenile delinquents expressed their confusion and frustration in acts of meaningless violence.

As in the 1920s, intellectuals denounced dullness and conformity. The successor of Babbitt was the Organization Man who was said to live and breathe in the cheerful, noncontroversial manner prescribed by the head office on the basis of personality research. To repudiate, defy, and outrage this monster seemed to a few serious people the main need of the hour. "Beatniks," bearded and bizarre, proclaimed a new religion of defeat and withdrawal rather than defiance.

To most Americans, however, Eisenhower prosperity and its genial symbol were apparently highly satisfactory. An unassuming president who left many administrative decisions to his subordinates, praised free enterprise, disowned corruption, and cooperated with a cautiously reformist Congress seemed to fit the needs of the hour. Surely one of these needs, though hardly the only one, was for reassurance and rest after decades of fierce controversy. Despite a heart attack in 1955, Eisenhower was renominated in 1956 and scored a landslide victory over a visibly less confident Adlai Stevenson.

FROM MASSIVE RETALIATION TO PEACEFUL COEXISTENCE

In 1952, many Republicans had denounced war, government spending, and appeasement. Some had promised in contrast peace, economy, and a rollback of world communism. The difficulties of this commitment were made greater by a change in the tactics of the opponent. In March, 1953, Joseph Stalin died. Nikita Khrushchev, who emerged as Russia's new leader, repeatedly proclaimed a relaxation of the Russian police state and a foreign policy of peaceful competition with capitalism. The main theater of this competition was to be the underdeveloped countries just emerging from colonial rule. In many of these countries the new, comparatively "soft" Communist line, coupled with unquestionable Russian technological achievement, seemed far more effective than Stalin's steamroller.

During most of Eisenhower's presidency, foreign policy was formulated, and to a large extent formed, by Secretary of State John Foster Dulles. Dulles, a tactless man of formidable knowledge and consistency, distrusted Russia's intermittent gestures of conciliation. American power, he believed, was sufficient to defeat, and not merely to contain, the Communist enemy. Sometimes alarming America's allies with statements about going to the brink of war, he was more aware than he sounded of the limits of possible action.

Anti-Communist militance plus Republican traditions of economy led to the proclamation of a new military policy. Instead of reacting to local Communist threats with expensive and indecisive ground wars, America, Dulles said, would from now on rely on "massive retaliation" at times and places of its own choosing. Expenditures and ground troops would be cut back, while nuclear weapons would be further developed and the air arm expanded. This would provide, as the newspapers soon put it, "more bang for a buck." Corollaries of this "New Look" in military policy were tight alliances and the development of a string of air bases abroad from Spain to Iran. NATO armies in Europe would be equipped with tactical atomic weapons.

The new policies drew heavy criticism abroad and at home. Critics charged that they would make American resistance to aggression impossible except in cases justifying all-out nuclear war. This became harder to contemplate as American tests made clear the colossal destructiveness of the H-bomb, and scientists made conflicting statements about the effect of fallout on cancer, leukemia, and birth deformities. In October, 1954, Eisenhower, who had seldom echoed Dulles' bellicose pronouncements, said that war had become obsolete under modern circumstances. Since the Russians were saying much the same thing, the world breathed a little easier.

The new military-diplomatic policies were severely tested in the Far East. Carrying out a campaign promise, the administration succeeded in negotiating a Korean peace on approximately the same terms Truman had been willing to accept. The massive retaliation policy may have contributed something to Communist willingness to sign, since Dulles announced that if war persisted it could not be confined to the Korean Peninsula. Prisoners of war were allowed, as both Truman and Eisenhower had insisted, to choose whether to go home or not, and a large number of Communist soldiers chose Formosa. The peninsula was left divided, leaving America committed to assist and defend an economically and politically shaky South Korean state.

With peace in Korea, attention shifted southward to Indo-China where since 1945 the French had been fighting a bloody and unsuccessful war against the Viet Minh independence movement, by now under solidly Communist leadership. At first the United States had been skeptical about colonialism here as elsewhere, but since the Korean War America had been supporting the French more and more heavily with money and material. In March, 1954, it suddenly became clear that northern Indo-China could no longer be held unless the United States committed at least its air power. Both Dulles and Eisenhower proclaimed that the loss of Indo-China would lead to Communist domination of all South Asia. Prospects of joint American-British intervention were explored by Dulles without success. Some of the administration's military advisers suggested the use of small atomic weapons.

Examined closely, American intervention in Indo-China seemed a dubious prospect. Dispatch of American troops to fight a jungle war, right after the unpopular Korean episode, would contradict administration pronouncements. Air power alone would be difficult to use in Indo-China. According to the new military doctrine, this seemed to make a clear case for massive retaliation against the centers of opposing power, presumably Moscow and Peking. This terrible alternative was not considered, and Eisenhower, overruling his military advisers, decided against even local air assistance to the French.

In May the fall of the fortress of Dienbienphu forced the French to move toward settlement of the war. Though the United States took no direct part in the Geneva Conference among Russia, China, Britain, France, and the Indo-Chinese states, Washington accepted its complex and fateful results. The Geneva agreements recognized the three states of Laos, Cambodia, and Vietnam. The last was divided at the Seventeenth Parallel, with the Viet Minh holding the north and the French-backed Saigon government the south. In two years, internationally supervised elections were to be held throughout Vietnam. Meantime, military forces were to be regrouped and populations exchanged. Military bases of any country, the introduction of new military forces, and adherence to military alliances were forbidden on both sides of the line. Observance of the agreements was to be supervised by a commission representing India, Poland, and Canada.

As had happened in the divisions of Korea and Germany, separate governments developed in both parts of Vietnam. The insecure government in the South refused to carry out the scheduled election, arguing that supervision in the Communist north was impossible. Of the new states, Communist North Vietnam was the strongest. Neutral Cambodia leaned toward friendship with China. Laos and South Vietnam, both weak and internally divided, were added to the long list of possible American responsibilities.

One of the administration's early acts was to carry out Republican promises to "unleash Chiang Kai-shek." The Seventh Fleet, patrolling the Straits of Formosa mainly to protect Chiang's Nationalists against mainland assault, was instructed to present no further opposition to attacks in the other direction. In 1954 the Chinese Communists loudly proclaimed their intention of capturing Formosa which, quoting the

Cairo Declaration of 1943, they insisted was part of China. It had long been clear that the United States would not allow Formosa to fall, and she had just assisted in the movement there of former Communist soldiers. American policy was less clear toward the tiny islands, within ten miles of the Chinese coast, which the Nationalists had garrisoned. When mainland batteries began shelling these offshore islands, the United States announced that America would defend them *if* the assault seemed to be part of an attack on Formosa itself. In a treaty with Chiang, the United States pledged herself to defend Formosa and the Pescadores, but Chiang promised not to invade the mainland without United States consent. Thus his brief "unleashing" was ended.

In September, 1954, the United States signed the SEATO treaty of military alliance, modeled on the Atlantic Pact, with Britain, France, Australia, New Zealand, the Philippines, Pakistan, and Thailand. A special protocol extended the treaty's coverage to Laos, Cambodia, and South Vietnam. Thus a Far Eastern policy not much unlike that of Truman had emerged. The United States had divided two crucial areas with the Communists and guaranteed the resulting *status quo*. The Formosa Straits now, like Korea in 1950, were an area of great danger where the limits of American commitment were not clear.

The Eisenhower policies were further tested in a new theater, the Middle East, whose problems to some extent typified those of the entire underdeveloped two thirds of the world. More and more, it began to be said that the outcome of the world struggle for power lay not in Europe or East Asia but in the vast, backward, impoverished, restless countries of Africa, Southern and Western Asia, and Latin America. Clearly, American power could not replace the European empires which had until recently provided most of these areas with one kind of stability. In many of the new countries governments were unstable and economies both unjust and unstable. An intensive effort to understand and assist them was widely urged. Yet America's whole past made it difficult for her to understand the needs and feelings of the most impoverished and oppressed people.

In the Middle East American policy was influenced by two special concerns. One was the region's immensely important oil resources, long defended by Britain and coveted by Russia. The other was a special kind of commitment to the new state of Israel. The American Jewish community contributed heavily to Israel's support, and most Americans admired the courage of the tiny state, which not only defended its independence against heavy odds, but welcomed all survivors of Hitler's massacre. Most of Israel's Moslem neighbors, particularly the displaced Palestinians, hated the Israelis as interlopers and refused to accept the new state's existence.

The United States fostered, but did not join, the Baghdad Pact signed in 1954 by Great Britain, Turkey, Pakistan, Iraq, and Iran. America agreed also to assist President Nasser, the Egyptian dictator who aspired to Pan-Arab leadership, to build a huge dam on the upper Nile. When Nasser seemed to bargain for Russian support as well, the American offer to build the dam was suddenly withdrawn. Nasser promptly seized this excuse to nationalize the French-built, British-and-French-owned Suez Canal which had been for generations the lifeline of the British Empire and was now a funnel for vitally needed European supplies of oil. At the end of October, 1956, Egypt was attacked by Israel, Britain, and France. Siding against her traditional allies, America condemned this use of force. American pressure, in strange combination with Russian threats of intervention, forced a humiliating British-French withdrawal.

Alarmed at declining Western prestige and strong signs of Soviet interest in the Middle East, the President, in January, 1957, persuaded Congress to endorse the "Eisenhower Doctrine." This authorized the President to provide military assistance to Middle Eastern nations requesting aid against Communist aggression. This pledge proved difficult to implement. Within two years crises occurred in Jordan, Syria, and Iraq. Each, however, involved the threat of a Communist coup from within, rather than that of external aggression, and American help was not sought. In July, 1958, the United States did send troops to Lebanon, whose president had requested them. At the end of the Eisenhower era, conditions in the Middle East seemed a little less dangerous despite the baffling dilemmas of American policy. So far, nationalism in this area seemed to be gaining on communism.

In Europe, where the President was personally popular, the program for collective defense ran into serious difficulties. The NATO scheme had been formulated when Stalinist threats and Far Eastern aggression had alarmed the European nations. Now, with the Korean peace and the new Russian tone of conciliation, immediate fear of communism subsided. In some circles, not all of them left-wing, fear of possible American rashness and consequent nuclear war took its place. More-over, Europeans, like many Americans, were more interested in their own burgeoning prosperity than in problems of defense.

In August, 1954, the European Defense Community scheme, a French suggestion heartily endorsed by the United States, was killed by the French parliament. Secretary Dulles threatened angrily an "agoniz-ing reappraisal" of American policy, which seemed to suggest with-drawal of American forces or perhaps a separate relation with Germany. Under British leadership, the European nations in 1955 developed a complex substitute. Germany was invited to provide a limited proportion of NATO troops. The (West) German Federal Republic received full sovereignty, was guaranteed by France, England,

and the United States, and promised not to pursue reunification by force. Yet West Germany still claimed the lost territories, West Berlin was still isolated, and no Central European settlement came near being acceptable to both sides. As yet, the dream of making Western Europe a single major military power was a failure.

Ironically, while America's relations with her European allies deteriorated, her relations with her major antagonist moved from unexampled harshness to unexampled mutual toleration. At the outset of his administration, Eisenhower announced that Russian goodwill could be demonstrated by a Korean peace and an Austrian peace treaty. Not only the first but, to everybody's surprise, the second condition was satisfied. In 1955 Austria was evacuated and became an independent, neutral, Western-oriented nation. Russia made peace with Yugoslavia without a Yugoslav return to the orthodox Communist fold and recognized West Germany. At a major Communist congress in 1956 Khrushchev denounced the crimes of the Stalin period in startling terms. Western skepticism about the new Russian line was lessened when the Chinese began to denounce it as a betrayal of Leninism.

In the summer of 1955, while the new line was still unfolding, Eisenhower consented to meet with the British, French, and Russian heads of government at Geneva. The conference settled no outstanding problems. Its most dramatic moment came with Eisenhower's suggestion of an "open sky" formula under which each side would receive full military information from the other and be free to verify it by aerial inspection. Acceptance of this proposal, either by Russia or by the American Congress, was doubtful. Yet an exchange of military information seemed a promising avenue toward peace and became a recurrent goal of American policy. The new "spirit of Geneva" seemed for a while more important than concrete negotiations, as America and Russia exchanged delegations of ballerinas, farmers, and other ambassadors of goodwill. The Dulles policy of massive retaliation was dead, and even the Truman policy of building collective resistance became harder to implement.

If the new Soviet line raised problems for Western policy, it raised still harder ones for Stalin's heirs, who had no thought of abandoning Stalin's East European gains. From Warsaw to Berlin people longed to test the limits of the new policies. Some remembered that Secretary Dulles had promised American support for liberation. In 1953 strikes and riots in East Germany produced no American action. In 1956, Poland, a country especially important to the United States because of immigration, daringly defied the Russians and established a regime which, while still Communist and part of the Eastern alliance, offered considerably greater liberty of expression. Taking the cue, and tragically taking it too seriously, the Hungarians revolted with greater violence and seemed on the point of leaving the Soviet sphere altogether. After considerable initial hesitation, Russian troops brutally suppressed the revolt. Later, its leaders were executed. Since the United States took no action, it seemed that liberation was as dead a policy as massive retaliation.

Despite these disturbing events, the country apparently entered Eisenhower's second term in a cheerful and optimistic mood. Within two years new threats at home and abroad made optimism far more difficult.

THE END OF COMPLACENCY, 1957–1960

The administration's troubles began with an economic downturn in late 1957. This recession, more serious than its postwar predecessors, focused attention on three problems. The first of these was unemployment which hovered around 5 percent, declining only slightly with economic upturns. The second problem was the rate of American economic growth, which was far slower than that of either Russia or Western Europe. The third was the American balance of payments. Declining European purchases and continuing American arms and aid programs were causing an outflow of gold and threatening American capacity to maintain her massive responsibilities.

Aside from these immediate problems, analysis began to show more and more clearly that Eisenhower prosperity, impressive as it was, had never spread to all the people. The war and the early Cold War periods, with their colossal new government expenditures, high taxes, and demand for labor, had benefited the lower economic groups most. The group considered poor by economists had shrunk from something like two-thirds of the people in the depression to about one-fourth in 1953. Since then, while the well-to-do group had grown sharply, the proportion of poor had remained about the same, and their share in the national income had decreased. The poor quarter of a rich society were too easy to overlook and neglect. Most were untrained and undereducated, and automation was rapidly lessening demand for unskilled labor. Many were old, and many were Negroes. Neither unions, social security, nor housing legislation seemed to reach the problems of these rejected people. Even an economic upturn might pass them by.

These moral, social, and economic challenges did not become clear overnight. Yet it was obvious enough that distress existed in some areas (like West Virginia coal fields and big-city slums) and that the economy had lost some of its drive. At the same time the administration was wounded when Sherman Adams, Eisenhower's chief administrative aide, was forced to resign after disclosure of his acceptance of improper gifts from favor-seeking cronies. Rumors of corruption, the fact of recession, and worry about foreign policy were registered in the election of 1958. Democrats, and especially liberal Democrats, scored their biggest gains since 1936. The President accepted this blow with good grace and continued to cooperate with the anything but radical Democratic leadership in Congress.

Abroad, challenges and disasters mounted dramatically from 1957. In October of that year, the Russians placed in orbit their "sputnik," the first man-made earth satellite. This was not only a major feat of applied science, but also a demonstration of military power. Russia had already boasted that she possessed an intercontinental ballistic missile capable of delivering a nuclear warhead anywhere. Now this claim seemed probably true. Sputnik set off a wave of American self-criticism which tended to exaggerate the achievements of Soviet education, science, and weapons as much as these had been underrated earlier.

Many tasks were quickly accomplished to remedy the American lag in rocket building and the penetration of space. In January, 1958, a small American satellite was put in orbit, and in November the Air Force fired a huge rocket six thousand miles. Probably the strongest American answer to the Soviet lead was the firing of a rocket from the "Polaris" submarine in July, 1960.

Like the competition between European powers from the sixteenth to the nineteenth centuries, the "space race" had both a peaceful and a warlike aspect. It was a new field for "peaceful competition" in which each country spent vast resources for scientific and exploratory prestige. It was also a sinister and complex struggle for military superiority and particularly for possession of mobile, hard-to-destroy, and infinitely powerful nuclear weapons. Whoever was ahead, it was clear that the terms for American foreign policy had changed. America's historic invulnerability was gone; war would mean immediate and vast destruction in the United States as well as in enemy territory.

In confronting the new threat the administration was handicapped by the fatal disease (1957) and death (1959) of Secretary Dulles. No new policy seemed at hand to replace his consistent though unsuccessful system. And the Soviet Union, full of self-confidence, intensified both the conciliatory and the belligerent phases of its offensive.

American-Russian negotiations about disarmament and an end to nuclear tests continued under immense pressure from alarmed world opinion. In 1958 both countries announced a temporary cessation of testing, but the Soviet Union, which acted first, got most of the credit. In November of that year Khrushchev renewed Russian pressure on Berlin. In the absence of an acceptable settlement, he announced,

Russia would in six months sign a peace treaty with East Germany. This would turn over the Berlin approaches to the most intractable and rigid of the satellite states. From time to time in the next years the deadline was extended, but the threat remained. Pressing hard for negotiations on the Berlin issue, Khrushchev secured an invitation to visit the United States in September, 1959. Once more nothing was settled, but an atmosphere of strained cordiality was maintained.

Making a further concession, Eisenhower agreed to meet Khrushchev in Paris in May, 1960, without the preliminary lower-level negotiations which the United States had earlier demanded. Just as the meeting was getting under way, the Russians shot down an American photographic plane 1,300 miles inside Russian territory. At first, American spokesmen denied the charge of espionage but the pilot, who had been captured, confessed. Contrary to international custom in such matters, the administration now acknowledged and justified the practice of secret photographic flights over Russian territory. Dramatically Khrushchev demanded an impossibly abject apology from the President and, in its absence, angrily broke off the Paris meeting and withdrew an invitation for a presidential return visit to Russia.

In Asia affairs went little better. Communist China bombed the offshore islands again in 1958 and bloodily subdued autonomous Tibet in 1959. Immediately after the Paris fiasco, an Eisenhower visit to Japan had to be postponed because of student riots against a Japanese-American security treaty. In Laos and South Vietnam, Communist guerrilla movements seemed to be stronger than non-Communist governments.

In Algeria prolonged insurrection absorbed the energies of France and threatened the United States with a difficult choice between anticolonialism and a traditional alliance. Further south in Africa, the French, British, and Belgian empires were liquidated with great rapidity, leaving in their wake many large and small nations, mostly lacking experienced leaders or viable economies. In one of the weakest and largest of these, the former Belgian Congo, disintegration threatened to spread East-West conflict to a new theater.

Most distressing of all to Americans were the developments in Latin America. Since the wartime triumphs of the Good Neighbor policy, little had been accomplished in this region by American diplomacy. Despite statements of democratic solidarity, both the Truman and Eisenhower administrations had made cordial gestures toward oppressive military regimes. The most spectacular action of the Eisenhower administration in the region, applauded at home but reviving memories of intervention among Latin Americans, had been to assist a right-wing coup against a pro-Communist government in Guatemala. No program like the Marshall Plan had been developed to complement political with economic action, and the region's desperate economic problems were steadily growing more acute. In 1958 Vice President Richard Nixon, touring Peru and Venezuela, was the target of violent hostile demonstrations.

In January, 1959, in Cuba, the guerrilla forces of Fidel Castro triumphed over the government of Fulgencio Batista. Many Americans sympathized with the Castro movement's program of needed economic reform and blamed American policy for close relations with the previous right-wing regime. But before long, executions and confiscations in the island seemed to indicate that Castro was drawing closer to the Communist bloc. By the end of the Eisenhower administration, American investments in Cuba were confiscated, American trade nearly cut off, and Castro's violently anti-American and by now pro-Soviet movement was threatening to attract support throughout the poorer regions of the hemisphere.

Probably the position of the United States in 1960, difficult as it was, seemed even worse because of the apparent lull of the mid-1950s. Straining for a vanished security, the American people still felt a deep affection for the immensely likable President, while at the same time they repudiated his party in Congress and increasingly criticized his policies.

This situation was dramatized, as so much of American history has been, in a presidential campaign. Richard Nixon, Eisenhower's vice president, received the Republican nomination and campaigned on the administration's record. Senator John F. Kennedy of Massachusetts, forty-four years old, able, rich, and Catholic, promised sweeping change and vigorous forward movement. The outcome of the election, a hairline Kennedy victory, proved difficult to analyze. It seemed to demonstrate that (1) the obvious ability, political skill, and vigor of Senator Kennedy impressed the public; (2) a great many people, though many fewer than in 1928, still voted according to historic ethnic and religious loyalty; and (3) the American people, though shaken from the complacency of 1956, were still not in the mood for large-scale new departures. This last point was underlined by the congressional elections. Democrats retained control, but Republicans and conservatives of both parties registered gains. Thus the Kennedy administration came to power in no position to implement the bold new programs it had promised.

In 1960, critics of the Eisenhower administration pointed out, correctly, that eight years of "Modern Republicanism" had failed to solve the critical domestic and foreign problems which faced the country. Its defenders argued, also correctly, that peace had been preserved, general prosperity maintained despite brief recessions, and the political atmosphere somewhat improved. In the tragic years ahead, Eisenhower's more vigorous successors were to achieve few more complete victories, and some of the unsolved problems were to become more intractable.

FOR FURTHER READING:

The most informative inside account of the Eisenhower presidency is E. J. Hughes, *The Ordeal of Power* (1963), and the most incisive criticism is R. H. Rovere, *Affairs of State* (1956). Robert L. Branyan and Lawrence H. Larsen, ed., *The Eisenhower Administration, 1953–1961* (1971) offers a sympathetic, documentary view; and Arthur Larson, *Eisenhower: The President Nobody Knew* (1968) is a personal portrait. Eisenhower's own memoirs* are less helpful than Sherman Adams, *Firsthand Report* (1961). Accounts of the administration's foreign policy include Richard Goold-Adams's sympathetic biography of Dulles, *The Time of Power* (1962), and Townsend Hoopes's critical *The Devil and John Foster Dulles* (1973). Richard E. Neustadt, *Presidential Power* (1960)*, offers interesting insights into the powers and limitations of the Presidency under Truman and Eisenhower. Stuart G. Brown, *Conscience in Politics* (1961)* is a study of the era's leading also-ran, Adlai Stevenson. N. V. Bartley, *The Rise of Massive Resistance* (1969), and Neil R. McMillen, *The Citizens' Council* (1971) chronicle southern reactions to the *Brown* ruling; and Benjamin Muse, *Ten Years of Prelude* (1964) is a good overview of the first decade of the civil rights struggle. The facts of the period's economic history are accurately and simply presented in Herman P. Miller, *Rich Man, Poor Man* (1964)*. Influential interpretations of the period's economic problems include J. K. Galbraith, *The Affluent Society* (1958)*, and Michael Harrington, *The Other America* (1962)*. The social and intellectual impact of American affluence is suggestively treated in David Potter, *People of Plenty* (1954). Samuel Lubell, *The Revolt of the Moderates* (1965)*, interprets the political situation just before Eisenhower's reelection and Theodore H. White, *The Making of the President, 1960* (1961)*, analyzes Kennedy's victory.

---

* Available in paperback edition.

THE KENNEDY-JOHNSON YEARS

Year	Negro Revolution	Other Domestic	Vietnam War	Other Foreign
1961	Freedom Riders	January Kennedy inaugurated.	December Kennedy pledges help to South Vietnam.	April Bay of Pigs. August Berlin wall.
1962	October Troops to Oxford, Mississippi.	April Steel price dispute. November Election; slight Republican gains.		October Cuban missile crisis.
1963	April–May Birmingham incidents. August March on Washington.	September Tax cut passed. November 22 Kennedy shot.	November Fall of Diem.	August Above-ground test-ban treaty signed.
1964	January Poll tax amendment. June 3 civil rights workers murdered in Mississippi. July Civil Rights Act.	August Economic Opportunity Act. November Johnson wins election.	August Tonkin Gulf incident.	October Chinese atomic bomb.
1965	August Voting Rights Act Watts riots.	July Medicare enacted.	February Bombing of North Vietnam begins. June U.S. troops in combat.	April U.S. troops to Dominican Republic.
1966	January Robert C. Weaver, first Negro cabinet member. Black Power movement	November Election; Republican gains.	June Bombing of Hanoi, Haiphong.	July France withdraws from NATO command organization.
1967	June Thurgood Marshall appointed to Supreme Court. July Riots in Newark, Detroit.		January U.S. offensive. September Elections in South Vietnam.	June Israeli-Arab War.
1968	April 4 Martin Luther King shot. April 10 Civil Rights Bill passed.	June 5 Robert Kennedy shot. November Richard M. Nixon elected President.	February Viet Cong offensive. May Paris peace talks. November 1 Bombing of North Vietnam ended.	August Soviet invasion of Czechoslovakia.

Promise and Frustration
1960-1968
31

In the first years of the 1960s, it seemed as though many of the promises of recent American history were to receive their fruition. While affluence increased, major efforts were made to alleviate the distress of the poor and to further the drive of the Negroes toward full equality. Abroad, the power of the United States seemed to increase and division among its enemies promised greater successes than ever. Yet, through the decade, doubts increased not only about victory in these goals but about many of the premises on which the efforts depended. By 1968, Americans were clearly casting about for new goals and new programs, and few answers were readily available.

IN SEARCH OF THE NEW FRONTIER

Despite Kennedy's hairline victory, his administration opened in an atmosphere of hope. Cool, rational, urbane, the President put together a brilliant staff and set about the task he had defined as "getting America moving again." More consciously than any predecessor, Kennedy with the help of his attractive wife tried to improve not only the political and economic order, but the American style of life, calling artists, writers, and intellectuals to the White House a little in the manner of a European monarch.

Kennedy's administration opened in a time of economic sluggishness, with 6 percent of the labor force unemployed. The President was thoroughly persuaded by his economic advisers that a strong drive for expansion was in order, including deficit financing if necessary. Here as elsewhere, however, he was limited by public and congressional opposition. He was further constricted by the less obvious problem, growing more severe during the decade, of the balance of payments.

American receipts from investment and export sales were falling short of expenditures, private and public, military and civilian.

Seeking to speed up the economy without impairing confidence in the dollar or unduly antagonizing the Congress, the administration began by pushing through bills of a kind familiar since the New Deal, such as assistance for slum clearance and increases in social security payments and the minimum wage. Federal expenditures, both military and civilian, were cautiously accelerated. Tax reform offered increased incentives for investment and modernization in industry. Finally, after an alarming stock slump in 1962, the administration succeeded in the following year in persuading Congress to pass a ten-billion dollar tax cut. This action, in a time of rising expenditures, marked a new degree of federal commitment to Keynesian policies. By 1963 the national growth rate had nearly doubled and employment, income, and wages had all risen sharply.

One major concern which went with business upturn was inflation. The limited powers of the administration to deal with this threat were supplemented by constant appeals for restraint both in wages and prices and by the issuance of "guide-lines" for industry. In 1962, a sudden price rise by United States Steel Corp. was followed by most other steel firms. Angrily, the President applied maximum pressure and the rise was rescinded. At the cost of considerable business resentment, price increases in general were held to a minimum.

While the administration's economic policies were moderately successful, Kennedy was less successful in attacking the country's persistent social problems, especially those connected with poverty. Administration bills for medical care for the aged under social security, for federal support for education, and for urban renewal were defeated. These and other antipoverty measures were seen by the President as a major goal for his second term.

In confronting the country's worst social problem, Negro inequality, Kennedy was sharply limited by the dominant congressional coalition of Southern Democrats and generally conservative Republicans. Defeated in several legislative battles, fearing to tie up all domestic and foreign action in a filibuster, the administration relied mainly on executive action. Negroes were increasingly appointed to office, pressure against discrimination was applied through government purchasing policies, and after some hesitation a presidential order forbade discrimination in federally financed housing. Robert Kennedy, the President's brother whom he appointed Attorney General, vigorously attacked the problem of Negro voting rights in the South.

As in the previous administration, the most important advances were made through the increasingly militant, though still nonviolent movement of Southern Negroes, now strongly supported by college students, clergy, and other white sympathizers from the North and opposed in the South by threats and mounting violence. By the end of 1962, the efforts of "freedom riders," supported by the Attorney General against violent white resistance, achieved the end of segregation in transportation. In October, 1962, federal troops were sent to Oxford, Mississippi when mob violence and the resistance of the governor of the state threatened to bar a Negro, James Meredith, from the state university. The threat of similar action prevailed the following year in Alabama and university desegregation was under way in all states.

The year 1963 saw the peak of the peaceful victories of the Civil Rights movement and the beginning of a new stage. Violent resistance sharply increased: in Birmingham police dogs were used against marchers and four Negro girls were killed in the bombing of a church; in Jackson, Mississippi, Medgar Evers, a moderate Negro civil rights worker, was killed in front of his house. In June the President, eloquently proclaiming a state of moral crisis in the nation, committed the government more fully than at any time since Reconstruction to the achievement of equality. A new Civil Rights bill attacking particularly discrimination in public accommodations was introduced in Congress as a major administration objective. In August, the nation seemed profoundly impressed by a peaceful march of a quarter of a million people in Washington, under the leadership of Martin Luther King.

Superficially, it seemed that great and peaceful progress was being made on this old and crucial front, and there was no doubt that opportunities increased for many Negroes, especially those with skills and education. Yet the economic gaps between most Negroes and most whites were not lessened, the city ghettoes remained almost unaffected, and there were signs that some Negroes were losing their patience with moderate leadership. It was also clear that a large and determined white minority was ready to fight with all weapons against real social equality for the black population.

KENNEDY AND THE WORLD

Perhaps the most important international fact of the whole decade of the 1960s was a steady deterioration of the two great alliances formed by America and Russia in the early Cold War period. In 1960, Russia withdrew technicians from China and during the rest of the decade Russian-Chinese hostility mounted sharply. From time to time, serious efforts to increase their independence appeared in Soviet satellites in

Eastern Europe, and in Russia itself intellectuals fought an uphill fight for freedom of expression. While neither party dictatorship in Russia nor Russian control of Eastern Europe was ended, Russian freedom of action was limited. This situation had some obvious advantages for American policy. It also meant, however, that Russian leaders felt the need of some major success, either peaceful or military, to consolidate their leadership in a divided Communist world.

The Western alliances put together under Truman and Eisenhower were at least equally insecure. Like his predecessors, Kennedy tried to promote European economic and military unification. Partly with this in mind, he persuaded Congress in September, 1962, to adopt a Trade Expansion Act, allowing the President to negotiate tariff reductions up to 50 percent in order to deal with the European Common Market. France, under General de Gaulle, insisted on maintaining an independent and highly nationalistic stance. In January, 1963, de Gaulle blocked England's effort to enter the European Common Market. Insisting on a separate French nuclear force, de Gaulle likewise resisted European military unification and refused to join in efforts for nuclear disarmament. England, generally loyal to her special relation with the United States despite many disagreements, found herself increasingly unable to play the role of Great Power, especially in the Far East. Japan, America's principal ally in that region, continued to prosper without arming, under American protection. Without solid alliances, a stable balance of power, or a really powerful international organization Kennedy, like his predecessors and successor, dealt with each crisis as it arose according to the means available.

In military terms the means increased. Robert F. McNamara, the spectacularly talented Secretary of Defense, imposed modern administrative techniques and the Kennedy policies on the massive military establishment with remarkable success. Whatever remained of Dulles's reliance on massive retaliation was scrapped in favor of a balanced development of the ability to respond appropriately to all kinds of threats, whether nuclear, conventional, or guerrilla. The mistaken impression of Russian superiority in missiles gave way to a clear American preponderance in most kinds of armament. Rocket development was further demonstrated by somewhat belated successes in putting astronauts into orbit. In the various theaters of foreign policy, both America's new might and its limitations were to be clearly shown.

Far more than its predecessors, the Kennedy administration turned its attention to the problems of the impoverished and unstable "Third World." The Peace Corps recruited young Americans for service in regions which needed their efforts, while, less successfully, the President tried to persuade Congress to provide massive aid for struggling economies. A special effort to promote unity, economic development and nonrevolutionary social change in Latin America was given the name of the "Alliance for Progress." Though only the barest beginning was made in the social and economic goals of the Alliance, goodwill was increased. Willingness to tolerate diversity and neutrality led to some other successes, especially in relations with African states. A Chinese attack on Indian borders in 1962 led India to turn a friendlier face toward America.

One of America's closest neighbors, Cuba, remained uncompromisingly hostile. In April, 1961, Kennedy reluctantly acquiesced in a project developed under the Eisenhower Administration for backing an invasion by anti-Castro exiles, recruited and trained secretly with American help. Misled as to the extent of support likely in Cuba, the administration provided logistical assistance but refused decisive military help. The resulting humiliating defeat increased Kennedy's suspicion of military adventure and expert military advice. On the other hand it raised the hopes of Cuba's Soviet ally for an easy success.

The truculent side of Khrushchev's changeable policy was shown at the West's most vulnerable point, Berlin. In a meeting with Kennedy in Vienna in June, 1961, Khrushchev refused to give up his threat to negotiate a treaty with East Germany which would have the effect of ending the occupation rights of the Western Allies. Kennedy let it be known that the defense of Berlin was an American commitment even to the extent of nuclear war. In August, 1961, Communist forces built a wall physically dividing the city in half, and preventing the escape of East Germans to the West.

In the opinion of Kennedy and his key advisers, an effort for a clearer victory in Berlin was one major reason for Khrushchev's next major challenge to America, which led the world nearer to major war than it had been since 1945. In August, 1962, American reconnaissance planes reported that the Soviet Union, contrary to repeated and specific assurances, was building in Cuba sites for offensive missiles which would be capable of striking the United States with nuclear warheads. Probably intended for bluff rather than actual use, these weapons, once operational, would have seriously changed the balance of power.

In a series of tense meetings the President and his advisers debated various responses ranging from pacific to belligerent. Characteristically Kennedy chose neither extreme. On the one hand, the administration was unwilling to propose, under pressure, the reciprocal withdrawal of Russian missiles from Cuba and American missiles from Italy and Turkey. (Actually, the latter bases, rated obsolete, were soon quietly withdrawn; missile-carrying submarines were regarded as less vulnerable.) On the other hand, Kennedy also rejected an immediate though limited airstrike recommended by his military advisers and others.

Instead he announced that he had ordered American warships to stop and search vessels coming to Cuba which might contain offensive weapons. In case this proved insufficient, he ordered military concentrations preparatory to possible invasion of the island, which might mean a direct clash with Russian personnel at missile bases.

To Khrushchev, Kennedy offered a pledge not to invade Cuba if Russian offensive weapons were withdrawn under inspection. To the world's relief, Khrushchev accepted Kennedy's terms. Russian ships heading for Cuba with missiles aboard were turned around and missiles already present were removed under American aerial surveillance. Gratifyingly, both the Organization of American States and America's European allies backed Kennedy's action. For the moment, it seemed as though American boldness, together with Russian realism, had produced not only an American victory but a better chance for peace. Refraining from any tendency to gloat over its success, the Kennedy administration increasingly stressed the advantages, to both sides, of Soviet-American disengagement.

The most urgent peaceful task was to end the threat of nuclear annihilation. In 1958, as part of the last rapprochement, both great powers had suspended nuclear testing pending disarmament talks. In the fall of 1961 the Soviet Union resumed it, exploding the largest bombs yet, and America felt it necessary to follow suit. In 1963, however, a complex and determined American diplomatic effort produced a treaty banning atmospheric, though not underground tests. Ratified by the Senate despite conservative fears, this treaty was signed by Russia, the United States, Britain, and many other countries, not including either France or China. Further measures of relaxation were promised, and in October the United States agreed to a large sale of wheat to the Soviet Union.

These important if limited foreign policy successes failed to end the world's tensions, which showed themselves in the most acute form in Southeast Asia, apparently a remote and peripheral concern of the United States and yet, the very place where the United States had challenged a potential enemy in 1941. In Laos, where neither Communists nor anti-Communists seemed fiercely determined, Kennedy abandoned Eisenhower's highly unsuccessful support of a right-wing faction for a policy, approved by the Soviet Union, of supporting a tripartite coalition. In Vietnam, however, even such a partial and unstable compromise was impossible.

In South Vietnam, the Eisenhower Administration had given diplomatic and military assistance to the relatively vigorous, though unpopular and dictatorial government of Ngo Dinh Diem, whose support came mainly from the landlords and the Catholic minority, swollen by refugees from the Communist North. In 1960 insurgents, led by the

Communist guerrillas who had fought France, formed the National Liberation Front (called by its opponents the Viet Cong) and North Vietnam announced its support of their cause. Unwilling to see the Communists win, the Kennedy administration increased American military aid to Diem. By 1962 progovernment officials were being assassinated by the Viet Cong, villagers were being removed to military hamlets by the government, guerrillas were being infiltrated from the North, and helicopters manned by American military "advisers" were firing on insurgents. In 1963 the American public suddenly began to realize that the United States had become involved in a peculiarly brutal war which her side was not winning. Following rebellion by the large and militant Buddhist faction against the South Vietnamese government, the United States withdrew its support and in November Diem was assassinated and his government fell, giving place to a series of governments which were neither more successful nor much more popular than his. The dilemma for American policy epitomized a question long awaiting answer: what should be done in the case of a Communist insurrection with considerable popular support, against a weak and unpopular government, in a militarily unpromising terrain?

Kennedy was not to decide this question, and there are indications both that he found the prospect of American defeat unacceptable, and that he thought further American commitment of troops to a failing cause a mistake. In the fall of 1963, his administration seemed to be characterized by great promise, resting on a limited record of solid accomplishment against odds. The Democrats had held their slim lead in the congressional elections of 1962, and the President's staff was planning confidently for his reelection. An increased margin of victory would, they thought, bring further advances against poverty at home and the threat of war abroad. On November 22, 1963, the President was shot dead in Dallas, Texas. This event, almost as traumatic as the death of Lincoln, seemed to bring to the surface all the shortcomings of American civilization.

THE GREAT SOCIETY

Nobody could have presented a greater contrast to the cool, rational, slightly aloof Kennedy than his successor, Lyndon B. Johnson. Tense, ambitious, hard-driving, gregarious, and earthy, Johnson had risen to wealth and political power through the hard school of Texas politics. His enemies considered him unscrupulous and coarse. In the opening days of his administration, however, most Americans were reassured by his emphasis on familiar programs of domestic reform. Modeling his approach on that of Franklin Roosevelt, clearly concentrating on domestic affairs and particularly on the problems of poverty, Johnson made clear his intent to build a new and workable consensus, the first since New Deal days. While courting business and Congress, the President hoped to retain the support of Kennedy liberals. The administration's brightest hope was that the first wholly Southern president since the Civil War could reconcile the South to the advancement of the Negro. Committing himself to this cause more eloquently than to any other, Johnson succeeded in pushing through in 1964 Kennedy's Civil Rights bill, which included further support for Negroes in voting rights, education, job opportunities, and above all, public accommodations. A further massive tax reduction gave rise to record economic advance. The Economic Opportunities Act spelled out Kennedy's proposal for a "War on Poverty" in terms of job training, grants to cities, and other measures. As the election of 1964 approached, Johnson gave the impression of masterful success.

Conservative Republicans, restive since New Deal days with moderate candidates of the Eisenhower variety, nominated Senator Barry Goldwater of Arizona in a convention whose highly organized antiliberal fervor alarmed many Republican liberals. Goldwater, a personally attractive and forthright man, had at various times proposed such measures as sale of the Tennessee Valley Authority, repeal of the Income Tax Amendment, and making social security voluntary. In the campaign he seemed to suggest that local military commanders be allowed to make independent decisions concerning the use of tactical atomic weapons. To cheering audiences, Goldwater denounced big government, the rising crime rate, and declining morals. The President campaigned on his record, presented as a reassuring combination of reform at home and steadfast, moderate resistance to aggression abroad. In the biggest landslide since 1936, Johnson carried all but six states.

With the Democratic majorities in Congress handsomely increased, it seemed that the power of the conservative Republican-Southern Democrat coalition had been broken for the first time since 1938. Unlike Truman or Kennedy, Johnson was able to push through a coordinated reform program. Laws passed in 1965 and 1966, too many even to list, centered around four crucial fronts. Negro equality was promoted by a stricter voting rights act and other measures. (Johnson also appointed the first Negro cabinet member and the first Negro Supreme Court Justice.) Kennedy's bill for medical care for the aged was successfully pushed through, breaking a long taboo against federal support of health care. Ancient sectarian opposition to federal aid to education was also overcome, and the President, largely self-educated, seemed to take special pride in bills to assist schooling at all levels. Finally, the complex problem of urban poverty was further attacked through such innovations as rent subsidies and demonstration cities. Not unjustly, the President claimed the most spectacular legislative record since Franklin Roosevelt's famous "hundred days" in 1933.

THE AGONY OF POWER

Despite these achievements, it was apparent by the middle of the decade that America, potentially a great society, was actually a divided and confused one. In both foreign and domestic affairs, the Johnson administration inherited the unsolved problems and shifting balances of the last decades. In both spheres, old policies were pushed to new lengths. In both, increased commitments seemed, by 1965 or 1966, to bring increased frustration.

The disintegration of the two great alliances continued to offer a strange mixture of menace and opportunity. By 1966 de Gaulle had announced France's withdrawal from the NATO military organization. China, at last a nuclear power but torn by domestic turmoil, was denouncing Russian revisionism almost as bitterly as she attacked American imperialism. And indeed the two greatest powers, Russia and the United States, seemed to be continuing their gingerly rapprochement. Johnson was able, in the wake of Kennedy's test-ban treaty, to push through a dubious Congress a consular treaty and finally, in 1968, to get Russian agreement to a treaty against the further spread of nuclear weapons.

To both great powers, the restless and impoverished Third World seemed to present impossible problems. The Alliance for Progress failed to solve Latin America's economic or political problems and in one instance the President reverted to older methods. In the Dominican Republic, where the liberal government was overthrown by a military coup in 1963, a revolt against the new military regime threatened civil war in 1965. Stating reasons ranging from protection of American lives to preventing a triumph of Castroism, Johnson sent 22,000 troops to the island. Fortunately a compromise among contending factions eventually produced a regime with some claim to legitimacy. Yet the Johnson action was denounced as high-handed both in Latin America and by liberals at home.

The problems of power were most tragically illustrated, however, in the bloody, baffling struggle in Vietnam. Coming to power in the aftermath of Diem's fall, with the South Vietnamese government weak, the NLF increasingly formidable, and North Vietnamese involvement increasing, Johnson in effect had only two possible courses: to increase the American effort or to accept an unfavorable solution. Like many American leaders before him, he seemed at first to hesitate to embrace either of these disagreeable alternatives. In retrospect, however, it seems clear that Johnson, however reluctant to be a war president, never contemplated the alternative of accepting real defeat.

In August, 1964, a U.S. destroyer cruising in the Tonkin Gulf in an area of recent South Vietnamese naval action, was attacked once, and according to contested evidence twice, by North Korean torpedo boats. Ordering retaliatory action, the administration requested and got from Congress authorization for whatever further military action might prove necessary to repel attacks on American forces or provide assistance to Southeast Asian states who requested it. During the campaign and after, Johnson emphasized the limited character of the reprisals taken. The Tonkin Gulf resolution provided, however, crucial justification for more drastic actions taken later. In February, 1965, an attack on an American barracks was made the occasion for retaliatory raids on North Vietnam. Gradually the aerial offensive against the North shifted from transport to factories and fuel dumps and included buildings in the center of large cities. At the same time the raids were defended less in terms of specific reprisals and more as part of an effort to stop troop infiltration into the South, or to force North Vietnam to negotiate by showing that victory was impossible. Partly in support of the air offensive, American ground troops were increased until, by 1968, they reached one-half million men engaged in an effort to search for guerrillas and destroy them throughout the country.

By 1967 it was clear that this massive effort was very far from successful. The South Vietnamese government, despite American efforts to broaden its base, was opposed by large parts of the population. Not only was the infiltration of Northern troops increasing, but American efforts to secure parts of the country and there promote agrarian reform were failing. Repeated and complex suggestions of negotiation failed to produce plausible compromise terms. To the North Vietnamese, the struggle in the South was part of a civil war in which the United States had no right to intervene. To the defenders of American policy, the war was the defense of an independent nation. Between these two premises, compromise proved impossible.

At home, as the casualties mounted (25,000 Americans had died in Vietnam by 1968) and the end seemed no nearer, the war was denounced more widely and more intensely than any American war since 1865. Opponents included powerful senators, much of the press, large sections of the liberal clergy, and a large number of fervent and articulate young people. On the left of the antiwar movement, some critics insisted that the Vietnam war was part of a long pattern of American aggression, that the administration had no intention of negotiating and desired permanent bases, and that the outcome would be war with China and possibly Russia. More restrained critics, some of whom by no means accepted all or even any of these statements, believed the war impossible to win, and incompatible either with the needs of domestic policy or the effort for worldwide stability. Still others were appalled by the very heavy bombing of both halves of Vietnam (by 1968 America had dropped a greater tonnage of bombs on Vietnam than had been dropped on Europe and Asia together in World War II), by the use of napalm and fragmentation bombs, by the forcible relocation of villages, and by the chemical destruction of crops and forests. The minimum demands of the growing antiwar movement were the end of bombing in the North, recognition that the NLF must play a part in the government of the South, and the scaling down of operations. Defenders of the administration, while insisting that they were willing to negotiate and denying any intention of carrying the war to the North, insisted that South Vietnam must be defended. Often using phrases which had been familiar for a generation, they insisted that Communist success in Vietnam would mean the spread of Communist power through Southeast Asia, the collapse of American efforts everywhere to prevent the expansion of communism, especially through Chinese-style guerrilla wars, and, immediately, bloody reprisals against government supporters in South Vietnam.

A TIME OF TROUBLES, 1966–1968

By 1967 it was apparent that the unsuccessful war in Vietnam was only one of a number of desperate and divisive problems facing the United States. Not one was new, though all were presented in newly acute form.

The most serious disaffection was that of the black minority. While both civil rights progress and violent resistance to it continued in the South, a series of cataclysmic events turned the nation's attention to the Northern Negro ghettoes. In August, 1965, a riot in Watts, a Negro section of Los Angeles, resulted in 34 deaths and 30 hours of looting and arson. For the next three years scenes of burning buildings, helmeted troops, and even tanks moving down city streets became almost commonplace on American television screens. The worst disturbances took place in Newark (23 killed) and Detroit (43 killed) in July of 1967, but few major cities escaped violence altogether. Immediate origins differed, usually involving some real or fancied action by police: the shooting of a fleeing petty criminal, or even the arrest of a Negro. Nearly always firebombs and sniping (whose incidence was usually exaggerated) were answered by drastic police action. As the smoke cleared, it always became evident that the dead and injured were mostly Negroes, and that property destroyed was in Negro slums.

In 1967 President Johnson appointed a commission, apparently of rather conservative cast, to investigate these disturbances, and early in 1968 the commission made a startling report. The underlying cause of the riots, it flatly declared, was white racism resulting in pervasive discrimination. In the ghettoes, unemployment, inadequate and humiliating welfare systems, and long experience of police hostility had resulted in complete frustration. To counter the threat of a completely and permanently divided society, the commission called for an unprecedented national commitment to a complex series of remedies, including further measures of education, employment and housing; and a shift from the welfare system to income support.

Many hostile and genuinely frightened whites, on the other hand—and especially those who lived on the outskirts of the black ghettoes—demanded instead new measures of suppression. Though most Negroes, according to the polls, still believed in integration, a growing minority of militants subscribed to the new slogan of Black Power, which could mean anything from bloc voting and separate economic development to outright separatism. In a few central cities, relations between police and black militants threatened to approach the level of civil war, and suburban housewives took up pistol practice in preparation for its spread. On April 4, 1968, Martin Luther King, the leading Negro advocate of nonviolence, was murdered by a white man in Memphis, Tennessee. The immediate results of this tragic event included a great outpouring of expressions of grief and guilt, riots in 125 cities including Washington, D.C., and the passage of a civil rights bill including an open-housing provision. The President decided, however, that the national mood made it inadvisable to appeal for the kind of comprehensive program called for by his commission.

A very different kind of disaffection which drew almost equal attention was that of certain articulate sections of youth. In the summer of 1964, a number of Northern university students had gone to Mississippi to take a militant part in the civil rights movement. The violence they encountered inevitably led to a loss of respect for all authority, and the success of nonviolent methods suggested new kinds of power. The University of California at Berkeley, in 1964, was the scene of the first major student sit-in, which grew out of an argument over limits on student on-campus political activity. Almost completely successful in securing its immediate objectives in Berkeley, the new student movement spread rapidly to other campuses throughout the country. Shifting objectives (free speech, student participation in control of university education, increased numbers of black students and faculty) were accompanied by increasingly militant tactics, sometimes resulting in violent clashes with police. More and more, grievances seemed to center on the Vietnam war, regarded by many articulate young people as an American aggression. Divided in their emotions about all these causes, most Americans at least understood their meaning. Far more baffling was a new youth ideology, partly shared with the still more militant students of Europe and Asia, far transcending politics, often expressed in bizarre gestures, and centering its attack on the frustrations inherent in all highly organized societies. Still more alarming than even the most extreme militance was its polar opposite, a widespread tendency toward withdrawal and passivity, often symbolized by a cult of drugs. Much of the public, however, concentrated its attention on such dramatic events as the clash between students and police which led to the temporary closing of Columbia University in the spring of 1968.

Riots in the ghettoes, demonstrations on the campuses, and a major rise in nonpolitical crime (its dimensions disputed but its reality undeniable) tightened the tensions of another disaffected minority: the right wing. Fears of social and moral breakdown, seen by some as part of a departure from traditional religious and political standards, led to a crescendo of demands for the restoration of "law and order," often seen mainly in terms of Draconian severity.

Fears and frustrations at home seemed to be accompanied by new dangers abroad. In February, 1968, the Viet Cong and North Vietnamese launched an offensive which produced heavy fighting and widespread destruction in the major South Vietnamese cities, including Saigon. As it became apparent that four years of increased American commitment had not made it possible even to secure the allied capital, and as Communist attacks and American counter measures completed the destruction of some "friendly" towns, the peace movement gained new recruits and overt demands for further military commitment seemed almost to disappear. Yet it was possible, as some observers pointed out, to see this offensive as a major, even a decisive defeat for the Communists. The people of South Vietnam did not, as expected, rally to their support, nor did the Saigon government collapse, and the losses of the attackers were of a size not long to be borne.

In June, 1967, the eruption of war between Israel and the Arabs threatened to produce another East-West confrontation, with Moscow supporting the attack on a country to which America was committed. A smashing Israeli victory prevented immediate disaster, but American powerlessness in this crisis seemed to demonstrate that the nation could not afford to commit its principal effort to the peripheral, frustrating war in Vietnam. In January, 1968, the American reconnaissance ship Pueblo was captured by North Koreans off the Korean coast.

Militant counteraction, demanded by a few, would have risked the opening of still another front.

So far, surprisingly enough, relations between Moscow and Washington had continued ever since the Eisenhower administration to combine conventional verbal hostility with some minimum measure of actual cooperation. In August, Soviet forces suddenly invaded Czechoslovakia, whose Communist government had been edging toward political and intellectual freedom, and the Soviet government forced Prague to reverse its program of reform. In the wake of this event, either a revival of great-power combination or a turn towards isolationism seemed possible. What was clear was that new priorities were needed: the foreign policy, which had been dominant since 1947, of limited response to Communist pressure anywhere in the world, was increasingly difficult to defend.

In times of crisis, Americans had usually turned to the White House, but this time the presidency itself seemed to be suffering a crisis of authority. Despite Lyndon Johnson's reputation as a political wizard, his popularity polls declined sporadically from a high 80 percent to a disastrous 35 percent in the fall of 1968. In 1966, Democratic election losses had reinstated the conservative Republican-Southern Democrat coalition in power in Congress. The new realities were shown by drastic cuts in foreign aid and in funds for such administration social programs as medicare and open housing. By the time of the 1968 presidential campaign, presidential appointments (including that of a new Chief Justice) were being rejected and even the treaty for stopping the spread of nuclear weapons was stalled in the Senate.

Thus the Johnson administration, which had brought to fruition many of the hopes of the New Deal and pushed to new lengths the foreign policy of resistance to communism, was ending in frustration on both fronts. Consensus had become deep division, and even the spectacular and unparalleled Johnson prosperity was being threatened by a sharp upturn in prices. With relief as well as trepidation, the people turned to the traditional electoral remedy.

A CHANGE OF LEADERSHIP

Despite his lost prestige, most people took it for granted that the President could command the nomination of his own party and that this would make him a formidable contender against Richard Nixon, the probable Republican nominee. This assumption was challenged first by Senator Eugene McCarthy of Minnesota who, sharply attacking the President's Vietnam policy, got 42 percent of the Democratic vote in the New Hampshire primary. A few days later, Robert Kennedy, already an outspoken critic of the war, announced his own candidacy on a program of opposition to the war and commitment to a drastic attack on ghetto poverty. The two antiwar candidates neatly divided the potential Democratic opposition. While McCarthy's courage and low-key style drew the ardent support of many students and intellectuals, Kennedy's name and record drew equally fervent crowds in Negro and other minority centers, and professional Democratic political leaders watched him with rapidly increasing interest.

The expected Democratic showdown, however, never materialized. Sensing the futility of his own candidacy, an increasingly unpopular Lyndon Johnson announced on March 31 a halt in the bombing of North Vietnam, called for a negotiated settlement, and declared he would not seek reelection. In June, Robert Kennedy, during a celebration of his important but narrow victory over McCarthy in the California primary, was murdered by an obscure assassin. Kennedy's death dealt a staggering blow to the party's antiwar forces. In August, Vice President Hubert Humphrey, a domestic liberal and staunch supporter of Johnson's war policies, easily defeated McCarthy on the first ballot for the Democratic nomination. In the streets outside the convention hall, angry and frustrated antiwar demonstrators, a few of whom hoped to disrupt the proceedings within, were clubbed by police while the world watched. Reflecting the growing polarization of American society, many citizens expressed shock and outrage at police overreaction, while many others applauded police containment of an unruly and unwashed mob of dissidents. Few could doubt, however, that the noisy melee contrasted sharply with the well-managed Republican convention in July. Amid apparent order and restraint, the GOP in Miami passed over such early contenders as George Romney, Nelson Rockefeller, and Ronald Reagan to nominate Richard Nixon and his running mate, Spiro T. Agnew, an obscure border state conservative favorite of the party's increasingly vital southern wing.

During the ensuing months, Nixon and Humphrey, neither of them a popular figure nor an eloquent speaker, engaged in a colorless campaign of partisanship and personality. Both candidates stressed "law and order" and supported the negotiations then proceeding unproductively with the North Vietnamese in Paris. Humphrey belatedly tried to dissociate himself from Johnson's war policies and Nixon spoke vaguely of a "secret plan" to end the fighting. But in the end, Humphrey had little choice but to run on the record of a discredited administration and Nixon fell back on his customary strategy of attacking his opponent without offering concrete proposals of his own. Faced with seemingly unattractive alternatives, many mainstream voters picked the least objectionable candidate. But a substantial body of alienated citizens elected to leave the two-party system. The articulate but impotent far-left minority either boycotted the election or cast protest ballots for radical candidates; the disaffected right, far more formidable, turned to American Independent party candidate George C. Wallace, a former Alabama governor and staunch segregationist. Advocating drastic action against black militants and student radicals, and saturation bombing of North Vietnam, Wallace and his ticket mate, retired Air Force General Curtis E. LeMay, developed remarkable strength outside the South, particularly among blue-collar workers and noncollege youth. Although he carried only five southern states, Wallace polled a larger percentage (13.5 percent) of the total vote than any third party candidate since 1912. The balloting was unusually close between the major party candidates. Humphrey, struggling vainly to shore up the crumbling Democratic coalition, commanded the Eastern cities and the minorities, especially Negroes. But he lost the upper South and the election to Nixon, who swept the traditionally Republican strongholds of the Middle and Far West. Yet despite the shattering of the Johnson consensus of 1964 and an apparent shift to the right, there was little cause for jubilation in the GOP. By election day, early predictions of an easy Republican triumph had eroded to a hairline victory. Nixon's share (43.4 percent) of the total popular vote was smaller than any president since Woodrow Wilson. For the first time since Zachary Taylor in 1848 a newly elected President faced an opposition Congress. Indisputably, a nation divided by war and tormented by fear of violence and race had repudiated the party in power. But the incoming administration faced seemingly insurmountable domestic and foreign problems without a popular mandate and without congressional support.

FOR FURTHER READING:

William L. O'Neill, *Coming Apart* (1971), is a splendid "informal" history of the 1960s. Two first-rate books by members of Kennedy's staff are A. M. Schlesinger, Jr., *A Thousand Days* (1965)*, and T. C. Sorenson, *Kennedy* (1965)*. Tom Wicker, *JFK and LBJ* (1968), offers balanced assessments of both presidents. Alfred Steinberg, *Sam Johnson's Boy* (1968), is an informative, hostile biography of President Johnson; while Hugh Sidey, *A Very Personal Presidency* (1968) is a penetrating critical essay on Johnson's presidential style. Johnson guardedly speaks for himself in *The Vantage Point* (1971)*. Rowland Evans and Robert Novak, *Lyndon B. Johnson* (1966) and Eric F.

---

* Available in paperback edition.

Goldman, *The Tragedy of Lyndon Johnson* (1968), are highly suggestive assessments. Marvin E. Gettleman and David Mermelstein, eds., *The Great Society Reader* (1967) is useful, but partisan. Analyses of the Johnson-Goldwater and Nixon-Humphrey races include Theodore H. White's *The Making of the President* studies for 1964 and 1968 (1965, 1969), and Lewis Chester, et al., *An American Melodrama: The Presidential Campaign of 1968* (1969). The judicial activism of the Supreme Court is assessed by John D. Weaver, *Warren: The Man, the Court, the Era* (1967); while Victor Navasky has dissected *Kennedy Justice* (1971). Benjamin Muse portrays *The American Negro Revolution* (1968); and Malcolm X has written a moving *Autobiography* (1966)*. Kirkpatrick Sale sympathetically analyzes *SDS* (1973) and Paul Jacobs and Saul Landau offer a collection of essays and documents on the New Left in *The New Radicals* (1966)*. Theodore Roszak charts the *Making of a Counter Culture* (1969)*. One chilling Cold War drama is presented in Elie Abel, *The Missile Crisis* (1966), and Robert F. Kennedy, *Thirteen Days* (1969). Perhaps the best overview of the Vietnam quagmire is Chester L. Cooper, *The Lost Crusade* (1970). Other highly suggestive statements include: Bernard Fall, *Two Vietnams,* 2nd ed. rev. (1967); J. William Fulbright, ed., *The Vietnam Hearings* (1966); David Halberstam, *The Best and the Brightest* (1972); Neil Sheehan, ed., *The Pentagon Papers* (1971); and Francis Fitzgerald, *Fire in the Lake* (1972).

THE NIXON YEARS

	Domestic	Southeast Asia	Other Foreign
1969	January Nixon inaugurated. June Burger replaces Warren as Chief Justice. August Family Assistance Plan proposed. October Vietnam mobilization demonstration.	Spring Secret U.S. bombing of Cambodia begins. April Peak U.S. troop strength in Vietnam. August Phased troop withdrawal begins.	July Nixon Doctrine proposes reduced American presence in Asia.
1970	May Campus disorders; Kent State killings. November Midterm elections; modest Democratic gains. June Pentagon Papers leaked to press.	April U.S. and ARVN force invade Cambodia.	
1971	January Nixon proclaims New American Revolution. August New Economic Policy announced; 90-day wage and price freeze imposed. November Phase II economic plan activated.	January–March U.S. supports ARVN incursion into Laos.	October Red China admitted to UN with U.S. support. August Ping pong diplomacy with Red China. December First devaluation of dollar.
1972	May Wallace assassination attempt. June Watergate burglary. October Revenue sharing bill enacted. November Nixon reelection landslide.	Spring Haiphong harbor mined; Hanoi bombed. October Kissinger announces "peace is at hand." December Renewed bombing of North Vietnam.	February Nixon's Peking summit. May Nixon's Moscow summit; SALT I.
1973	May–August Senate Watergate hearings. October Agnew resigns; Nixon fires Special Prosecutor; agrees to surrender tapes.	January Paris accords end U.S. involvement in Vietnam. August Bombing of Cambodia halted.	September Kissinger becomes Secretary of State. October Arab-Israeli War.

New Directions

32

A veteran of both houses of Congress, a two-term vice president well versed in the system and process of American politics, a widely traveled expert in foreign affairs, Richard Milhous Nixon was indisputably well qualified for the presidency. Although he was the most conservative occupant of the White House since Herbert Hoover, he proved, nevertheless, to be a remarkably flexible, pragmatic, and strong chief executive. Breaking with traditional Republican policy, he moved toward disengagement from Indochina, pursued détente with the Communist powers of Europe and Asia, advocated briefly a guaranteed annual income, and experimented reluctantly with Keynesian economics. Such bold departures inevitably angered his party's right wing, but conservatives were generally pleased with most Nixon policies. A tireless spokesman for such traditional values as self-reliance and hard work, a harsh critic of judicial activism and "the permissive society," Nixon took a tough stand on "law and order," endeavored to remake the Supreme Court in his own conservative image, and reversed his Democratic predecessors' policy of executive engagement in the civil rights struggle. Tentatively at first, then with growing confidence following his landslide election to a second term, he preached the doctrine of the "New Federalism" and appropriated the radical slogan "power to the people" in order to reverse the twentieth-century trend toward big government. The success of his efforts, however, were threatened early in his second term by the opposition of a Democratic Congress and a scandal of unparalleled dimensions that imperiled not only presidential programs but Nixon's hold on the office itself.

THE NEW FEDERALISM

Nixon's public personality and presidential style contrasted sharply with those of his post-World War II predecessors. He did not share

Harry Truman's identification with the common man and he lacked Dwight Eisenhower's affability and personal charm. He was unblessed by either John Kennedy's urbanity and wit or Lyndon Johnson's disarming folksiness. Usually reserved and formal, by nature reclusive, he was a political loner and one of the most aloof and isolated presidents in American history. Although he was undeniably the nation's leading sports fan and the self-styled apostle of Middle America, he was a politician strangely ill at ease with people. Suspicious of the news media, he rarely held press conferences; uncomfortable in the public eye, he maintained a low presidential profile and spent much of his time away from Washington and the demands of bureaucracy, press, and Congress. Intense and hard-working, he preferred to labor in the isolation of Camp David, Maryland, the presidential retreat, or in the privacy of his sun-washed villas in San Clemente, California and Key Biscayne, Florida. Generally concentrating on one large issue at a time, he made decisions alone or in the select company of a few trusted aides. Not an avid reader, he neither skimmed newspapers nor watched network television news programs. His major source of outside information was a daily news summary produced by members of his staff. He chose a predominantly conservative and reasonably competent but undistinguished cabinet and, with the exception of Attorney General John Mitchell, generally denied it access to the Oval Office. Although he delegated power and responsibility in enormous blocks, it fell not to the heads of the traditional executive departments but to an inner circle of highly trusted subordinates led by presidential assistants H. Robert Haldeman and John D. Ehrlichman. Derisively called the "Disneyland Mafia" and "The Germans," even by White House staffers, these political amateurs had few contacts with either party or Congress, and little knowledge of, or experience in, public affairs. In the end, it seemed apparent that their most conspicuous qualification was intense personal loyalty to the President. Jealously protective of his time and energies, they erected around him a "Berlin Wall" that was rarely penetrated even by cabinet members, top Republican officials, or congressional leaders. As one disgruntled speech writer observed late in Nixon's first term, the thirty-seventh President operated in a "soundproof, shockproof bubble."

Even before assuming office, Nixon revealed that foreign affairs would be his principal concern. "I've always thought this country could run itself domestically without a President," he said during the campaign. "All you need is a competent cabinet to run the country at home." True to his word, he gave international issues, particularly the war in Vietnam, top priority throughout his first term. But one other legacy of the Johnson administration, a runaway economy, required an enormous amount of presidential attention. Having promised the nation both "guns and butter," the Democratic President had refused to seek a tax increase to finance the rapidly escalating war in Southeast Asia. The result by 1968 was a raging inflation that threatened not only the value of the dollar, but the nation's role as a great power and the quality of life in the United States.

The Republican administration's response to this economic crisis was a cautious monetary and fiscal "game plan" that proved disastrously inadequate. By tightening the money supply and balancing the budget, the President and his advisers hoped to curb inflation without economic controls or even wage-price guidelines. Instead, inflation continued unabated, while unemployment rose sharply, the stock market sagged, and corporate profits fell. Taking note of the seemingly impossible—simultaneous recession and inflation—Democratic critics and outside economists labeled these policies "Nixonomics." Not until August, 1971, did the administration abandon its free market measures for a bolder "New Economic Policy." Then, proclaiming himself a Keynesian, the President briefly froze prices and wages, adopted budgetary deficits (the largest in peacetime history), and pursued a fitful course that moved from stringent controls, to voluntary restraints, to a second price freeze, and renewed controls. Thus, lurching from one policy to the next and back again in what one eminent economist called "schizoid economics," the administration failed to slow inflation or restore stability. Although a temporary respite in 1972 deprived the Democrats of an election issue, economic problems reached crisis proportions early in Nixon's second term. By mid-1973, as the President imposed his second price freeze in fifteen months and prepared to reinstitute stringent price controls, corporate profits and wages were soaring, the stock market was in a prolonged slump, and consumer costs, especially for food, were spiraling at a rate unequaled since the early post-World War II period. By that date, the administration had already twice devalued the dollar in a desperate attempt to offset mounting trade deficits by improving the competitive position of American goods on foreign markets.

In large part, the administration's erratic economic policies were rooted in the President's own stalwart republicanism. Despite his use of economic activism, he remained to the end a devoted free marketeer. That same traditional conservatism also placed him directly at odds with the liberal social programs of his Democratic predecessors. Although administration spokesmen periodically urged tough antistrike legislation and Nixon vetoed a minimum wage bill (1973) there was no serious threat to New Deal programs. But early in his first term it was clear that Nixon viewed many Great Society programs as both unwise and unworkable.

When the democratically controlled Ninety-first Congress convened, the Republican administration offered it broad policy aims rather than specific programs. In good Republican fashion, the President proposed to decentralize authority over federal programs and emphasized local solutions for local problems. But acting upon the advice of Daniel Patrick Moynihan, his urban affairs adviser, he delayed immediate action. A liberal Democrat who served as Assistant Secretary of Labor under both Kennedy and Johnson, Moynihan argued that a wholesale dismantlement of the Great Society would further divide a nation already torn by an unpopular war, a rising crime rate, and domestic unrest. Lacking a program of his own and accepting momentarily the argument for continuity, Nixon gave the Great Society a reprieve. To the astonishment of critics and supporters alike, bills authorizing the extension of Johnson's antipoverty programs, including such favorite conservative targets as Job Corps and Model Cities, won presidential support and were enacted by Congress.

The President sent additional shock waves through his party's right wing in August, 1969, when in a television address he unveiled his Family Assistance Payments plan to provide every American family with a guaranteed annual income of at least $1,600. Although cloaked in conservative rhetoric, FAP was a remarkably liberal scheme developed largely by Moynihan. Months later, the former Harvard professor's influence was felt once again when Nixon appealed for "a decade of government reform such as this nation has not witnessed in half a century." Embracing reform as his "watchword," the President urged congressional consideration of tax and welfare reforms, a full-employment budget, and new federal initiatives against hunger and environmental decay. In his State of the Union message in January, 1971, he proclaimed the advent of a "New American Revolution . . . as profound, as far-reaching, as exciting as that first revolution 200 years ago."

But it was not revolution but counterrevolution that Nixon seemed to favor. Clearly he would not be Moynihan's Disraeli, implementing domestic programs that even liberals dared not touch. Whatever his watchword, his personal instincts and political philosophy favored retrenchment and consolidation, not innovation and reform. He signed a limited Tax Reform Act of 1969, but he resisted a modest and successful congressional effort to reduce the oil depletion allowance. He created the Environmental Protection Agency and signed the Water Quality Improvement Act (1970), but administration policies, particularly its support of the supersonic transport and the Alaskan pipeline, frequently enraged environmentalists both in and out of Congress. Moreover, in the face of mounting conservative opposition, he quietly dropped FAP and his proposal for a modest national health program.

Indeed, at midpassage, the administration's first-term course was firmly fixed. Having drifted uncertainly at first, it now moved with growing confidence away from the "New American Revolution" in the direction of the "New Federalism."

Offered early in 1970, as a framework for the administration's policies, the "New Federalism" promised "to reverse the flow of power and resources from the states and communities to Washington." To begin the process, the White House proposed the "sharing" of federal revenues with city, county, and state governments. Congressional leaders, fearing a dilution of their powers to control the federal purse, hesitated at first. But in October, 1972, under heavy pressure from the administration, Congress enacted a measure to return to local governments over a five-year period $30.2 billion in federal revenues. As he signed the bill at a ceremony in front of Philadelphia's Independence Hall, a deeply satisfied President declared that with this enactment the New Federalism began the "renewal" of the federal system. The nation's financially hard-pressed city governments, however, quickly learned to their dismay that revenue sharing was not a windfall. In his budget proposals for fiscal 1974, a frugal Republican chief executive moved to slash previously budgeted federal grants for social services and community development.

But well before he offered his austerity budget of 1974, Nixon was already battling congressional spending. To cut federal expenditures and reduce federal commitments he spent much of his first-term domestic energy beating back appropriation bills for social programs. When he failed he used his veto (nineteen times during the Ninety-second Congress alone); and when his vetoes were overridden, he simply refused to spend congressionally authorized funds. Nevertheless, as his first term ended, Richard Nixon continued to preside over a social service state. During four years of his leadership, the nation's food stamp program more than quadrupled; loans to small businesses more than tripled; subsidies for the arts and low-cost housing grew markedly; and new service agencies, including the Office of Child Development and the Office of Consumer Affairs, proliferated.

The contours of the administration's conservatism although emerging slowly in legislative areas, were immediately apparent in areas largely outside congressional control. Fulfilling a campaign promise to appoint a no-nonsense attorney general, Nixon named John Mitchell, his campaign manager and former law partner, to head the Department of Justice. Gruff and taciturn, Mitchell served until his resignation in 1972 (to manage Nixon's reelection campaign) as the stern symbol of the administration's unwavering devotion to "law and order." With one eye fixed on the nation's soaring crime rate and another on the mood of the electorate (particularly on Wallace's 13 percent), he sponsored a controversial "no-knock" crime law for predominantly black Washington, D.C.; advocated preventive detention and stop-and-frisk laws; claimed an unrestricted government right to eavesdrop electronically on suspected security risks; dealt harshly with antiwar demonstrators; and prosecuted a motley body of radicals and political dissidents on charges ranging from conspiracy to espionage. Although the Supreme Court ruled against unrestricted electronic surveillance and civil libertarians objected to the "no-knock" statute and the apparent harassment of political dissenters, many Americans, perhaps most, believed that severe measures were required to stem the rising incidence of criminal violence and civil disorder.

Fear of crime was but one facet of a pervasive national malaise that had emerged gradually in the late 1960s as the nation's most salient political issue. However troubled by the stalemate in Vietnam, the American people seemed more deeply disturbed by such domestic ills as drug abuse, racial disorder, and violent protest. Identified originally as the Wallace "backlash" but later more accurately described as the "Social Issue," this widespread dysphoria portended, some analysts believed, a fundamental national political realignment. Indeed, White House strategists viewed the Social Issue as the cement for a majority Republican coalition of the unyoung, the unpoor, and the unblack. In the first test of that strategy, the midterm elections of 1970, the results were inconclusive. The administration's campaign to unseat the "Radical-Liberals" of the Democratic party produced some truly memorable vice presidential billingsgate (critics called Spiro T. Agnew's colorful epithets "Agnewisms") but not a Republican Congress. However much they disliked "scroungy student dissenters," "pusillanimous pussyfooters," "sniveling hand-wringers," and the "effete corps of impudent snobs," the voters themselves seemed as concerned with runaway inflation as with the Social Issue. On election day the GOP won two new seats in the Senate but lost a total of nine congressional seats and eleven governorships. Despite White House claims of a stunning victory, the Democrats remained firmly in control of both houses of Congress.

In the administration's grand design for a new Republican coalition the conservative white voters of the South were of central importance. Increasingly disenchanted by the liberal, "pro-Negro" policies of the national Democratic party, white southerners admired Nixon more than any president since World War II. He did not sweep the region in 1968, but he dominated the Upper South and without Wallace in the running, could easily have carried every southern state except Texas. Thus, mindful of the obligations of the past and not unaware of the possibilities of the future, the administration moved to absorb Wallace's strength by openly courting the troubled South.

The imperatives of this "Southern Strategy," of course, ran directly counter to Afro-American aspirations. Despite the race chauvinism of youthful black militants and a growing black emphasis on separate economic and cultural development, the vast majority of the nation's Negro minority still dreamed of assimilation in a colorblind society. Black fears were aroused by Nixon's blistering attacks on "forced integration" and "busing"; and widespread black skepticism met his preinaugural promise to do "more for the Negro than any President has ever done." Negroes expected the worst from this Republican administration and their suspicions were not altogether without foundation. In 1969, for the first time in modern civil rights history, the Justice Department sought court-ordered delays in southern desegregation. It relaxed government compliance standards and shifted the burden of civil rights enforcement to the courts. Perhaps most telling of all, it attempted, though without success, to block the extension of the most efficacious federal civil rights statute, the Voting Rights Act of 1965. Still there was no major rollback of Negro freedoms. The New Nationalism mirrored increasing white impatience with black demands for rapid social change. Yet during its dispensation, the achievements of the past remained secure and all but the most persistent vestiges of lily-white public education vanished from the South. Moreover, Nixon supported an act extending the life of the Civil Rights Commission and resisted southern pressures to restore federal tax exemptions for all-white private schools. His pledge to curb federal spending took precedence over his pledge to promote "black capitalism" through federal loans and subsidies. But in his Philadelphia Plan of 1970, he boldly exercised executive authority to impose racial quotas on traditionally all-white construction unions. These were modest achievements. Ironically, however, the administration's performance in the area of civil rights was stronger than either the President or his critics cared to admit.

In his judicial appointments Nixon broke more sharply with the policies of his immediate predecessors. Although he failed in two attempts to appoint conservative southerners with segregationist records to the Supreme Court, he filled four high-court vacancies with judicial conservatives. Joined by one and sometimes two of the other five justices, the Nixon appointees (perhaps only one of whom was a genuine "strict constructionist") were expected to reverse nearly two decades of Warren Court liberal activism. Once again, however, there was more continuity than seemed immediately apparent. The decisions of the reconstituted court neither expanded nor eroded basic civil liberties and rights. Contrary to White House wishes it ruled in favor of abortion and against state aid to parochial education. Its principal departures from earlier high court rulings came in a tougher attitude toward criminals and pornography.

TOWARD A GENERATION OF PEACE

The caution and ambivalence that so often marked Nixon's domestic policies found no parallel in his bold handling of international affairs. Promising a "full generation of peace" through negotiation, not confrontation, he moved quickly to "normalize" relations with the Peoples' Republic of China and the Soviet Union. In both cases, détente was complicated by the President's reputation as an intractable cold warrior. A vigorous Red-hunter during his congressional career, he had often found his political opponents "soft" on communism. As Vice President, he engaged Khrushchev in "kitchen debates" in Moscow and Camp David, and in 1954 urged massive air strikes in defense of beleaguered French forces at Dienbienphu. Yet, though initially viewed by Kremlin leaders as the most belligerent in a long line of anti-Communist presidents, he proved more sophisticated and flexible than any of his post-World War II predecessors in his dealings with Communist nations. Placing ideology aside, he pursued a policy of realism based on the ancient maxim that nations have no permanent friends or enemies, only permanent interests. In this exercise in *Realpolitik*, Nixon was to an extraordinary degree his own Secretary of State. He was assisted at every turn, however, by Henry Kissinger, a former Harvard professor, director of the National Security Council, and perhaps the most remarkable foreign policy adviser ever to serve the White House. Kissinger did not formally become head of the Department of State until 1973, but he was in fact the nation's chief diplomat throughout the first term.

The most spectacular examples of the new realism in American diplomacy came in 1972. In February of that year, while a nation of television viewers watched via satellite, the President journeyed to Peking to lay the groundwork for a resumption of Sino-American relations. Although denied recognition by the United States and its western allies since the rise to dominance of Mao Tse-tung in 1949, mainland China was a major power armed with nuclear weapons and populated by one-fifth of the world's people. In 1971, the Peoples' Republic was admitted to the United Nations with American support, and over ineffectual American opposition Chiang Kai-shek's Nationalist regime was ousted. In a second internationally televised summit meeting, Nixon became the first president ever to set foot on Soviet soil when he conferred in Moscow in May, 1972, with Soviet party leader Leonid Brezhnev. A year later, a second Nixon-Brezhnev meeting occurred in Washington amid rising hopes of a permanent "thaw" in the Cold War. Seasoned diplomatic observers cautioned that other summits had been followed by deteriorating relations, and ultraconservatives, Vice President Agnew among them, were alarmed by the open camaraderie between the nation's chief executive and the leaders of its postwar adversaries. But the President declared that "1972 has been a year of more achievement for peace than any year since the end of World War II," and most Americans believed him.

The Peking-Moscow summits, although enormously important as symbols, were less important than the substantive agreements they represented. As Nixon's second term began China and the United States had not exchanged formal diplomatic recognition but relations between the two nations were vastly improved and a cultural and economic exchange was underway. The first phase of the Strategic Arms Limitation Talks with the Soviets brought no agreement on the control of offensive nuclear weapons, but a Salt I agreement limiting defensive or antiballistic missile systems was signed. Moreover, the two nations had signed a massive trade agreement, as well as agreements of cooperation in such areas as cancer research and space exploration, and were negotiating a "Mutual and Balanced Force Reduction" for Europe.

Spectacular breakthroughs in East-West relations, however, could not obscure the administration's failure to stop the fighting in Vietnam. Elected on a campaign pledge to end the war and win the peace by a "secret plan," Nixon sought an early conclusion to the fighting through negotiations in Paris with the North Vietnamese. When these talks, underway since the autumn of 1968, proved unproductive, the President shifted to a policy of "Vietnamization." Designed to "de-Americanize" the war by transferring American combat responsibility in Vietnam to ARVN soldiers, the policy reversed a decade of accelerating troop strength by gradually withdrawing American forces. Although the success of Vietnamization and the future of the wobbly Saigon regime remained in doubt, troop withdrawals continued throughout the first term. From a peak strength of 550,000 in April, 1969, the number of American soldiers fell to 27,000 in early 1973, and American annual combat deaths dropped from a 1968 high of 14,592 to only 300 in 1972.

Yet even as American involvement in Vietnam declined, the war was carried to other theaters in Southeast Asia. In secret missions unknown to even congressional leaders and the Secretary of the Air Force, American aircraft bombed communist "sanctuaries" inside Cambodia throughout most of 1969 and well into the spring of 1970. On April 30, 1970, United States and South Vietnamese soldiers invaded Cambodia and the following winter ARVN troops with

American air support moved into Laos. Although defended by military brass and White House spokesmen as necessary to disrupt enemy supply lines and purchase time for Vietnamization—and therefore vital to American withdrawal—these limited but much criticized incursions provoked domestic disorders in tragic proportions. The antiwar movement, recently lulled by massive troop withdrawals and falling casualty figures, erupted in protest against the Cambodian invasion. On campuses across the country students picketed and struck, and at riot-torn Kent State four of them were killed by Ohio national guardsmen. The bloodletting at Kent, soon followed by a similar though unrelated tragedy at all-black Jackson State College in Mississippi, brought a sense of renewed urgency to the peace movement. But a substantial majority of the voters remained steadfast in support of the President's conduct of the war. To the dismay of a growing body of congressional "doves," the people evidently accepted Nixon's argument that he could shorten the war by widening it.

In the end it was negotiation, not Vietnamization, that ended American participation in the struggle. Fresh from stunning triumphs in Peking and Moscow, Dr. Kissinger returned from Paris in October, 1972, to announce that "peace is at hand." Yet, though popular hopes and the stock market soared, the carnage continued for three long months. During the Christmas season, when it appeared that the October agreements had unraveled, the President dispatched wave upon wave of B-52s to rain bombs in unprecedented tonnage on Hanoi and Haiphong. At last, however, late in January, 1973, the longest war in United States history ended. The Paris Accords, signed by the United States, North and South Vietnam, and the National Liberation Front, provided for a supervised cease-fire, complete American withdrawal, and a prisoner exchange. Yet even as the nation celebrated Nixon's "peace with honor," the United States air war over Cambodia continued. Not until mid-August, 1973, after Congress moved to terminate funds for all military operations in Southeast Asia, did the commander in chief halt the round-the-clock bombing sorties against the enemies of the military regime in Phnom-Penh.

A CRISIS OF CONFIDENCE

The administration's foreign policy successes offset early Republican fears of a one-term Nixon presidency. The President's popularity had slumped markedly following the midterm elections of 1970. Early in 1971, opinion pollsters revealed, he trailed Senator Edmund S. Muskie of Maine in public esteem. Popular enthusiasm for Nixon's "peace initiatives" abroad and favorable developments at home, however, soon brought renewed hopes. During the early months of 1972, the good news from Peking and Moscow was matched by a dramatic, though temporary, economic upswing that brought new jobs and stablized prices. Soon thereafter Muskie's bid for the Democratic nomination was crippled by a feeble showing in the hotly contested Democratic primaries; and in May Wallace's threat to Nixon's southern support was eliminated when the Alabamian was critically wounded in an assassination attempt. Then in July, an army of enthusiastic and idealistic amateurs seized control of the Democratic convention to nominate Senator George McGovern, a left-leaning South Dakotan whose issues were immediate peace in Vietnam, reduced military spending, and sweeping tax and welfare reforms. In a campaign effort remarkable only for its blunders, McGovern was quickly branded by Republicans and conservative Democrats as the candidate of "amnesty, acid, and abortion." As many of his party's traditional leaders feared, he led the Democrats to their worst humiliation in half a century.

On election day only half of the eligible voters (some 55 percent) turned out, but among those who did Nixon was a clear favorite. Awarding him every state but Massachusetts and the District of Columbia, the electorate submerged Nixon's opponent in a sea of electoral (521 to 17) and popular (60.7 percent) votes.

It was a triumph almost without precedent. Except for Lyndon Johnson's landslide of 1964, no President ever polled a larger popular majority; and except for Franklin Roosevelt's record-shattering sweep of 1936, no President ever won more electoral votes. Indeed, Nixon ran so well among blue collar workers, union members, ethnics, and Catholics that he carried fully 37 percent of all the votes cast by Democrats—a record unequaled even by Dwight Eisenhower. Still, Nixon's was a personal rather than a party victory. As they had in 1968, ticket-splitting voters returned solid Democratic majorities to both houses of Congress. Losing only twelve seats in the house (243–192), the Democrats gained two additional Senate seats (57–43) and a majority of the nation's governorships. Clearly McGovern had lost, but the Republicans had not won.

But if the mandate of 1972 was uncertain, Richard Nixon's second term intentions were not. Having built a "structure of peace" through détente abroad, he would now restructure the nation's domestic priorities by diffusing federal responsibilities for local problems and decreasing federal spending for social programs. Although perhaps not sounding a full retreat from the Kennedy-Johnson "war on poverty," he was surely advocating a drastically revised battle plan. "Visionary" and "inherently unworkable" federal programs for urban renewal, manpower training, vocational education, and housing subsidies must be eliminated or sharply curtailed. The nation's rudimentary health-care program for the aged could stay, but such Great Society agencies as the Office of Economic Opportunity and such programs as Model Cities, Job Corps, Community Action, and Neighborhood Youth could not. By so economizing, the government could hope not only to ease mounting inflationary and tax pressures, but free additional monies for revenue-sharing grants to hard-pressed city halls and state houses.

To the surprise of no one, least of all the President, the New Federalism proved no more appealing to the democratically controlled Ninety-third Congress than it had to the Ninety-second. Indeed, the dominant mood in Washington as the new Congress convened was one of combat. Lawmakers from both parties were angered by apparent executive usurpations of legislative prerogatives. In the tradition of a succession of strong chief executives, Nixon, despite his self-styled strict constructionism, had governed in the grand manner. Without either the advice or consent of Congress, he had invaded Cambodia and Laos, mined the harbor of Haiphong, and resumed saturation bombing of Hanoi. He had invoked executive privilege to shield White House policymakers from congressional inquiry and impounded congressionally authorized funds slated for programs he opposed. Although precedents for such extraordinary assertions of presidential authority were numerous, aroused congressional leaders were now urging redress of the imbalance of power. There was, then, every indication that the executive-legislative stalemate of the first Nixon administration would become in the second a power struggle of historic importance. At stake, it appeared, was the doctrine of checks and balances itself.

As it turned out, however, the overriding issue of Nixon's second term was the abuse, not the accretion, of executive power. During the campaign of 1972, two White House aides were arrested for their roles in a conspiracy to burglarize and implant illegal wire taps in Democratic National Committee headquarters in Washington's elegant Watergate Building. Although Democrats accused the White House of "political espionage," the President and his chief spokesmen denied executive involvement and dismissed the incident as a "third rate burglary attempt." The voters, for the most part, showed little interest; in November the unseemly affair, like the presidential aspiration of Senator McGovern, was buried in the Nixon landslide.

Or so it seemed until early in 1973, when congressional investigators, aided by a courageous federal judge and a vigorous press, began exposing a sordid family of White House scandals that shocked the nation and raised profoundly disturbing questions about Nixon's capacity and fitness for leadership. Almost daily throughout the spring and summer evidence of official misconduct and lawlessness mounted. By autumn Nixon's immense popularity had collapsed and for the first time in more than a century there was serious talk in Congress of the impeachment of a President.

At the heart of the Nixon scandals lay, of course, the Watergate break-in and subsequent efforts by highly placed administration officials to limit the investigation and conceal or destroy evidence. But there were also allegations that the White House, or its Committee for the Re-Election of the President, engaged in: (1) unethical and illegal campaign practices ranging from "dirty tricks" against Democratic hopefuls to the solicitation of illegal contributions from corporations and interest groups desiring government favors; (2) efforts to politicize such nominally independent and traditionally nonpartisan government agencies as the FBI and the Internal Revenue Service; and (3) illegal and wide-ranging domestic security and intelligence gathering operations. Additionally, there were charges that Nixon's income and property taxes were not in order, that his estates in California and Florida were acquired under questionable circumstances, and that federal funds (totalling nearly $10 million) spent on improvements for these private dwellings often had little to do with presidential security.

Initially the White House tried to ignore the uproar, then it issued a series of general denials of executive wrongdoing. But even Nixon loyalists acknowledged that each presidential statement seemed to raise more questions than it answered. There was, moreover, little discernible White House cooperation with the several investigations into its alleged misconduct. Invoking the doctrines of separation of powers and executive privilege, Nixon at first refused even to permit his aides to testify before the Select Senate Committee on Presidential Campaign Activities. Under mounting congressional pressure, he reversed this position but refused investigators access to secret White House tape recordings of selected presidential conversations and telephone calls. When these were subpoenaed by the Justice Department's independent special prosecutor, the President fought compliance through two federal courts, promising obedience only to a "definitive" ruling of the Supreme Court. After months of negotiation and litigation, Nixon agreed to turn over the disputed material—but not before he had fired the special prosecutor and forced the resignation of Attorney General Elliot Richardson, and not before Congress moved toward his impeachment. To the nation's astonishment, however, the surrendered tapes did not contain two of the conversations presumed by investigators to be most relevant to the inquiry. The President's lawyers attributed these critical gaps in the evidence to inadequacies in White House recording equipment. But critics in growing numbers accused the President of withholding evidence and obstructing justice. To a people grown increasingly cynical of its political leadership, it was not inconceivable that the administration had something to hide.

Thus, as the first year of his second administration closed, Nixon faced a staggering crisis of confidence. Few expected that he would resign and fewer still expected that he would be forced from office by a diffident Congress. But it seemed unlikely that his administration could ever regain its lost authority and public support. Indeed, events themselves seemed to conspire against the beleaguered chief executive. In October, 1973, Vice President Agnew, under federal investigation for bribery and extortion, resigned his office and pleaded guilty to a lesser charge of income tax evasion. That same month détente with Russia was threatened by the outbreak of a fourth Arab-Israeli war. Meanwhile the cost of living continued its dizzying spiral, and for the first time since World War II, consumers faced shortages in food, energy, and other basic resources. Although the position of the dollar in the world's money markets had improved, domestic wholesale and credit costs were at record highs, the average annual increase of food prices threatened to exceed 20 percent, and many economists predicted a recession for 1974.

Faced with similar crises, a less stable society could expect domestic upheaval. Yet, though the sources of their traditional optimism had been gravely challenged, most Americans looked confidently toward the bicentennial of their nation's birth. However unpredictable the twists and turns of history, they had reason to believe in the essential worth of their basic institutions, in the resilience of their economy, and in their own capacity to survive as a free and united people.

FOR FURTHER READING:

Rowland Evans and Robert D. Novak have written authoritatively about *Nixon in the White House* (1971). Jules Witcover, *The Resurrection of Richard Nixon* (1970); Ralph De Toledano, *One Man Alone* (1969); and Garry Wills, *Nixon Agonistes* (1970)* offer varied assessments of the man and his politics. John Osborne's several *Nixon Watch* studies (1970, 1971, 1972) are often incisive. Nixon tells his own story in *Six Crises* (1962). Books by disgruntled "insiders" include: Leon E. Panetta, *Bring Us Together: The Nixon Team and the Civil Rights Retreat* (1971), and Richard J. Whalen, *Catch the Falling Flag: A Republican's Challenge to His Party* (1972). James Keogh's *President Nixon and the Press* (1972) supports the administration's views on media bias. Theo Lippman, Jr. provides an unflattering portrait of *Spiro Agnew's America* (1972); and Daniel Moynihan writes knowingly of *The Politics of a*

Guaranteed Income (1973). Kevin Phillips candidly, but unofficially, discusses the administration's election strategy in *The Emerging Republican Majority* (1969); and Richard M. Scammon and Ben J. Wattenberg analyze the mood of the electorate in *The Real Majority* (1970). Reg Murphy and Hal Gulliver offer an unfriendly appraisal of *The Southern Strategy* (1971); and George Tindall, *The Disruption of the Solid South* (1972), places that strategy in its proper historical perspective. Nixon's efforts to remake the Supreme Court is analyzed by James F. Simon, *In His Own Image* (1972), and Louis M. Kohlmeier, *"God Save This Honorable Court!"* (1972). Henry Kissinger, *American Foreign Policy* (1969), outlines the administration's objectives in a formulative stage. It should be supplemented by Virginia Brodine and Mark Selden, eds., *Open Secret: The Kissinger-Nixon Doctrine in Asia* (1972)*, and David Landau, *Kissinger: Uses of Power* (1972). Theodore H. White reports on *The Making of the President, 1972* (1973); and Arthur M. Schlesinger, Jr. comments critically on the development of *The Imperial Presidency* (1973). Lewis Chester *et al.* offer a British view. of *Watergate* (1973).

Name Index

Subject Index